T0408098

FRENCH AND FRANCOPHONE STUDIES

*Precarious Sociality, Ethics and Politics*

FRENCH AND FRANCOPHONE STUDIES

# *Precarious Sociality, Ethics and Politics*

## *French Documentary Cinema in the Early Twenty-First Century*

Audrey Evrard

UNIVERSITY OF WALES PRESS
2022

*www.uwp.co.uk*

*British Library Cataloguing-in-Publication Data*
A catalogue record for this book is available from the British Library.

ISBN    978-1-78683-842-1
eISBN  978-1-78683-843-8

FSC
www.fsc.org
MIX
Paper from
responsible sources
FSC® C013604

Typeset by Gary Evans
Printed by CPI Antony Rowe, Melksham, United Kingdom

# Contents

# Series Editors' Preface

This series showcases the work of new and established scholars working within the fields of French and francophone studies. It publishes introductory texts aimed at a student readership, as well as research-orientated monographs at the cutting edge of their discipline area. The series aims to highlight shifting patterns of research in French and francophone studies, to re-evaluate traditional representations of French and francophone identities and to encourage the exchange of ideas and perspectives across a wide range of discipline areas. The emphasis throughout the series will be on the ways in which French and francophone communities across the world are evolving into the twenty-first century.

Hanna Diamond and Claire Gorrara

# Acknowledgements

First, I want to thank the film-makers and producers whose work and dedication to the documentary practice have inspired me to write this book. I am particularly grateful that many have authorised me to reproduce stills from their films in chapters and were very generous and supportive of the project. I had the privilege of meeting Marcel and Julien Trillat during their visit to Fordham and The Johns Hopkins Universities in October 2019. I fondly remember the conversations we had while walking the streets of New York City and Baltimore.

Many people, friends, colleagues and students helped me shape this book over the years, reading chapters, attending talks I gave, inviting me to present parts that were still works-in-progress and encouraging me to deepen my analyses. I will most likely forget to mention some of you, so please accept my apologies if I do. Maggie Flinn, Patrick Bray, Lise Schreier, Joshua Schreier, Carl Fischer, Gwenola Caradec, Robert St-Clair, François Massonnat, Masano Yamashita, Brian Reilly, Yiju Huang, Arnaldo Cruz-Maldave, Francesca Parmeggiani, Carey Kasten, Andrew Clark, Cynthia Vich, Shoshana Enelow, Thomas O'Donnell, Jordan Stein, James Kim, Grace An, Catherine Witt, Derek Schilling, Alison J. Murray Levine, Martin O'Shaughnessy, Sarah Waters, Jeremy Lane, Martine Guyot-Bender, Sam DiIorio, Kathryn Parker, Paulo Coelho and the students of *French Documentary in Action* (Fall 2019) and *French Films d'Auteur: Agnès Varda* (Fall 2020), thank you.

I would be remiss not to thank my editor Sarah Lewis at The University of Wales Press as well as Claire Gorrara and Hanna Diamond, the editors of the French and Francophone Series, for their enthusiastic response. I also want to thank Fordham University for providing me with the resources to complete this book, as well as the large and small institutions that allowed me to discover and access the films presented in these pages over the years.

Finally, I thank my parents and Vincent for their unconditional and loving support over the years.

# Illustrations

Figure 1. *Fragments sur la misère* (Christophe Otzenberger, 1998)

Figure 2. La Maison du Peuple in Saint-Nazaire. *Il suffira d'un gilet* (Aurélien Blondeau and Valerio Maggi, 2019)

Figures 3, 4 and 5. The long final dissolve. *Rêve d'usine* (Luc Decaster, 2003)

Figures 6 and 7. The employees of the Epéda factory in Mer. *Rêve d'usine* (Luc Decaster, 2003)

Figure 8. The industrial geosystem. *Silence dans la vallée* (Marcel Trillat, 2007)

Figure 9. The gutted factory. *Les hommes debout* (Jérémy Gravayat, 2010)

Figure 10. Clandestine footage recorded aboard Queen Mary 2, *Les prolos* (Marcel Trillat, 2002)

Figure 11. Laurent Hasse as a child, playing movies, home movies archives. *Sur les cendres du vieux monde* (Laurent Hasse, 2002)

Figure 12. Film poster, *Retour à Forbach* (Régis Sauder, 2017)

Figure 13. Noah, waving from his new bedroom. *Retour à Forbach* (Régis Sauder, 2017)

Figure 14. Family portrait, *Fils de Lip* (Thomas Faverjon, 2007)

# Notes to readers

Official translations of French texts and film dialogues have been used whenever available. In other instances, translations were done by me.

A freestanding version of the section devoted to *Rêve d'usine* (Luc Decaster, 2003) from chapter 1 was previously published in the 2018 special issue, 'Work in Crisis', of *Modern and Contemporary France* in 2018 as '*Rêve d'usine* (Luc Decaster, 2003): Presenting the Vanishing Workplace'.

An early version of chapter 2, 'French Documentary Perspectives on the Collective Politics of the Atlantic Shipyards, A Global Workplace', was included in a 2014 special issue of *Working USA: The Journal of Labor & Society*.

# Introduction

---

À l'origine de ce livre, il y a un air du temps irrespirable, une suffocation, une colère contre la précarisation des vies ordinaires à laquelle nous assistons, impuissants, sommés de justifier l'entrée dans la précarité par l'adhésion à de nouvelles formes idéologiques.

Guillaume Le Blanc, *Vies ordinaires, vies précaires* (2007).[1]

In 1998, Christophe Otzenberger walked around Paris, with his camera, asking strangers: 'Comment vivez-vous la misère?' In English, this question can either translate as 'How does living on the street or being unemployed affect you personally?' or 'How do you feel about seeing so many destitute people around you?' He had been commissioned by the French TV channel ARTE to make a film about social exclusion, a timely issue in French society.[2] By the late 1990s, the concepts of *précarité* and exclusion had fully entered public discourse, thanks to the activism of many people unemployed and homeless, undocumented immigrants, public figures and artists.[3] Otzenberger decided to approach the subject of injustice and indifference to knock down prejudices – which he did.[4] Otzenberger's *cinéma vérité* style bluntly and brutally calls people out when they would rather disappear in the background.[5] Many people found his methods 'upsetting', 'disrespectful' even, and refused to answer his questions. Others took the time to reflect on the film-maker's question.

Two scenes, edited in sequence at the film's midpoint, illustrate the film's imbrication of politics and ethics. The first sequence starts near the Montparnasse railway station, during the morning rush hour. Suddenly, amid the continuous flow of people hurrying down the street, a man, silently kneeling in the middle of the pavement, his back to the camera, appears. He seems to be holding a cardboard sign, asking for money or food to no avail. Nobody stops or acknowledges him (see Fig. 1).

Figure 1. *Fragments sur la misère* (Christophe Otzenberger, 1998)
© courtesy of Nathalie Rigaux-Otzenberger.

The film-maker moves towards a young man walking his way, a book under his arm, and accosts him: 'May I ask how you feel when you see this man, on his knees like this?' Visibly uncomfortable, he glances back towards the man, low on the ground, signalling from his demeanour that he will answer. Giving him time to collect his thoughts, the film-maker repositions the camera to face him before he starts speaking:

> — I don't know; it depends on the day. Your question is embarrassing.
> — I know!
> — One day, I want to help him. The next day, I think he stinks. On the third day, I want to invite him for a drink

… It's not easy to be confronted by poverty daily. For instance, you see fifteen or twenty people begging on the subway every day. You give money to three or four of them, it adds up, and the last one yells at you for not giving anything. I don't know what to do. It kills me.

After the man has answered the question, the film-maker thanks him, ready to let him go. Then, the young man glances back once again towards the man on his knees. When Otzenberger's voice-over asks if he wants to say more, the young man retorts, a smile on his face: 'If I do, it will be a long conversation!' 'I am in no rush', the film-maker replies, implicitly inviting him to go on. After another reflective pause, the man starts speaking again, this time seemingly oblivious of the camera's presence:

— It's important to get one's bearings in life or society [...] It's hard for everyone, even if I have more money or wear nicer clothes … (*pause*). But I prefer to be in my shoes. (*pause*). It's a personal issue, I have some difficulties positioning myself. So, I can't help him. It would not help me. I would need to figure things out for myself, first. (*pause and smile*). This is such an embarrassing question!
— Yes, I know!
— You ask me how I feel about seeing this man here. It is like asking me how I feel about our society.
— That's exactly what I am asking you!
— Well, it's such a crazy society we live in! The only way to survive is to be a little selfish until we get our bearings and then we work together. Some days, we want to be alone; other days, we want to collaborate with other people. When I see him, I don't even want to empathise with his situation; I just want to keep walking … (*still looking at the man kneeling*). Otherwise, we start talking to him, and we never leave.

As he finishes this sentence, the editing returns us to the image of the homeless man, surrounded by morning commuters (see Fig. 1). Holding the shot for a while, Otzenberger now calls the viewers out, implicitly asking us, as he did the strangers he stopped on the street, to consider our attitude towards homelessness and others who lack social and economic security. Where do we stand in (relation to) this 'crazy society'? The question remains the same whether we are in front of his camera or looking at the screen.

In the next shot, the camera brings us face to face with a homeless man. At first, we look down on him, adopting the film-maker's point of view, who is standing, whereas the man is sitting on a public bench. Their conversation, which is already under way, naturally enacts what the young man previously envisaged – 'we start talking to him, and we never leave.' When we join, the man explains that he lives one day at a time. Otzenberger's voice asks: 'aren't you exhausted?'

— Of course, I am! My way of life is, let's face it, pathetic.
— So why did you say earlier that you like living on the street if you now say it's a hard life?
— Because I am 61 years old, and I cannot be employed, Sir. Because I have a postgraduate diploma in accounting, I worked for a reputable company, and now, I am unemployed. I am truly sorry; I was laid off shortly after I started my job. I have been out of a job ever since.
— How long ago?
— Ouh (*suggesting it has been many long years*).
— Do you sleep on the street? In hotels? In shelters?
— I sleep on the street. I never sleep in shelters.
— How about during the winter?
— I sleep outside. It's my right. Let's be honest, it's not my choice. It's not my choice, but I sleep outside. Because I don't like shelters. I hate promiscuity. I go here and there; I sleep in front of a building entrance door. I make do … I think that people who live on the street, in extreme poverty, are indeed a bit crude. It can be a good thing, but one should not take advantage of them.
— Who takes advantage of them, Sir?
— Ah, who takes advantage of them? (*scoffs at the question*)
— Do you think I take advantage of them?
— I am not talking to/about you, Sir.

— So, who takes advantage of them?
— So, who? I ask you the same. Who? I will leave you with this question.

The man adds a brief remark about the RMI (*Revenu Minimum d'Insertion*) – a small welfare allowance introduced in 1988 by the French government to support people who have been unemployed long-term and are without an income – before signalling he is ready to leave. He has said enough. He stands up. The camera angle tilts up as he makes one more declaration: 'I have no future; I only have my past. My future is behind me. And it's not much. Let's see, I am 61 years old, I may still have ten years to live.' The camera levels up, bringing us to the man's eye level. He continues: 'If all goes well, I can hope to get ten more years. I don't deserve more.' He starts walking away before returning for one last remark: 'In conclusion, instead of giving me the RMI, I wish they'd given me an apartment. I don't need their money!'

These sequences present public sympathy and governmental assistance as two sides of the same coin: both responses to precarity and exclusion are nothing but transactional. They make the bystander and the government feel good, but they do not return to the person on the street their humanity and dignity. They do not answer a homeless person's true needs, which, in the second instance, are described as feeling recognised as another human being, as an equal in that sense, and being granted the security of a home. The film does not pass these judgements; it powerfully interrogates the acts of looking at, and filming, poverty and social vulnerability. *Fragments sur la misère* uncomfortably probes documentary cinema's capacity, or failure, to address precarious subjects and mediate a response in the viewer that is *just*. It also uses the camera to confront people with their ethical contradictions and responsibility.

Therefore, it is concerned about moulding 'a non-violent visual relation to others, especially the culturally de-idealised [...] and show[ing] us how we might valorize such others rather than subject them to a culturally-informed gaze of disdain', what Sarah Cooper posits as a foundational dilemma in the redefinition of post-war French documentary's ethics. Otzenberger's understanding of the camera's moral force is central to the film's 'subjective dynamics of social engagement' and 'the rhetorical force of [his] argument about the world we inhabit', critical principles of documentary cinema's ethics for Bill Nichols.[6] At the same time, the film aims to provoke people into 'finding the way in which I am tied to "you", and therefore a reason to care for those who are regarded with contempt because they (can) no longer conform with society's rules'.[7] What is at stake in this film, and I will argue in the rest of this book, in many films produced in the past two decades in France, is a double agenda: to cast light on a range of social, economic and affective experiences produced by the systemic precarisation of work, sociality and life, and to mobilise documentary cinema's unresolved/unresolvable ethical dilemma as a relational counterforce. In *Film and Ethics: Foreclosed Encounters*, Lisa Downing and Libby Saxton state that 'ethicizing the cinematic experience means conceptualizing it in terms of responsibility and desire (where these are not straightforward opposites), rather than simply in political or moral terms'.[8] The question for this study will thus be to see how French film-makers have rearticulated these two sets of intentions, reasserting responsibility and the desire to be in community with another being as the core engine of a political and moral commitment to justice, recognition and radical equality.

## Precarity, precarisation, precariousness

A key concept of French sociology since the late 1970s, precarity started receiving much broader attention from the late 1990s onwards. In the past two decades, it has become a central concept of a vast cross-disciplinary critical undertaking of neoliberalism as a system of interconnected economic and political forces pressing on individuals' social, affective and subjective being.

In a famous essay, 'Job insecurity is everywhere now', published in *Contre-feux* (1998), Pierre Bourdieu argues that work, or its scarcity, has been turned into a 'mode of domination'.[9] Maintained in a 'state of insecurity', workers are forced to comply with exploitative practices to stay employed, not to 'fall lower into the subproletariat', forsaking 'all the values of solidarity and humanity, and sometimes produc[ing] direct violence'.[10] Building on these assessments, Isabell Lorey remarks that while 'precarity involves social positionings of insecurity [...] it implies neither modes of subjectivation nor the power of agency of those positioned'.[11] Hence the importance of considering the role 'governmental precarisation' plays, since its primary role consists of 'legitimising the protection of some [...] striating the precarity of those marked as "other"' by constructing precariousness as a threat, while neoliberalism and post-Fordism normalise precarisation.[12] As such, 'governmental precarisation' contributes to 'not only destabilisation through unemployment, but also destabilisation of the conduct of life and thus of bodies and modes of subjectivation.'[13]

In France, debates about precarity have intersected with reconceptualisations of work and raising awareness about suffering in the workplace, on the one hand, and reformulations of ethics of care in a French context. Still in 1998, two books, *Souffrance en France. La banalisation de l'injustice sociale* (1998), and *Le Harcèlement moral* (1998), respectively authored by Christophe Dejours and Marie-France Hirigoyen, both psychiatrists, sparked many discussions and contributed to new labour laws in the years that followed their publications. They documented correlations between the managerial models widely implemented in the workplace and systemic patterns of physical and emotional suffering. Two years later, Hirigoyen further examined harassment as a phenomenon increasingly present in the workplace in *Malaise dans le travail* (2001). For Dejours, the rise of work-induced pathologies, severe occupational stress and, in most extreme cases, suicides were symptoms of new forms of alienation. No longer an 'individual process embodied in individuals', alienation must be understood in more abstract terms, as the product of 'an orientation toward the negation of the human species-being' to which people 'give their willing consent'.[14] People's dis-eases manifest their 'struggle against their alienation' from (their) humanity, and, in that regard, they should be seen as a good thing and attended to as such.[15] In a workplace where work resources are rationed and expectations raised, people feel abandoned, isolated and helpless. As a result, fear has become a dominant affect, impeding social relations and formal solidarities. Even if, to all appearances, many of these employees have the security of a home, employment and social attachments precarious workers and non-working people lack, their experience nonetheless amounts to 'subjective precarity', according to Danièle Linhart.[16]

During the first two decades of the twenty-first century, social unrest has been a recurring feature in France. Insecurities about unemployment, the privatisation of several public services, repeated governmental austerity plans announcing cuts to social protections have mobilised retirees, youths, cultural workers, healthcare professionals and other categories. Other protests have brought awareness to the gendered and racialised stratification of precarity, with movements giving visibility to the exploitation of migrant and immigrant workers and bodies in hospitality, care and food industries and in the emerging gig economy. A few examples are addressed in chapter 2. Whereas some protests have followed fairly traditional patterns (*manifestations*), several others have ushered in new protestation and collective organisation modes.

Isabell Lorey remarks that precarity is inextricable from capitalism, and therefore not a new phenomenon per se. However, what is peculiar to neoliberalism is its 'democratiz[ation]' of precarisation, which, in turn, generates new political desires.[17]

> The temporality of the protests of the precarious is located in the present; it is a presentist democracy [...] Presentist democracy is currently the opposite of representative democracy and is for example practiced in the moment of the assembly [...] The assembled precarious exchange ideas, talk together about common concerns in the context of the present political-economic situation, and enter into a process in which aspects begin to crystallize. They not only have in common all their differences due to the governmentality of insecurity, but also share ideas of how a 'better society' could be built. They try to realize the approach of openness to everybody but also of equality [...] These presentist democratic practices based on contingency and precarious bodies show that there is no singular 'we' founded in common precariousness but a contingent coming together that invents and practices forms of solidarity.[18]

The *Intermittents* (2003) and Nuit Debout (2016) are early examples of this, despite their primarily urban base. A better embodiment of this 'presentist' democracy took shape on 17 November 2018, twenty years after the release of *Fragments sur la misère* in theatres. A wave of Gilets Jaunes rolled across France, as over 280,000 protesters wearing high-visibility safety vests blocked intersections, roundabouts and toll roads in more than two thousand different locations nationwide.[19] The protests, sparked by recent governmental decisions to reduce speed limits (from 55 to 50 mph) on secondary roadways and introduce an ecotax on top of already rising petrol prices, were largely coordinated through petitions and posts shared on social media. Protests quickly morphed into broad-ranging rejections of President Macron's economic and social policies, enacting the most vociferous resistance to 'governmental precarisation' to date. On 1 December 2018, many demonstrations in Paris and other French cities turned to chaos, storefronts were vandalised, and public monuments defaced.

While condemning the violence, intellectuals and film-makers looked away from major urban centres and towards the roundabouts to understand what galvanised so many people into action, often for the first time in their lives. In an op-ed, published on 3 December 2018, in French daily *Libération*, sociologist Dominique Méda, law professor Pascal Lokiec and economist Eric Heyer stated that the Gilets Jaunes mobilised a general despondency with two decades of neoliberal policies, austerity plans and growing socio-economic inequalities.[20] Ludivine Bantigny described this 'event' as 'an act of resistance [...] to false presumptions' and to 'the precepts that enjoin us to adapt to this new world, to be more flexible, open to precarity, accept to be exploited at will and disposable', in other words, to a reality that 'shatters solidarities, and, at times, people's dignity'.[21] Jeremy Lane recently noted that the Gilets Jaunes seem to have embodied

> the long drawn-out crisis of the French republican-corporatist post-war model – the proliferation of precarious forms of employment, the increasing polarisation between prosperous metropolitan centres, and a marginalised periphery, the tertiarisation and feminisation of the labour

market, the declining importance of the 'intermediary bodies', the growing rift between the promises inherent to French republican citizenship and the lived realities of precarious subjecthood.[22]

For Joseph Confavreux, a journalist with Mediapart, the movement brutally *collided* with the entire society, destabilising existing sociological and political frameworks.[23]

If nothing could have predicted the timing of such a social outburst, Serge Paugam nonetheless found that 'sociological survey had long shown signs of a broad malaise' brewing; 'all the conditions for the resentment expressed by the gilets jaunes today' were already latent in Pierre Bourdieu's *La Misère du Monde* (1993).[24] In 2014, Christophe Guilluy outlined the socio-demographic contours of 'la France périphérique', home to 60 per cent of the population, warning that future social and political unrest would erupt in these regions. 'Voices are rising against a model that privileges an oligarchy sitting at the top', he wrote; 'they are not interested in the debates between "left" and "right", "progressives" and "populists", "Good" and "Evil". They want a different model to return them their full economic, political, and cultural agency.'[25] Traditionally, this other France had been primarily viewed in geographical terms, not as a social and political force in and of itself.

In fact, many of the Gilets Jaunes heard in *J'Veux du Soleil* (François Ruffin and Gilles Perret, 2019) and *Il suffira d'un gilet* (Aurélien Blondeau, 2019), two documentaries on the movement, expressed similar feelings. In this second film, a former schoolteacher bluntly declares that people have simply had enough of 'living in disgusting conditions', 'eating disgusting stuff', only 'to end their lives in lousy nursing homes, dying of a disease caused by capitalism'.[26] In *J'Veux du Soleil*, François Ruffin asks a young woman met on a roundabout near Privas, a small town in south-central France, if she has felt this outraged for long. 'Years!', she responds. 'I've been waiting for this for years.' Both films capture the infectious energy that powered the movements for almost a year and stress the significant presence of women. The Gilets Jaunes' desire for a 'presentist democracy' is more directly manifested in *Il suffira d'un gilet*. A few minutes into the film, as we watch a few protesters build a makeshift hut on a roundabout near Saint-Nazaire, in north-western France, a voice-over reads a text:

> We practise true democracy on roundabouts. It takes place neither in television studios nor in the pseudo-roundtables convened by Macron. After he insulted us and treated us like nobodies, he now describes us as a heinous, fascist and xenophobic crowd. We are the complete opposite; we are neither racist nor sexist or homophobic. We are proud to stand together, with our differences, to build a new society and be in solidarity with one another.[27]

Reclaiming 'true democracy' is the centripetal force that moves the yellow-clad subjects of the film, and the viewers, into the Maison du Peuple in Saint-Nazaire (see Fig. 2). Local Gilets Jaunes appropriated the empty abandoned building in late 2018, turned it into a squat where protesters held assemblies and hosted various events. On 5, 6 and 7 April 2019, regional delegations congregated for a General Assembly, the second to be held after the inaugural *Assemblée des Assemblées* in Commercy in late January 2019.

Figure 2. La Maison du Peuple in Saint-Nazaire. *Il suffira d'un gilet* (Aurélien Blondeau and Valerio Maggi, 2019)

For Sandra Laugier and Albert Ogien, another 'France périphérique' becomes visible thanks to the movement's neon-coloured rallying: the care economy.

> These past few weeks, we have all had this experience: we see someone who is simply doing her job (help children to cross the street, collect garbage, work on a construction site) on the street or the bus, wearing a yellow vest. All of a sudden, these jobs and their importance become visible. This industrial army ensures our daily life can go on; yet, the rest of the time, it remains unseen. The movement taught us how to see them. It is not surprising that, even though those who go to Paris on the weekend are mainly men, the Gilets Jaunes are predominantly women, involved in political action for the first time in their lives. Many are care workers (nurses, health aides, social workers, house cleaners, part-time workers, retirees …), the first victims of the government's 'reforms' … *Care*, caring for others, is about protecting those who are vulnerable against those who are powerful. It is about recognising everyone's value and contributions, whether they are 'winners' or losers. This uprising is about fighting politics of *carelessness* and practices that misconstrue *care* as poor people taking care of the rich. By putting on this yellow vest, these people have been given *attention* (another synonym for *care*): 'We need this yellow vest to exist in front of a man who cannot see the people. Do you realise? We need to wear neon colours to be visible.'[28]

Their vision illuminates French society's ordinary but vital fabric and evokes Judith Butler's insistence that 'precarity exposes our sociality, the fragile and necessary dimensions of our interdependency', hence the urgency of 'rethinking social relationality'.[29] Lauren Berlant puts it slightly differently, asking what it would mean and yield if 'life' were 'not a drama of *earning* a place in it but a zone of generously configured social relations'.[30]

Initiated before the Gilets Jaunes' eruption, this book presents films that offer different insights into the complex reconfigurations of social, political and affective experiences during the twenty years that separate *Fragments sur la misère* and *Il suffira d'un gilet*, between a film-maker's anger at his contemporaries' indifference to other people's distress and the violent incursion in the social space of thousands of people outraged by 'governmental precarisation'. The chapters address different manifestations of this 'emergent present' shaped by neoliberalism, globalisation, precarity, exclusions and insecurities, focusing, among other concerns and locations, on local labour struggles, work-induced pains and anxiety, the effects of post-industrial decline in Lorraine, or social precarity in Marseille. The films *Les hommes debout*, *On a grévé*, *Un monde moderne* or *On vient pour la visite* confront the heterogeneous corporeality of contemporary labour struggles. In chapters 1 and 3, *Silence dans la vallée*, *Retour à Forbach* or *Sur les cendres du vieux monde* attend to the 'depressive modernity' of a post-industrial valley. In chapters 1 and 4, *Rêve d'usine*, *Ils ne mouraient pas tous mais tous étaient frappés* and *Rêver sous le capitalisme* reveal the physically and emotionally ailing 'subjective precarity' of white- and blue-collar workers alike. The corpus assembled here makes palpable the profound, differentiated damages of an ethos that exhausts resources, bodies and time. As a whole, the study expounds on how film-makers have mobilised documentary cinema as a site where social relations may be reconfigured more generously, revealing embodied praxes of (precarious) sociality.

## Documentary cinema as an embodied praxis of (precarious) sociality

Gérard Leblanc asserts that to transform humankind and bring about social change, cinema must transform its spectators, meaning it must transform how spectators view cinema.[31] Historically, this has been the project of so-called political and militant film-making. Paul Douglas Grant estimates that, by the mid-1970s,

> the majority of the films placed under this rubric [were] extremely low-budget productions, created predominantly collectively and/or by filmmakers working outside the mainstream (meaning both mainstream industry as well as

mainstream auteurist filmmaking) and which employ various strategies of contestation, particularly against the dominant systems of representation [...] the factory and the political vicissitudes this domain experienced.[32]

The concurring resurgence of 'the political' in French cinema in the 1990s with a 'documentary renaissance', which many scholars have addressed separately and conjointly, reignited debates about cinema's relationship with politics.[33] In 2000, Van Kelly and Rosemarie Scullion observed 'social commitment, *le social*, resurfacing [in French and Francophone cinema] within a politics less militant and more individual, a politics oriented toward smaller communities of interest and constellated around questions of interpersonal identity as much as the greater collective.'[34] More books have since described narratives poised in time, 'between the elaborated politics that was and the politics yet to come', as Martin O'Shaughnessy puts it.[35] In recent conversations, ethics has gradually replaced ideology as a third denominator, echoing contemporary political philosophy debates.

In direct dialogue with these debates, this book brings light to films and film-makers rarely featured in scholarly works published in English on contemporary French cinema, while deliberately blurring the lines between social and *auteur* documentary cinemas. As such, it provides a companion study to Alison J. Murray Levine's recent *Vivre Ici: Space, Place, and Experience in Contemporary French Documentary*, further asserting French documentary film-makers' lasting contributions to the creative evolution of this cinematic practice and the theoretical debates it provokes.

If Jacques Rancière states that 'there is no politics of cinema', he encourages us to stay attuned to the 'political effect' of 'documentary fictions':[36]

Aesthetic experience has a political effect to the extent that the loss of destination it presupposes disrupts the way in which bodies fit their functions and destinations. What it produces is not rhetorical persuasion about what must be done. Nor is it the framing of a collective body. It is a multiplication of connections and disconnections that reframe the relation between bodies, the world they live in and the way in which they are 'equipped' to adapt to it. It is a multiplicity of folds and gaps in the fabric of common experience that change the cartography of the perceptible, the thinkable and the feasible. As such, it allows for new modes of common objects and new possibilities of collective enunciation.[37]

This exploration of contemporary French documentary cinema is premised on this differentiation between politics and political density. Each chapter takes this task seriously, reclaiming dissolution, dislocation and disjunction, key operative principles of precarisation, as generative and constitutive engines of 'documentary radicality' in the face of a systemic precarisation of social relations.

Jane Gaines understands 'documentary radicality' as the relation 'between *evidence* and *aspiration*, the evidence of material conditions and the aspiration to transform the world'.[38] Building on Jacques Derrida's definition, she explains that 'the radical would then seem to require the genealogical. But also, these are the conditions of the hauntology, the goings and comings, which means that the question of documentary radicality is inevitably a study in elusive appearances, legacies, and finally returns.'[39] The book starts in the factory's economic, social and material ruins, and even more deliberately with its digital muddying and erasure by the end of *Rêve d'usine* (2003). This visual effect resignifies the bodies of the factory's employees we see at the beginning of the film, silently standing, gazing directly at the camera/the viewer, as spectral figures, in a Derridean sense. Patrick Cingolani reminds us that Marx understood workers' reconciliation with their spectrality as always already precarious subjectivities to be a fundamental engine of social change.[40] The book's intervention is thus premised on the assumption that early twenty-first-century French documentary cinema's 'radicality' stems from its dis-identification from politics to embrace political differentiation, a vital step towards 'new possibilities of collective enunciation'. Luc Decaster's resetting of the film's cinematic narrative thus operates as an example of internal *'political mimesis'* – a movement that 'energize[s] "body back" effects, translated into actions in and on the world, into the production of new events'.[41]

Absorbed in a work of 'critical inheritance', another Derridean concept central to this study, the film-makers we follow do not intend to rebuild collective solidarities as they existed in the past.[42] Neither are they interested in turning new forms of militancy into a spectacle and figuring the spectral silhouette of a precarious people. Instead, the detailed readings offered in each chapter reveal these film-makers' shared investment in Judith Butler's call for 'figur[ing] a sense of political community of a complex order [...] by bringing to the fore the relational ties that have implications for theorising fundamental dependency and ethical responsibility'.[43] Once reaffirmed as precarious, life becomes a binding force in an otherwise 'groundless ground of being'.[44] While presenting different forms and figures of vulnerabilities, invisibilities and sufferings rooted in the transformations of the French/global economy, the films most poignantly *address* their subjects as human, social and affected beings. Plumbing the 'precarious humus' of more localised social fabrics and situations, these film-makers unearth voices, histories, experiences and affects, creating a 'bridge between an ennobled past, shaped by silent struggles and victories, and a future, maybe uncertain, but at last open onto future voices and revolts'.[45] To this end, the book gradually widens its scope, covering a wide range of social, economic and geographical locations, moving into new sites of struggles and allowing different voices to resound, to trace an arc from the obsolete dramaturgy of masculinist, industrial antagonisms to differential politics and ethics of affiliations, care and communality.

This progression aims to problematise what is understood as the 'return of the political' in French cinema in the late 1990s, by loosening the historical entanglement of social and political cinema with work, labour struggles and social protests, without entirely losing sight of them. Examining Jacques Derrida's, Jean-Luc Nancy's and Maurice Blanchot's interrogations of the notion of community, Stella Gaon remarks that these texts offer 'a deconstructive take on community that is radically different from any classic conception of the community': 'at stake in them each [...] is not a politics but rather an interrogation of the political – a questioning that is itself "communal" or "social" in a certain sense of those terms.'[46] This book's main argument is that similarly confronted with 'a world whose grounds ha[ve] become fungible' documentary film-makers have re-envisaged their practice as a communal and social exploration of the 'contingent, temporary, conflictual, and plural grounding of *all* social relations'.[47] To this end, I draw from the work of Jacques Derrida and Jean-Luc Nancy to think through film-makers' aesthetic interventions. I propose that, in the specific context addressed here, French film-makers' embodied praxes of sociality redirect documentary cinema's engagement towards the promise of a democratic ethics. Overall, what is at stake in the paths that these chapters open is an exploration of the political value of documentary cinema's aesthetic and ethical practices as part of a project to rethink social relationality differently.

## Chapter overview

As already mentioned, chapter 1 starts with the material and symbolic dissolution of the factory, an iconic site of class struggles central to the political dramaturgy of militant cinema. In *Rêve d'usine* (Luc Decaster, 2003), *Silence dans la vallée* (Marcel Trillat, 2007) and *Les hommes debout* (Jérémy Gravayat, 2011), the disruption caused by *en masse* closures of manufacturing sites around France in the late 1990s serves as a point of departure for a renewed twenty-first-century political aesthetics of precarious labour struggles. In *Rêve d'usine*, the factory is on the brink of closure, and its workers are confounded by the absurdity of today's labour disputes. *Silence dans la vallée* reveals the economic and social disruption of an entire geosystem, the industrial valley. Finally, *Les hommes debout* depicts the factory as gutted and reclaimed by real estate developers eager to replace it with luxury flats. Mixing documentary, archival militant footage and fictional sequences, Gravayat imagines the factory as a heterotopia where the dreams of immigrant workers, squatters, migrant day labourers and white gentrifiers are interlocked. These three films trace the methodical erasure of industrial memory from landscapes and the early twenty-first-century French political imaginary. However, they resist impulses to fix the vanishing factory into a *site of memory*. By imprinting the vanishing factory as a lasting watermark on the documentary image instead, these films engage in what Svetlana Boym calls 'reflective' nostalgia and generate an alternative visual trope to the closure narrative commonly found in social documentary film-making by the mid-2000s. Furthermore, they establish disjunction from past class identities as the condition for social recognition in a post-industrial global economy that erases all workers to facilitate new (af)filiations between local, declassified industrial workers and a growing, transnational precarious labour force.

Chapter 2 considers the ethical and aesthetic challenges film-makers face when documenting the ambiguous status of migrant and immigrant labour in industries relying heavily on interim and subcontracting. The Atlantic shipyards and the cleaning industry are introduced in this chapter as exemplars of how companies exploit the disconnect between national labour legislation and the transnational reality of the workplace. Several films have brought attention to the exploitative nature of these activities and the activism of employees wronged by shady third-party contractors. The first three films examined take place in shipyards, *Le dernier navire* (Jean-Marc Moutout, 2000), *Les prolos* (Marcel Trillat, 2002) and *Un monde moderne* (Sabrina Malek and Arnaud Soulier, 2005), whereas the second set, *Remue-ménage dans la sous-traitance* (Ivora Cusak, 2003), *On a grévé* (Denis Gheerbrant, 2014) and *On vient pour la visite* (Lucie Tourette, 2009), document employees of the cleaning industry organising and defending their rights. The bodies of migrant workers, while lacking political representation and legal protections, reignite localised, tactical power struggles in response to the strategic global dismantlement of collective politics. Attention is also given to the film-makers' presence and positions amid these dislocated, ad hoc and tactically reactive labour struggles with no clear, predetermined dramaturgy. The chapter thus explores the possibility for documentary cinema to enact and foster affective solidarity between the films' viewers and the people on strike, between French workers and employees and migrant labour, between users of these industries and the invisible hands that sustain them.

The second half of the book examines documentary cinema's legitimation of precarious voices in a wider array of post-industrial, rural and urban spaces. Chapters 3, 4 and 5 present our contemporary precarious sociality as an ambivalent social ontology poised between experiences of vulnerability in a negative sense (as the result of the damaging economic logic of our times) and efforts to reclaim its constructive force as a condition that binds all (human) beings (as the product of an ethical work). These chapters grapple more specifically with film-makers' embodied mediations of different precarious subjectivities, as well as the distance that may stand between these subjects and the viewers. Like the first two chapters, they envisage various ways to be in community with *one an/Other*, reclaiming documentary cinema as an active praxis of sociality.

Chapter 3 follows film-makers who return home to document the economic and social devastation a long industrial decline has brought to these communities. Their ambivalent status as film-makers and native sons enables them to become privileged *passeurs* (facilitators) between the viewers and the precarious voices and experiences they record. I follow the philosopher Guillaume Le Blanc when he states that a precarious voice can no longer lay claim to any social, political and, as a result, ontological attachments. In *Fils de Lip* (2007), *Sur les cendres du vieux monde* (2002), and *Retour à Forbach* (2017), Thomas Faverjon, Laurent Hasse and Régis Sauder respectively use their embodied cinematic subjectivities to provide crucial attachments that post-industrial precarity gradually suspends. They simultaneously enact, through their work, complicated filiations that upset the political status quo. In *Fils de Lip*, Faverjon reconnects his mother's rejection of Lip's official story with other silenced voices, mainly women's, that raised questions about the direction of workers' struggles in the 1970s. In doing so, he rewrites social and political film-making from the perspective of these discordant voices that social history failed to account, and reformulates the legacy of this history for present times in such a way that it now stems from its failures and not its so-called triumphs. Back to their homeland (Lorraine), now riddled with unemployment and rising xenophobia, Sauder and Hasse also set themselves the task of turning documentary film-making into a way of honouring debts to their native communities. While both film-makers entwine the histories of immigration and industrialism,

Sauder's visual and narrative economy intimately conjoins post-colonial and post-industrial identities and territorialities in the present. At the end of *Retour à Forbach,* we watch eleven-year-old Noah wave at us from the window of what used to be Sauder's old bedroom. Noah's family, of Moroccan descent, recently bought Sauder's childhood home. He, his sister and their mother decided to sell the house after his father passed away from Alzheimer's disease during the film's preparation.

Chapter 4 moves us further away from post-industrial and precarious labour struggles while engaging with French society's broader crisis of work. This close analysis of Sophie Bruneau's sustained interest in these questions presents us with the psychosomatic effects and affects of the contemporary workplace, an environment that increasingly places competitiveness and cost-effectiveness over collegiality. Inspired by Christophe Dejours's clinical research in the psychodynamics of work and work-related pathologies and Charlotte Beradt's book *Rêver sous le 3ème Reich* (*The Third Reich of Dreams*, 1968), Bruneau makes speech the primary material of documentary. Tending to individual somatic and unconscious manifestations of physiological and psychological dis-ease, *Ils ne mouraient pas tous mais tous étaient frappés* and *Rêver sous le capitalisme* point to the noxiousness of neoliberal capitalism and drastically altered social relations. Her reliance on the dissonance between image and sound, bodies and voices, evokes a militant account of industrial workers' social alienation caused by hours spent on the assembly line, such as Bruno Muel's *Le sang des autres* (1973) and *Reprise du travail aux Usines Wonder* (1968). In the few decades that separate these films from Bruneau's, such pain has stopped being class-specific, becoming increasingly diffuse and rampant across the private and public sectors, crippling blue-collar and white-collar professionals alike. Bruneau's engagement with work, the workplace and the (non-)working subject is positioned across this chapter as a practice that intersects, on the one hand, with sociological, political and ideological critiques of neoliberalism focused on its destructive impact on individual subjectivities and collective solidarities, and, on the other hand, with ethical considerations that posit care as an act of resistance and a condition for the protection and renewal of sociality.

Finally, to conclude this study, chapter 5 reconnects the work of care and consideration undertaken by social documentary film-makers since the late 1990s with ethics of hospitality and friendship that characterise Agnès Varda's, Raymond Depardon's and Denis Gheerbrant's *auteurist* documentary practices. Focusing on Raymond Depardon and Claudine Nougaret's *Profils paysans* (2001; 2006), *La vie moderne/Modern Life* (2009) and *Les habitants* (2016), *La République Marseille* (Denis Gheerbrant, 2009) and *Visages villages* (Agnès Varda and JR, 2017), this last chapter embarks the viewers on journeys across social geographies that have been romanticised, neglected or disparaged. Raymond Depardon sinks into '*la France profonde*', intending to crack open what lies behind vague territorial constructs. His embodied ambulation, his *errance*, is central to his ethic of encounters with others and with the natural landscape. Taking us to Marseille's northern *quartiers* and *cités ouvrières*, Denis Gheerbrant delivers in *La République Marseille* his most ambitious film. This seven-part portrait of *la cité phocéenne* excavates fading social values and solidarities, as it presents us with two incarnations of the *cité populaire* (the housing estate) – the older working-class women of the Cité Saint-Louis and the stranded youths of the Cité des Rosiers. If *La République Marseille* strives to encapsulate 'La Totalité [de ce] monde' *marseillais*, the juxtaposition of 'Les femmes de la Cité Saint-Louis' (part 4) and 'Le centre des Rosiers' (part 5) draws attention to a gaping hole at the core of Marseille's deep-rooted proletarian identity: its shared, yet differentiated, precariousness at the beginning of a new century. Finally, the perhaps surprising collaboration of ninety-year-old Agnès Varda and thirty-three-year-old street artist JR invites viewers to envisage the village, not simply as a geographical place, but also as a regenerative and artistic ethos, grounded in the openness to difference and hospitality. If these settings convey a sense of *empaysement* in a nostalgic vision of France, their film-makers' *errance(s)* uncover pathways that promote genuine communality, friendship and hospitality.

Writing about contemporary French documentary cinema inevitably requires making choices that can only present a glimpse of how broad and diverse this production has been, leaving out of its purview many films that contribute to the discussion initiated in these preliminary readings. Therefore, this corpus should be seen as one suggested entry point among many more available. It nonetheless reflects my attempt to blur the boundaries that often isolate the work of a small number of film-makers recognised as *auteurs* (in this case, Raymond Depardon and Agnès Varda) from broader creative synergies, to bridge often separate concerns between cinema's political interventions and artistic work. I do not start with an overview of the French documentary production context, since other scholars have recently done such work, to dedicate more space to individual films.[48]

# Chapter 1
# The vanishing factory

At the end of Luc Decaster's 2003 documentary film *Rêve d'usine*, a long white dissolve slowly erases the Epéda mattress factory whose closure has been the subject of the film. Turning the documentary image into pure digital matter, this striking visual effect brings the spectators to witness the disintegration of the 294 employees' shared dream of preserving their jobs as their workplace ends up dematerialised before their eyes (see Figs 3–5). In doing so, *Rêve d'usine* powerfully draws the spectators' attention to the role that cinema, as a medium and a discourse, continues to play in the in/visibility of industrial labour.

Central to the politics of workers' movements since the late nineteenth century, the factory provided film-makers with an iconic site where the workers' subjective empowerment could be dramatised, defined and refined. In the 1930s, *cinéma engagé* constructed a political subject, the collective body of the working class, from crowds of workers on strike. Together, these men and women marched in solidarity with one another and in support of the Popular Front, filling up the streets of French towns. Later, in 1968, cinema's militancy became more individualised as film-makers found themselves witnessing and recording dissenting voices bursting out of these same crowds, drawing attention to the repression of singular affects in the name of class solidarity. Film historian Tangui Perron explains that, because they were forced to stay outside of the factory during the strikes of 1967 and 1968, film-makers creatively reinvented militant cinema as a practice committed to capturing the subjectivity, and subjectivities, driving working-class struggles:

> Aligning itself with work and workers, [militant cinema] remains at the factory gates often due to executive orders

Figures 3–5. The long concluding dissolve in *Rêve d'usine* (Luc Decaster, 2003) © Courtesy of 24Images.

refusing filmmakers the right to shoot inside the shops or, when it does make its way inside, work is often stopped, the factory occupied by workers on strike. Work is then told orally, with interviews, represented by tired bodies and a few symbolic shots often filmed under cover or diverted away from their original purpose [...] The camera must therefore penetrate the 'restricted area'.[1]

Whereas mines, ports and factories – three crucial cornerstones of working-class political activism – started shutting down in the 1980s, what was true about the militant cinema of 1968's relationship with the workplace still applies to the social documentary practice that resurged in the 1990s. Film-makers continue to stumble upon closed gates when seeking to document strikes, as chapter 2 illustrates. As a result, they are either forced to trespass into restricted areas or to rely, more than ever, on oral testimonies as they continue to cast light on working conditions, support various labour struggles and use their films as sounding boards for voices otherwise unheard.

Certainly, for film-makers, staying close to local struggles long-term is crucial. Film-makers like Luc Decaster pride themselves on being present before TV cameras arrive and on staying long after they have left. It demonstrates their ethical commitment to 'filming people rarely represented, with as much respect for their dignity as possible'.[2] True to the practice's long-standing political inclinations, this focus reflects their individual and collective efforts to give visibility to industrial conflicts that result from the geographical redistribution of the economy. In that regard, focusing on the growing Kafkaesque judicialisation of factory closures has built national momentum around very localised work conflicts by making more explicit connections between such instances and broader critiques of neoliberalism's global expansion. Reacting against the logic of sensationalism governing television newscasting, documentary film-makers have resisted the mainstream media's demonisation of workers and local union leaders. Instead, they have made them key voices of their counter-narratives.

Today, a couple of decades into a new century, work is stopping, or has already stopped, for many employed in the industrial sector, leaving both workers and film-makers at a loss. As Western Europe and North America face deindustrialisation, can film-makers reclaim the emancipatory value of the factory? Can they resist the systemic crushing of subjectivities in the workplace and the global economy? Can workers' struggles (*la lutte ouvrière*) still aesthetically anchor a socially and politically committed documentary practice when they no longer take place inside the factory? Can the industrial workplace still provide a stage where a more just politics can be imagined? The position I defend in this chapter is that the workplace, even when it is no longer operational, still holds significance, particularly in a context where work, and its absence, continue to organise social relations and the economy, serving as the ultimate, yet abstract, measure of a person's worthiness.

The three films analysed in this first chapter, *Rêve d'usine*, *Silence dans la vallée* (Marcel Trillat, 2007) and *Les hommes debout* (Jérémy Gravayat, 2011) introduce factories at three different stages of this vanishing process. The first bears witness to the end of industrial activity; the second considers the value of industrial ruins in France's regional landscapes, and lastly the third film follows the gentrification process that converts manufacturing sites into residential neighbourhoods and erases the political struggles of past labouring bodies from the social and geographical fabric of a place. Across these three films, the vanishing workplace is not fashioned into a *lieu de mémoire*, which Pierre Nora describes as 'the ultimate embodiments of a memorial consciousness that has barely survived in a historical age that calls out for memory because it has abandoned it'.[3] Instead, I argue that the three featured vanishing factories become vessels through which living and spectral memories re-actualise a present that is otherwise already in the process of being historicised, 'suppress[ed and] destroy[ed]'.[4] These workers' precarious subjectivity, as well as their chance to reclaim presence, lies, therefore, in the very spaces of disjunction and dislocation that deindustrialisation has generated, spaces that hold possibilities for new kinds of political solidarities.

While the workers in *Rêve d'usine* have remained attached to the *lutte*, the lasting currency of this collective practice seems highly compromised. In the last fifteen years, affects have become more central to a documentary practice historically driven by an action-based dramaturgy. As a result, we observe a greater investment on the part of film-makers in an aesthetic of loss, nostalgia and dislocation. However, in this chapter, these terms will not be seen as markers of resignation and defeat.

As a trope, the vanishing factory calls into question common affects about place, time and community. Considered together, in the sequence that I am laying out across this chapter, these three films certainly manifest their film-makers' nostalgia for a militant praxis, but such disposition should not be confused with nostalgia for past representations. The attention of film-makers to presence, in particular, distinguishes *Rêve d'usine*, *Silence dans la vallée* and *Les hommes debout* from a longing for a lost dramaturgy revolving around working-class activism. Following Svetlana Boym's distinction here, the nostalgic impulse found in these films is not 'restorative': it is, I contend, 'reflective'.[5] 'Reflective' nostalgia stems, in Boym's account, from 'defamiliarization and a sense of distance' that individuals and communities experience when their 'home' has been 'shattered'.[6] She was most directly concerned with the difficult, complex process that Russians underwent to reconstruct their personal and national identities after the collapse of the Soviet Union. Having lived in the United States for a while, she described her experience of returning home and standing by her home 'in ruins or, on the contrary, [having] been just renovated and gentrified beyond recognition'.[7] Notwithstanding the fact that Boym referred to post-Soviet Russia – a specific, and very different, shattered home – her words resonate almost perfectly with industrial workers' experience, as they stand by their factories, empty, in ruins, or in the process of being gentrified. Filming the factory in the process of decaying and fading out of our view plays into this necessary 'defamiliarisation' and 'distance', while maintaining a connection to what its presence still means for the people and locales whose lives and identities have been defined by it.

*Rêve d'usine* films the exhaustion of working-class activism and the erasure of working-class history from our collective memory. *Silence dans la vallée* uncovers one of the many industrial ruins that persist in the social and environmental landscapes of French regions. Meanwhile, *Les hommes debout* audaciously '[re-]awakens multiple planes of consciousness' while tackling the last stage of this effacement, gentrification.[8]   This last film weaves together an 'impure history of ghosts', that of successive generations of migrant labourers called upon to do the dirty work of industrial production or post-industrial reconstruction.[9] In doing so, these migrant workers are perversely charged with doing the work of erasing their own history as workers, or that of their predecessors.

In these films, Luc Decaster, Marcel Trillat and Jérémy Gravayat – themselves representatives of three generations of socially and politically committed documentary film-makers – shift their focus from the event of closure which has dominated mainstream media and, to some extent, social sciences. Conjuring Jacques Derrida, I propose that their films actively 'hauntologise' the prevailing 'discourse of the end' as well as 'the discourse about the end' of the industrial working class.[10] Each film contributes in its own way to a broader narrative that, as Boym suggests in the context of post-Soviet Russia, reflects the immediate response individuals feel, individually and collectively. When confronted with their own loss, the primitive scene of militant cinema, they 'narrate the relationship between past, present and future'.[11] Most significantly, they do so by envisaging 'non-teleological possibilities' and unveiling new, radical 'collective frameworks of memory'.[12]

### Screening industrial decline

Since the 1980s, more French manufacturing sites have closed than new ones have opened, and many production activities have been relocated abroad. In an early 2013 study, Trendeo, a national survey agency specialising in business investments, reported over one thousand locations closed since 2009. Additionally, relocations abroad caused the loss of up to 8.5 per cent of industrial jobs in France during the same time.[13] About five hundred more closures were added in 2013 and 2014, once again exceeding the number of new active sites of production in France.[14] Politicians have not missed an occasion to use this sombre economic trend to score quick victories and publicly exhibit their sympathy with French workers. In 2012, ArcelorMittal's two Lorraine sites in Florange and Gandrange took centre stage in the presidential campaign between

Nicolas Sarkozy, the incumbent president, and François Hollande, who eventually won the election.[15] More recently, in 2017, Marine Le Pen's parking-lot photo op with the employees of Whirlpool in the northern town of Amiens, while Emmanuel Macron was meeting with their representatives inside the factory, made international headlines.[16]

Since the late 1990s, several violent conflicts have opposed the employees of high-profile companies to management – Cellatex and Moulinex (2000–1), Metal Europ (2003), Goodyear (2006–12), Molex, New Fabris, and Continental (2009), and more recently, PSA-Peugeot Citroën (2012) and Air France (2014–16). Over sixty films dedicated to conflicts like the ones listed here, and to many others overlooked by national media, were produced between 2000 and 2010, including *Ex-Moulinex: Mon travail, c'est capital* (2001), *Moulinex, la mécanique du pire* (Gilles Balbastres), *MetalEurop: Germinal 2003* (2003), *Conflit MetalEurop* (2004), *Les Conti, Gonflés à Bloc* (2010), *Molex, des gens debout* (José Alcala, 2010), *Au prix du gaz* (Karel Pairemaure, 2011) and *La saga des Conti* (2012).[17] Still growing, this now established sub-genre of post-1995 French social documentary saw a production peak between 2003 and 2009, a short period during which over forty films were released.[18] Unlike the two-minute video snippets headlining local and national newscasts, these films were typically shot over several months, sometimes years, giving workers and local union representatives a chance to explain at greater length their anger, actions and defiance of politicians, mainstream media, business leaders and, at times, even national union leaders thought to be working in alliance with the government. In the opening sequence of *Au prix du gaz* (2011), for instance, director Karel Pairemaure refers to the New Fabris's 2009 occupation strike in Châtellerault, which took place just a few miles away from his home, as that 'summer's saga'. The use of this phrase, echoing a radio bulletin heard in the background, underlines the broad vulgarisation of labour struggles in mainstream media, and the reduction of months-long social conflicts to background noise and political spectacle.

Aesthetically, film-makers have also had to adjust, and most of these films follow, for the most part, fairly predictable narrative patterns. When film-makers start filming, the conflict is typically under way, workers occupy their factory even though production has already been halted, and union delegates (or, in some cases, representatives of the employees) and management are engaged in negotiations. Film-makers thus have to find ways to render lengthy periods of waiting cinematic, and to maintain some sort of dramatic tension where every struggle is almost guaranteed to conclude with the closing of the factory or its geographical relocation, typically abroad.

Some, like Marcel Trillat in *300 jours de colère* (2002), focus on the chronology of the struggle, alternating between individual interviews and scenes where we can understand the group dynamic (meetings and local actions). Other film-makers have experimented with different modes of characterisation as a way to empower the *ouvriers en lutte*. In *MetalEurop: Germinal 2003* (2003), for instance, Jean-Michel Vennemani cleverly leverages the literary reference to Emile Zola's nineteenth-century social novel, *Germinal* (1885). In 2003, Metaleurop, one of the largest French steel mills, founded in 1894, announced imminent closure, threatening over 800 metalworkers with unemployment in a region already depressed. As his title suggests, Vennemani harks back to a common national literary repertoire to repoliticise Zola's heritage, ironically dismantling the 'apolitical aesthetics of spectacle' displayed in Claude Berri's 1993 film adaptation of the novel *Germinal*, a film commonly cited as an exemplar of the consensually 'reactionary' French heritage cinema of the 1990s.[19] Like Zola, Vennemani concentrates on one family, the Bertrands: Jean-Pierre, forty-eight years old, his wife, their five children and grandchildren. Generation after generation, Metaleurop has been the main employer of the Bertrand family: fathers, sons and now daughters have worked there, so when the foundry closes, the entire family will be affected. Jean-Pierre's determination to fight for his job and the industrial memory of the region conflicts with his wife's resignation. Adapting Zola's late nineteenth-century literary naturalism in modern video-reality style, Vennemani creates a family saga, with dramatic family disputes.

More recent, *Florange, l'acier trompé* (Tristan Thil, 2012) recounts the long political fight of Lorraine's steel workers (2008–12). Drawing from his dual background in graphic design and film-making, Tristan Thil punctuates sequences of recorded footage with animated vignettes that universalise the struggle fought by the steelworkers of ArcelorMittal. Through animation, the struggle gets rehabilitated as what structures these men's actions, and restored as a carefully thought-out political strategy unfolding in seven steps: 1. *révolte*/revolt, 2. *couler*/sink, 3. *veiller*/keeping watch, 4. *agir-réagir*/act-react, 5. *résister*/ resist, 6. *dominer*/dominate, and 7. *esquiver*/dodge. This intermedial weaving of live footage and animation allows the film-maker's narrative impulse to coexist with the personal and collective struggle(s) of Florange's steel workers. In 2014, Thil published *Florange, une lutte d'aujourd'hui*, a BD-reportage or documentary graphic book, inspired by and developed from the materials recorded for the film.

Perhaps too predictably, many documentary films chronicling processes of industrial relocations and dislocation leave us with defeated characters. This trend contrasts with past militant cinema which turned seemingly ordinary workers into popular heroes and heroines, best illustrated in the political becoming of Suzanne Zedet in *Classe de lutte* (Medvekin Besançon, 1969).[20] A few recent films have resisted general assumptions about the hopelessness of work-based struggles, however: *Brukman, une usine sans patron* (Valeria Selinger, 2004), *Les 28 de Morlaix* (collectif, 2010) and *Lutte des FRALIB, 1336 jours de combat* (Plus belles les luttes, 2014) give the spectators happy endings.

Because of its focus on a local conflict between the 294 workers of the Epéda mattress factory and their employer in Mer, a small town located in western France, *Rêve d'usine* resembles many other social documentaries produced during the first decade of the twenty-first century to document the country's massive downsizing of its industrial workforce. Though emblematic of the broad cinematic focus on redundancy plans in the 2000s, *Rêve d'usine* uniquely submits the 'factory closure' sub-genre to self-reflexivity. By revealing the current process of in/visibility affecting working-class struggles in contemporary France, the film foregrounds some fundamental tensions at the core of the social documentary practice: while denouncing the excess of neoliberalism, on the one hand, it stays true to social documentary's commitment to its subjects, their dignity and their subjective affirmation, on the other. What makes this film particularly worthy of attention for the present study is the layering throughout the film narrative of the inevitability of the closure with a powerful spectralisation of the struggle carried out by the soon-to-be-defeated employees of Epéda-Mer.[21] I argue that, through this process, Decaster is able to restore a sense of justice for these workers. *Rêve d'usine* received several awards and was screened at various festivals, before being eventually released in theatres in early 2003 and receiving critical praise in *Cahiers du Cinéma*, *Les Inrockuptibles*, *Le Monde*, *L'Express* and *Télérama*.[22]

## Conjuring workers' struggles: *Rêve d'usine*, or the Dreamed Factory

When a friend informed him of the situation that was taking place at the Epéda mattress factory in Mer, Luc Decaster, who grew up in Saint-Nazaire, a major seaport home of the Atlantic shipyards and a bastion of working-class militancy, packed up his camera and spent six months inside the idling factory filming. In April 2000, after months of failed legal actions and stalled negotiations, the employees of Epéda-Mer resolved to vote almost unanimously to end their struggle, accepting the terms of their layoffs and the financial compensations offered to them. Despite its record productivity levels, the site closed for good. The machines were removed and most likely transferred abroad to another factory owned by Slumberland, the multinational company which had acquired Epéda just a few months before the decision to close the company's original site in Mer was announced.

The film's cinematography and editing strategies carefully encapsulate the surreal quality of these workers' situation. Facing the absence of interlocutors, they stay focused on establishing their presence in the workplace. Despite dwindling orders, they return back to the factory, every day for months, until their defeat is undeniable. Except for a few scenes and the final dissolve already mentioned, Decaster's camera remains inside the assembly rooms, where he films employees left to kill time: some knit, some chat, others discuss the ongoing situation and share their concerns about the future. Little time is spent on making mattresses. Management intentionally slowed down production, so their strike fails to create meaningful disruptions of the production process. The theatricality of the struggle, as it was established in past militant films, is, therefore, completely reversed. Fighting to stay in the global system of productivity instead of challenging it, these workers' *lutte* leaves them caught in between two temporalities, two theatricalities.

In the second half of the film, two executives finally show up at the factory to meet with the workers, after having ignored their request for weeks. The visual and narrative progression of the scene uncannily recalls the political drama of *Citroën-Nanterre*, a militant film directed by Guy Devart and Edouard Hayem in 1968. In this earlier film, we can see the director of the Citroën factory in Nanterre walk through the picket line, entering the workplace controlled by the workers. A confrontation ensues, with leftist students and union representatives joining in the heated discussion to point out that immigrant workers face pressures and discriminations by both union representatives and management. Most of the scene consists of arguments and disagreements between the site director and his 'factory cops' (that is, the supervisors and administrators), and representatives of the labour force, unions and student activists. The workers on strike hardly get to speak for themselves in that scene, their voices covered by union representatives' and leftist students' voices. In 1968, ideological conflicts were carefully staged, and roles strictly defined; the extent to which film-makers rendered the tensions on the ground visible, as *Citroën-Nanterre* illustrates, enabled them to build a distinctive dramaturgy for militant cinema. *Rêve d'usine* reveals, at least as far as the employees are concerned, a desire to replicate similar confrontations, if only to get answers from M. Guérin: 'Why? Why? But why?' one employee pleads. 'Do you have any children who are unemployed M. Guérin?', another asks. They never do.

Months after the events depicted in *Rêve d'usine*, Decaster returned to Mer and shot a short film. It consists exclusively of long takes crawling along the empty walls and rugged floors of what used to be a factory.[23] In the audio commentary to these images, Decaster and his producer, Anne Toussaint, discuss his intentions for *Rêve d'usine* and the political impact of his cinematography and editing choices. Toussaint explains that, in her opinion, the whole film revolves around the notion of confrontation, reiterating a fundamental principle of militant cinema. She considers the scene between Josiane, surrounded by her colleagues, and M. Guérin, to be central to the film's dramaturgy. Slightly bothered, Decaster rejects this focus on confrontation. He adds that he similarly cut shots of crying workers, to avoid facile melodrama. In his view, such images undermine the political force of the film.

For Audrey Mariette, *Rêve d'usine* is about the end of the working class, poised between a past that is lost and a future that will no longer be. It thus conforms to *l'événement-fermeture*, a central trope of French documentary production in the early 2000s.[24] In another reading of the film, Samia Moucharik remarks on the film's split temporality and its significance regarding the workers' subjectivity. She thus argues that Decaster's presence with a camera permits the 'coexistence' of three present times – the closure, the struggle, the workers' pursuit of normalcy, a sign that they are collectively in denial of the situation. Her conclusion that the factory is the only place where this process of subjective affirmation can take place is, however, highly problematic when we consider that such struggles are already foreclosed in the future. Instead, I propose that we consider Decaster's cinematic emphasis on the stretched-out vanishing of this industrial workplace as a way to capture these workers' spectral *presence*.

In the final sequence of the film (see Figs 2–4), these workers' dream – preserving their workplace as an active site of production – literally evaporates in front of our eyes. Through this final dissolve, Decaster directly draws attention to cinema's role in what Jackie Clarke has described as 'the new forms of working-class invisibility' in French politics and the media since the 1980s:[25]

> [N]ot only has industrial labour ceased to occupy the place it had in politics and the media [...] but the new representations of workers and factories that have come to the fore, notably in the coverage of factory closures, often operate in such a way to elevate these people and places to a time and space outside the contemporary social world [...] it is not because there are no factories left that industrial labour is less visible in France; rather, it might be argued the discourse that consigns factories and those who work in

them (or used to work in them) to the past is itself one of the most common mechanisms by which a *France ouvrière* that does exist is conjured away before our eyes.[26]

Initially following the dismantling of the machines inside the assembly rooms, Decaster eventually repositions the camera on the outside, at a distance from the factory. Our eyes can catch the company's slogan, 'Je veux mon Epéda!' (I want my Epéda) painted across the back of a truck parked on the left side of the frame. At this point in the film, this exclamation sounds ironic as we have witnessed these workers' struggle fail to keep the factory open. On several occasions, we hear them refer to the factory as theirs: 'Cette usine, c'est nous, c'est *notre* usine!' (This factory, it's us, it is *our* factory); 'On était chez nous en fait! On était chez *nous*!' (It was our home! It was *our* home!). Notably, editing produces a subtle disjuncture between the consumer's individuality (highlighted in the slogan, 'Je veux mon Epéda!'/'I want *my* Epéda!') and the workers' collective identification with their factory (This was *our* factory; *our* home).[27]

Had it stopped there, *Rêve d'usine* would be just another film that documents the sadness and resignation of workers facing yet another factory closure. But it continues. As we hear the first voice-over comment – 'On était chez nous en fait! On était chez *nous*!' – the image of this factory, still filmed slightly at a distance, starts disappearing very slowly into a white dissolve. After several minutes, the materiality of the image has washed away into a uniformed flat tint. Contrary to fades-out to black that commonly signal an end or an abrupt transition, the white dissolve accentuates the long, drawn-out process that workers experience, and makes the vacuity they endure residually palpable. As the image becomes increasingly hard to discern, a male voice-over explains that starting from scratch again is hard. It belongs to an employee of Epéda, who, after the factory in Mer closed – that is, in a visually unrealised future at this point of the film – found a new manufacturing job. This ageing worker does not refer to physical pain, however. His testimony points to the humiliation of resetting his career (twenty-five years' worth of work), of not feeling challenged in his new job and of simply waiting it out until he can retire with a full pension. His last

Figures 6–7. Employees of the Epéda factory, *Rêve d'usine* (Luc Decaster, 2003) © Courtesy of 24Images.

few injunctions, for himself and others in the same situation, are to 'hang on' and 'fight mentally'; but these words fail to fully overcome the feelings of dispossession and insecurity that his testimony conveys. Only after he has finished talking does the screen go dark.

By the end of the film, this last image of dissolution invites the viewer to see the prologue of the film anew, turning the film's narrative into a reflexive time warp. The first minute of *Rêve d'usine* showcases the actual work performed by these employees; the camera, extremely mobile, films as close as possible to their hands, highlighting the precision and efficiency of well-rehearsed skills. An employee's voice-over comments, 'we'd got the message: "do better than the competition!"' The fast-paced sequence offers the spectator a quick, efficient summary of the multi-step process involved in the manufacturing of a quality mattress. Other voice-over captions iterate these workers' pride in the company's productivity and their own *savoir-faire*. Seen separately, this first minute and a half could easily be mistaken for an industrial film commissioned by Epéda or Slumberland to promote their brand, 'the world's leading mattress manufacturer!' – the voice-over of an employee exclaims. Suddenly, this well-oiled machinery is brought to a stop, and Decaster's fast-paced editing switches to longer still shots, revealing human faces and bodies standing behind machines brought to a standstill (see Figs 6–7).

The only reminder of the production process at this point comes from the soundtrack: non-synchronous sounds of gearwheels producing and turning metallic coils. These men and women face the camera, holding the spectators' gaze for as long as they can. Finally, the camera starts to pan slowly to the right, revealing piles of unfinished mattresses and coils accumulated in the warehouse. The sound of machinery is now replaced with thumping sounds. This prologue ends with a slow-motion, low-angle circular leftward pan of the employees, who stand before us as a collective presence (see Fig. 6). Congregated together, they stare at the camera silently, with stern looks on their faces.

In filming these workers present in their factory, Decaster significantly stages, as early as the prologue, the possibility for this *presence* to acquire a spectral quality, and as such, to raise the question of social and economic injustice as a fundamental lacuna of late-closure narratives. The political force of these human bodies' silent, spectral presence is reinforced by the final cinematic erasure of the industrial workplace. What we can now see in retrospect are not workers staring at us but the spectres of these workers. Indeed, this sequence acquires a Derridean quality as 'presence is enjoined, ordered, distributed in the two directions of absence, at the articulation of what is no longer and what is not yet'.[28] The workers' cinematic presence and their present struggle are in that very moment conditioned both by the absence of work and the lack of recognition for their value as workers, and by the future erasure of the factory and their own selves from this location and, more broadly, our collective social and political imaginary.

In *Specters of Marx* (1994), Jacques Derrida distinguishes the spectre from a spirit. The spectre, he says, is 'a paradoxical incorporation, the becoming-body' of a spirit.[29] But most significantly, the spectre is 'this thing [that] meanwhile looks at us and sees us not see it, even when it is there'.[30] Of course, in *Rêve d'usine*, this non-reciprocity of the gaze operates at different levels. In the context of the neoliberal enforcement of optimal profitability and perpetual growth, workers are reduced to figures – shadowy, abstracted silhouettes and statistics – for employers who do not see them, often because they themselves are absent from the scene. Mainstream media outlets focus on big-impact news. In September 1999, Michelin's decision to lay off several thousands of employees across Europe, for instance, caused an uproar in France.[31] In response, several senators proposed a motion to amend the French Labour Code and protect employees from redundancies that would be prompted by a company's liability to its shareholders' contractual return on investment, and not by financial urgency.[32] The fate of the 294 employees at the Epéda factory in Mer was the consequence of a similar business strategy, but they failed to receive attention in the media. Luc Decaster decided to film this more modest struggle because he wanted to cast light on the many micro-events that go unnoticed every day.[33]

The spectrality effect created in the opening sequence of *Rêve d'usine* promotes a 'spectral asymmetry [that] interrupts here all specularity' – as well as the possibility for identification and empathy – between the film's subjects and the spectators.[34] If we follow

Derrida, *Rêve d'usine*'s disjoining of workers' and spectators' subjective experiences paradoxically opens up a space where these workers can receive justice. For Derrida, justice can only be true when it operates outside a teleological understanding of history, thus taking the form of a gift that thwarts economies based on exchange, retribution, restitution or reparation.[35] Justice is about time, about offering the gift of presence independently from a predetermined framework, narrative or horizon of expectations. As is the case for Derrida, justice in Decaster's film is not, cannot be and will not be about giving this factory back to these workers. Instead, the film-maker provides these men and women with space and a time that do not historicise them, memorialise them or assign them to a (new) social, economic or political place at the very moment that they face their own 'impossible state of being'.[36] In the past, militant cinema aimed at abstracting political icons, producing subjects that embodied class consciousness. The possibility for economic and social justice, embedded in Decaster's disjunctive cinematography, realigns his film-making praxis with a militant gesture grounded in the ethos of justice, but it also unwaveringly rejects the ideological dogmatism that militant film-makers endorsed in the 1960s.

Contrary to Mariette's claim that, in the early 2000s, documentary cinema reduced workers to tragic characters to benefit a broader critique of neoliberalism, Decaster's cinematography signals a continued commitment to maintaining these subjects' precarious agency.[37] By thwarting the *événement-fermeture*, Decaster escapes the dominant narrative economy that erases these persons as it prescribes the extinction of the working class as inevitable. Instead, his film grants them representation as characters in a cinematic narrative. In other words, by means of this spectral asymmetry, which 'de-synchronises' and 'recalls us to anachrony', *Rêve d'usine* redirects the 'factory closure' narrative by substituting the 'aneconomic gift of presence' for a closed logic of rupture between past and future.[38] Rather than simply affirming the 'end' of a working-class narrative, as Mariette sees it, this analysis emphasises the friction that Decaster creates in the last minutes of *Rêve d'usine* between a teleological narrative, punctuated by the final black screen and very factual conclusions, and a temporal suspension

that enables the spectral presence of these otherwise already
forgotten and invisible bodies and voices to reveal themselves to
the viewers, as such. Here, the vanishing workplace acts as the site
of a cinematic resistance against a teleological impulse that negates
these workers' present being. Luc Decaster's successful attempt to
reclaim the affirmative power of disjunction is obviously contingent
upon the film's editing and its narrative construction. While *Rêve
d'usine* de-materialises the self-sufficient, contained industrial space,
*Silence dans la vallée*, which I consider in the next section, markedly
reterritorialises it. This film, by veteran film-maker Marcel Trillat,
deeply roots the loss of the working class in a memorial landscape
that resists fixity.

## Industrial landscapes in *Silence dans la vallée*

Marcel Trillat's 2007 documentary film *Silence dans la vallée* takes
place in the Ardennes, a region in north-eastern France that borders
Belgium. Well-known for its steel mills, the region still accounts
for 30 per cent of France's foundries, despite numerous factory
closures in recent decades.[39] This film takes us to Nouzonville,
a small town of no more than 7,000 residents and, until the late 1970s,
a major industrial hub for steel manufacturing. In 2006,
Nouzonville's last foundry, Ateliers Thomé-Génot went bankrupt,
shortly after being purchased by an American hedge fund. Its last
317 employees were left jobless. The closing of ATG – founded in
1863 by two local blacksmiths – marked a symbolic turn for the
region's industrial history.

Though *Silence dans la vallée* is concerned with factory closures,
the film does not present them as an event in and of itself. Instead,
it successfully underscores the dismantling of an entire 'geosystem'
– geographer Simon Edelblutte uses this term to describe the
integration of several geological and geographical elements into a
coherent composite.[40] The temporal disruption that *l'événement-
fermeture* assigns to a single factory is here spatialised; history
becomes geography. A similar dynamics structures and supports the
original, coherent spatial system that organises industrial towns
around the factory. An economic engine, the latter also acts as the

social heart of the valley. Back in the late nineteenth and early twentieth century, industrial capitalists embraced their roles as paternalistic benefactors for their local communities.[41] Marcel Trillat's documentary narrative reconstructs the industrial 'geosystem', by imbricating three distinct sites obeying different temporalities. Each factory is carefully embedded within the topographical limits of the factory-valley circumscribed in the opening aerial shot (see Fig. 5).

This chapter previously examined the closing factory, as depicted in *Rêve d'usine*, as a disjointed experience unfolding in three coexistent present times. This section considers the temporal scission that structures *Silence dans la vallée*. The first location we visit early in the film closed in 1996 after a brief takeover by Italian investors and is now an abandoned wasteland. The second, the Aciéries Thomé-Génot (ATG), is now a contested site, legally and physically. Verdicts from the lawsuits against the US holding company that took over before declaring bankruptcy are still pending. Meanwhile, former employees continue to clash violently with police forces sent to protect the buildings and machinery. Finally, the film-makers go to Ateliers Arthur Clausse, a small stamping foundry down the river that appears to be doing fine at the time of filming.[42] Tracking the vanishing workplace across these three separate sites and timelines, *Silence dans la vallée* draws a composite view of industrial decline, entwining past, present and future to depict the vanishing *vallée-usine* and roots the struggle of the ATG employees to receive financial compensation from their former employer and denounce their mismanagement in a nexus of geographical, historical and cinematic topoi.

Born in 1940, Marcel Trillat's film career and political activism bridge the militant cinema of the 1960s and the revival of social documentary from the 1990s onwards in a prolific body of work.[43] His films bore witness to both the triumph and the demise of the French working class, from the controversial *Le 1er mai à Saint-Nazaire* (with Hubert Knapp, 1967) to the trilogy *300 jours de colère* (2000), *Les prolos* (2002) and *Femmes précaires* (2005), released at the turn of the century. In 2011, Trillat collaborated with his friend Maurice Failevic on *L'Atlantide, une histoire du communisme* (2011) and, in 2014, he gave his 1970 militant film, *Etranges étrangers*, a

Figure 8. The industrial geosystem. *Silence dans la vallée*
(Marcel Trillat, 2007) © Courtesy of Jean Bigot and Marcel Trillat –
VLR Productions.

modern-day sequel with *Des Étrangers dans la ville* (2014). In *Silence dans la vallée,* Trillat returns to a more traditional industrial milieu, geographically and sociologically rooted in late nineteenth- and early-twentieth-century industrial paternalism. He follows the decline of regional entrepreneurial dynasties and the rise of amorphous, transnational corporate investment shareholders to reveal this changing landscape's social and economic violence.

*Silence dans la vallée* opens with a long aerial take, set to the sound of Marc Lublat's accordion score, flying us over Nouzonville, nestled along the sinuous banks of the Meuse river and surrounded by the hilly and woody terrain of the Ardennes (see Fig. 8). As the camera gradually travels away from the river up the hill, Trillat offers a voice-over homage to the generations of steelworkers who have lived and worked in this dense, green and rolling landscape: 'They have forged steel since Henry IV's times in the heart of the Ardennes' woods. They manufactured connecting rods for the Republic's trains, gearwheels for combine harvesters, alternators for our cars. They were the blacksmiths of modernity.'[44] In just a few sentences, the film-maker traces a centuries-old lineage of artisans – blacksmiths, metal and steelworkers – whose craft and skills have served the development of so many other industries, from farming to transportation. His use of the phrase 'forgerons de la modernité' (the blacksmiths of modernity) at the end echoes the nation-building metaphors commonly used in early militant films, particularly in the Ciné-Liberté trilogy: *Sur les routes d'acier* (Blaise Peskine, 1937), *Les Métallos* (Jacques Lemare, 1938) and *Les Bâtisseurs* (Jean Epstein, 1938).[45] Margaret C. Flinn traces these films' influence on the social construction of the working class as a collective body during the 1930s in *The Social Architecture of French Cinema, 1929–1939*, highlighting the cohesive role trade unionism and industrial paternalism played at the time.[46] Using the example of *Les Métallos*, she shows how the workplace and workforce were fused into one symbolic entity in the film's credits, as the title referring to the corporation espouses the contours of the factory.[47] *Silence dans la vallée* goes against this grain, ending with the dissolution of the local social fabric rather than its construction. By the end of the film, we are not so much left with a working *class* as with struggling individuals and families slipping into social and financial precariousness and surviving thanks to welfare aid and local charities. Subjects of national pride in the 1930s, metal workers are now disenfranchised, and the factories that granted them a living wage abandoned, reduced to landfill waste.

A sequence at the Aciéries Thomé-Génot immediately follows the opening aerial survey of the valley (see Fig. 8). A squad of policemen in riot gear guards the foundry's front gate. A few more shots of the office buildings and the courtyard reveal substantial material degradations, more police presence, and picketers whose faces convey despair and resignation, more than anger at this point. Following this quick introduction of the tense local situation, Trillat visits the Dury family. They owned the closing factory until they sold their shares to a US hedge fund in 2004. The conversation provides some useful context about the region's economic history and its social structure. As we leave the Dury family, the film cuts to a view of the woods overlooking Nouzonville before a downward camera pan brings us back downtown, where Marcel Trillat meets with the current left-wing mayor. The shot reveals large construction projects in progress in the background – street renovations, new buildings going up and widened pedestrian areas. Trillat asks the mayor to recall his memories of the town from when he was a child, at which point a black and white photograph of the local industrial skyline appears on the screen. The soundtrack layers his voice over sounds of sirens and drop-forge hammers, which he remembers as constant at the time. More archival black and white photographs show workers standing in front of one of the 'forty-to-fifty factories' that used to be open around Nouzonville alone. He explains that, instead of competing, the smithies worked cooperatively, serving each other's material needs and supporting each other's long-term survival. These photographs, dating back to the early twentieth century, judging from the women's dresses, give evidence of a bustling town, where workers crowded the streets and train platforms – an image that contrasts with present-day Nouzonville, where over a thousand industrial jobs have been lost in thirty years.

The film quickly exceeds the narrative constraints of a film documenting a factory closure, devising a subtle and complex local geo-politico-aesthetics centred around the valley. If other films have highlighted industrial valleys in decline, the originality of Marcel Trillat's film lies in its cinematic replication of the industrial geosystem.[48] As early as the first shot, the Ardennes valley and its vanishing industries are presented as a site to be remembered, its topography reshaped into an affective landscape. For Simon Edelblutte, the sudden 'landscapisation' of industrial regions, starting in the late 1980s–early 1990s, coincided with the acceleration of industrial decline across the country.[49] As local identity and community integrity came under threat, attachment to the local landscape compensated for the loss of a tightly ordered and organised spatial system centred around the factory. With the transition from industrial paternalism to financial capitalism, social support structures (housing, childcare, health services) were dismantled, which further exacerbated the loss of economic revenues for individuals and local municipalities already diminished by the interruption of all production activities. Yet, the film's cinematography maintains the valley as a geographical system, reshaping it as a subjective landscape as its material reality disappears.

Just a few minutes into the film, a long leftward lateral travelling reveals the old Thomé-Crombacq foundry; filmed from across the river, the shot emphasises the monumentality of this abandoned factory. Marcel Trillat's voice-over resumes: 'Standing on the side as we approach the town, a ghostly foundry inhabited by the memories of five or six generations of workers, now entirely given over to time's effects.'[50] This introduction turns the industrial wasteland into a perfect *lieu de mémoire*, a place where the singularity of personal memories and collective history become one and the same. However, the following two interview sequences, filmed on the disused grounds, gradually move us from history to memory, from the often glorified past of industrial paternalism, the matter of institutional patrimony, to a more recent past, difficult to remember without feeling resentment, bitterness and pain. Slight variations in the cinematography across both sequences endow the vanishing workplace with a dual aesthetic value; it simultaneously appears as a vestige of the past and the still life of present economic spoliation.

Filming in these abandoned grounds, Marcel Trillat meets two men successively. Didier Bigorgne, born in Nouzonville and the son of steelworkers, is now a historian specialising in nineteenth- and twentieth-century social and political working-class movements. Eric Baudun, who grew up in Nouzonville in a family of steelworkers, owns a local pizzeria. Before getting into the restaurant industry, he worked at the Thomé-Crombacq foundry for several years until it closed in 1996 – at the time, he was also a union representative. Quite similar at first glance, these two juxtaposed scenes nonetheless reveal different emphases. The staging of Didier Bigorgne's interview is static for the most part. Cued by Trillat's questions – which we hear off-frame – the historian and local native focuses primarily on his recollections of the family history, his parents' working conditions, as well as the social role the factory system played in providing for the workers' families (summer camps, generous pensions, rewards and recognition for meritorious workers). Workers, supervisors and the boss were all a part of a symbolic community, from childhood to retirement. Both Didier Bigorgne and Mrs Dury, who oversaw the transition from a paternalist mode of management to the investment-driven foreign takeover with her sons, recall that class struggles and political divergences were central, though a non-issue, to the functioning of the local 'geosystem'. In his interview, Didier

Bigorgne recalls: 'I remember that my father had a lot of respect for his boss, which did not prevent him from complaining, but that was part of the class struggle' (8"34). Later, Marcel Trillat and Mrs Dury have the following exchange:

> — Among these supervisors, some were very far from you politically. They were rather 'red', as one would say, it didn't bother you?'
> — Ah, not at all! [...] Absolutely not. You know in Nouzonville, we would not talk to many people if this was a problem (*laughter*).' (Marcel Trillat and Claudie Dury, 30"19–31"02)

Black and white photographs from Didier Bigorgne's family archive, illustrations supporting his recollections, reinforce his reminiscences of a bygone era defined by the convergence of a locally invested industrial paternalism, working-class solidarity and social-minded Catholicism. In 1938, these same markers of social progress (social security, health provision, vacations, professional development, children's programmes, cultural associations) were already celebrated as major victories of organised trade unionism in films such as *Les métallos*, the twenty-three-minute militant documentary commissioned by the metal workers' CGT union and produced by Ciné-Liberté. Seventy years later, the workers' struggles seem all but erased in a history that remembers a benevolent form of capitalism promoted by the local bourgeoisie, calling for the end of a cycle and neutralising the political significance of class struggles as anecdotal workplace politics.

The second interview with Eric Baudun is more mobile than Didier Bigogne's: the camera follows Trillat as he wanders across the old industrial site. Along this walk, Baudun shows us around what used to be his old workplace, pointing at what used to be where. This peripatetic return to the remains of the factory echoes other films, including *Ex-Moulinex: Mon travail, c'est capital* (Marie-Pierre Brêtas, Raphaël Girardot, Laurent Salters, 2000) and *Plan social: et après* (Laurent Lutaud, 2010), where former employees visit their old workplace, in the company of film-makers.[51] Typically, the subject's recollections, spontaneously shared with the film-maker and the audience as they come up along the way, fill up the empty/emptied space. For a brief moment, the viewers get access to an absent yet embodied factory that symbolically shapes up as former workers share their intimate knowledge and living memories of the place.

Baudun seconds Didier Bigorgne's emphasis on steel workers' collegiality and pride in local *savoir-faire*, but his testimony addresses the transition that occurred in the late 1980s–early 1990s more directly. The nostalgic undertone of the first interview gives way to a strong resentment against foreign investors' condescending attitudes to the workers, a sentiment echoed in many films documenting redundancy plans and closures.[52]

> — We didn't know how to work, in their mind … In the end, they showed nothing at all. They left with the manuals, blueprints, licences … but they also left with … '
>
> — … the savoir-faire?'
> — Exactly, they took everything from us! They took everything!'
> — And the customers as well?'
> — Ah, everything, even our dignity, when I say everything, it's everything. They had us good, slowly, gradually. But they got us. But anyway, their goal was not to invest money here; what they wanted was to steal. That's it!'
> (Eric Baudun and Marcel Trillat, 13"19–13"56)

These concluding remarks indict the symbolic and actual violence that a now anonymous, internationalised capitalism, and the geographical dislocation it caused, exert at a local level. Italian investors are doubly marked as foreign. First, they embody the introduction of international financial interests within the national and regional economies. Second, and most importantly, they are foreign insofar as they failed to understand local social values which, for decades, cemented the base of a productive relationship (though one certainly not devoid of compromises) between the local industrial bourgeoisie and the working class.

The shift is perceptible in the subtle variations that affect the visual *mise en scène* of the vanishing workplace across both sequences. Though Marcel Trillat adopts a conventional set-up to film Didier Bigorgne's interview (medium shots, with the decrepit buildings visible in the background), close-up travelling shots crawling along rusty, crumbling walls and cracked windows confer upon this sequence a muted poetic quality that reflects and enhances the affective value of this decommissioned factory. The earthy colour palette and delicately textured surface of images of gently rippling water reflections of metal structures and blurred stems quivering in the foreground turn these industrial waste sites into organic matter. As time passes and nature starts reclaiming the grounds, the industrial wasteland morphs in front of our eyes into a landscape.

At the end of this first testimony, a travelling shot, moving laterally to the right this time, along a retaining wall covered with graffiti murals, reconnects this memorial landscape to the present town sitting above road level. There, we meet Eric Baudun, the former Thomé-Crombacq employee, working in the kitchen of his restaurant, before quickly returning to the Thomé site with him. In this second sequence, the use of wider landscape shots paradoxically de-naturalises the industrial landscape previously constructed for us. Hard lines, material degradations and gutted structures replace the organic texture and colours visually enhanced in the first sequence. We are now contemplating the scene of the wreckage, the leftovers of global capital's spoliation of Nouzonville's industrial identity and heritage, while regional commuter trains, built with parts once manufactured in that foundry, pass by, oblivious of the spectacular obsolescence of industrial manufacturing.

As France undergoes a rapid and massive industrial decline, closing and closed factories become de facto *lieux de mémoire* of 'the memorial heritage of [the French industrial working class]'.[53] If we adopt Pierre Nora's conception, this visual recurrence of industrial wastelands and disused factories in recent French social documentary films reinforces a general 'sense of rupture with the past'. However, the juxtaposition of the two testimonies recounted in the previous paragraphs problematises Nora's *lieu de mémoire*. Contrary to the *événement-fermeture*, the vanishing workplace presents itself as a place that can be revived as a *milieu de mémoire,* if only it were not fossilised by a 'rather teleological view of modernity'.[54] The persisting influence of such a view on Nora's nonetheless 'innovative rewriting of the French past from a non-linear, "site-specific" perspective' is, for Michael Rothberg, a highly problematic and hindering aspect of the *lieux de mémoire*.[55]

*Silence dans la vallée* insists as much upon the geographical dimension of the vanishing workplace as *lieu de mémoire* as it does upon the 'play' Pierre Nora underlines between 'memory and history'.[56] *Lieux de mémoire*, Nora claims, are produced in reaction to 'an acceleration of history'. In Marcel Trillat's film, this acceleration unquestionably collides with a rapid deceleration of the same modernity that steelworkers helped set in motion and pushed further for centuries. In other words, it is as a symbol of 'depressive modernity' that Trillat recasts the vanishing workplace as *lieu de mémoire,* not as a reflection of its triumphant past as Nora's interpretation would define it. Jani Scandura uses the phrase 'depressive modernity' to identify a subjective experience of modernity at times, such as the Great Depression in the United States, when 'modernity [is] in and out of place, therefore does not refer to a separate strain or oppositional modernity; instead, it might best be seen as modernity at a standstill.'[57] This 'depressive modernity', she writes, 'is the lived and symbolic reality of a modernity that idles; like an idling car, like a video on a still, it moves neither forward nor backward, but shimmers in place.' Scandura adds, 'a depressive mindset acknowledges […] the melancholy of not being able to forget' and '[a depressive location] is not just [a location] that remembers; it is [a location] that is haunted by and produced spectrally through an inability to forget that has been.'[58] Poised in such a way between the past and the present, progress and idleness, this 'depressive modernity' contradicts any discourse that relegates this industrial heritage to the past and ignores the presence of industrial workers out of convenience.

As in Luc Decaster's *Rêve d'usine*, the vanishing workplace once again serves in *Silence dans la vallée* as a vessel through which the film-maker acknowledges the historically negated presence/present of once *modern* subjects while coming to terms with documentary film-making's role in their negation. Trillat and Decaster similarly mobilise the vanishing workplace to highlight the critical limits of the 'factory closure' narrative. Their practice is invested in keeping workers' struggles and narratives alive and relevant in the current political context. However, both films can arguably only go as far as to suggest the possibility of restoring the vanishing workplace as a *milieu de mémoire* to save it from its historical negation. The dual aesthetic value the vanishing workplace acquires in the film gestures, without fully engaging with it, towards Svetlana Boym's attention to the temporal fluidity of nostalgia and its grounding in the 'loss of collective frameworks of memory'.[59] *Silence dans la vallée* promotes a meditation on the subjective spatiality of history; but much as it transcends the teleological determination of the *événement-fermeture*, the aesthetic experience of 'collective devastation' that we are given to see unfortunately fails to revitalise this memorial landscape into something more than a 'shattered mirror' of what the valley represents for this community.[60]

In *Les hommes debout* (Jérémy Gravayat, 2011), the last film discussed in this chapter, the dislocation of the industrial workplace and its effacement from the urban landscape are almost complete. Situated in the heart of the Gerland neighbourhood, in Lyon, the Peñarroya factory, a notorious symbol of immigrant labour exploitation in the early 1970s, is undergoing demolition and will soon be replaced with 'a brand-new neighbourhood' – as promised by a giant billboard. Production activities were moved to another town about thirty miles away in the late 1970s. Since then, the Gerland site has been left vacant and unattended, becoming a haven for homeless people, undocumented migrants and transient squatters in the late 1990s and early 2000s. The voices and bodies that our society fails, and often chooses not to hear and see, haunt Gravayat's filmography: migrants braving everything to wind up in the infamous Jungle of Sangatte (*Un autre jour sur la plage*, 2002; *L'Europe après la pluie*, 2006), undocumented immigrants (*Vivre ici*, 2007), and more recently, slum dwellers (*Planches, clous, marteaux*, 2013; *A Lua Platz*, 2019).

In *Les hommes debout*, Gravayat offers us a different kind of hauntology from what we see in *Rêve d'usine* and *Silence dans la vallée*. In lieu of highly localised sites and industrial workers confined to the residual spaces of working-class dramaturgies, the former Peñarroya factory becomes an intersecting point for a multiplicity of trajectories that traverse both space and time. Hauntology and inheritance are intimately connected in the narrative and visual fabric of the film, in which past, present and future, as well as documentary and fiction, continuously intermesh. Unlike the other films that invite us to see the spectral embodiment of a present already made past, *Les hommes debout* 'undo[es]' what Derrida postulates as 'this opposition, or even this dialectic, between actual, effective presence and its other', in other words 'between the specter of the past and the specter of the future, and the past present and the future present'.[61]

## The vanishing factory, a precarious heterotopia in *Les hommes debout*

In 2008, Gravayat spent several months in the Gerland neighbourhood of Lyon as an artist-in-residence at Les Inattendus, a local cultural organisation. For him, the area epitomises the profound economic and social shifts that have affected urban landscapes since the late 1980s.

> Until 1990, there was almost nothing else but factories, workshops and public housing estates in the old working-class neighbourhood of Lyon, Gerland [...] It had become a home for different waves of immigrant workers since the early twentieth century. In the last ten years, public authorities in Lyon engaged a vast urban renewal program to transform the neighbourhood, attract research and educational institutions to the area and build new residential amenities for middle- and upper-class residents. Traces of the neighbourhood's working-class past are slowly getting erased. Therefore, I decided to probe a terrain, in the literal sense of the term, where we could still see a factory, though inactive, and observe how this ground changes and mutates when the factory is demolished and new housing built. But I also wanted to study the different types of people who have worked and lived in this place.[62]

In the film, the materiality of the factory matters less than the stories, voices and bodies that its demolition conjures up.

Doreen Massey dismisses 'synchronic closure', a dominant perspective in historiography and the social sciences in recent decades, as politically unproductive. Space, or 'the spatial', acts, in her view, as a much more useful reconnective tissue that can help regenerate the political texture of time.

> [Synchronic closure] robs 'the spatial' (when it is called such) of one of its potentially disruptive characteristics: precisely its juxtaposition, its happenstance arrangement-in-relation-to-each-other, of previously unconnected narratives/temporalities; its openness and its condition of always being made [...] It is this crucial characteristic of 'the spatial' which constitutes it as one of the vital moments in the production of those dislocations which are necessary to the existence of the political (and indeed the temporal).[63]

Considering Massey's rejection of synchrony in the specific context depicted in *Les hommes debout*, I argue that the film takes a different approach from what is seen in many contemporary social documentary films, as it performs through the featured vanishing workplace a conscious rearrangement of conveniently 'unconnected narratives/temporalities'. As the film gradually reveals, these turn out to be intimately contiguous in time and in a space virtually constructed by cinematic means as heterotopia and defined by 'dynamic simultaneity'.[64] The Peñarroya, as Gravayat reconstructs it, aligns with several of the principles that Michel Foucault assigns to heterotopias in his famous essay 'Of Other Spaces' (1967).[65] Foucault's third, fifth and sixth defining principles are particularly relevant to this analysis. Heterotopias can host 'several spaces, several sites that are in themselves incompatible', they function as 'a system of opening and closing that both isolates them and makes them penetrable', and finally 'their role is to create a space that is other, another real space, as perfect, as meticulous, as well arranged as ours is messy, ill constructed, and jumbled', and serve a function of 'compensation'.[66]

Defying traditional genres, the film continuously crosses over between documentary and fiction, as militant cinema (by way of archival footage) permeates the poetic aesthetic of the essay. Fragmentation and dislocation become dominant narrative and aesthetic principles that intertwine the journeys and histories of three male figures. The first of these characters and, in fact, the only real subject in the film, Amor, worked at Peñarroya-Gerland after he arrived from Tunisia in 1968. There, he also served as a union delegate and was directly involved in the strike of 1972. The other two are fictional characters: a young squatter, a composite character based on stories and testimonies that Gravayat collected from various people he encountered during his residency, and a young migrant of Algerian origin, an entirely fictional creation.[67] Beyond the social experiences these two characters embody, Gravayat gives them symbolic functions in the film. The vagabond, while giving us access to various clandestine spaces, acts as a surrogate for the film-maker and becomes a repository for diverse narratives: a literary excerpt from Kafka's *La Muraille de Chine* (1923); first-person recollections shared by random encounters with marginalised individuals, including Roma people, undocumented immigrants and squatters; and official narratives, including an eviction notice requiring all squatters to vacate the premises before demolition is ordered. Like the watchman in Kafka's story, he and his recording machine bear witness to an invisible presence. As a migrant living clandestinely, the young man's journey recalls Amor's a few decades earlier. Only this time, stable industrial jobs – dangerous and exploitative as they used to be – are no longer available to young men like him. Surviving on day jobs at the Peñarroya demolition/ construction site, he sleeps outside, on the other side of the railway tracks. Like the vagabond, this migrant character serves as a threading device for Gravayat: his voice and endless peripheral ambulations weave together a cinematic material that resists chronological prescriptions and narrative linearity.

As these three men's journeys intersect in and around the now inactive Peñarroya, the factory stands as a centripetal locus through which all these temporalities and journeys converge and reorient one another. Each of these three characters invokes a different temporality: Amor reminisces about the past, the squatter grounds us into the present, while the young migrant appeals to some unrealised future. Immigration, migration and nomadic mobility provide the film-maker with lenses that enable him to restore the centrality of the industrial workplace in a politically committed documentary practice, while gradually dissociating it from traditional working-class teleology. Yet, because their three trajectories are so tightly and inextricably enmeshed throughout the film, no temporality is ever fully asserted. Instead, viewers are constantly maintained in the midst of destabilising tensions between past, present and future that underscore the aesthetic interconnectedness of their experiences.

Triggered by his visit to Peñarroya, Amor's narrative is at once personal and collective, nourished as much by his relationship to the homeland he left in the late 1960s as it is by the 'home' he created with the other immigrant workers he worked and fought with in 1972. This new home that is now 'in ruins', soon to be 'renovated and gentrified beyond recognition', to use Boym's words once again, has little to do with the factory itself, especially the barracks they were assigned to as 'their home' when they arrived.[68] This home is the political community he and other immigrant workers/dreamers built for themselves. Boym continues:

> Collective memory will be understood here as the common landmarks of everyday life. They constitute shared social frameworks of individual recollections. They are folds in the fan of memory, not prescriptions for a model tale [...] National memory tends to make a single teleological plot out of shared everyday recollections. The gaps and discontinuities are mended through a coherent and inspiring tale of recovered identity. Instead, shared everyday frameworks of collective and cultural memory offer us mere signposts for individual reminiscences that could suggest multiple narratives.[69]

There is no intention in *Les hommes debout* to 'mend' a 'teleological' and 'coherent' narrative, be it evocative of national history or a unified working-class narrative. On the contrary, the film seeks to reveal the 'gaps and discontinuities' that tend to be omitted in memorial projects such as Pierre Nora's *lieux de mémoire*.[70] The film's dislocation of working-class culture and industrial modernity produces a new form of memory, conditioned by differentiality rather than identity.

Amor's presence brings up memories of a time marked by the dissolution of the left's grand ideals in the aftermath of May 1968 and imbued with new aspirations on the margins of a social movement remembered by and from its centre.[71] In 1972, inspired by an earlier strike at the Peñarroya factory in Saint-Denis, a suburb of Paris, the workers based in Lyon, mainly immigrants from the Maghreb, sub-Saharan Africa and Portugal, organised with the help of local unions to draw attention to the horrid conditions in which they not only had to work but also live. Social historian Laure Pitti observes that the Peñarroya strike of 1972 remains a seminal moment in the history of immigrant workers' social movements; this event turned immigrant workers into political subjects and, most importantly, their demands critically challenged the direction undertaken by European workers' movements at the time:

> Working conditions, when treating lead, are by definition difficult. In that case, Peñarroya's production sites stand out as being particularly dilapidated [...] [and] labour legislation seems to have been entirely ignored by the company: work-related accidents and professional diseases are under-reported, hygiene and security committees are characterised by utter negligence and inertness.[72]

In 1971 and 1972, Peñarroya workers did not fight for their share in the capitalist system; they did not seek to increase their purchasing power and gain greater access to the range of material commodities newly available to the working classes. They fought for their fundamental rights: to be respected as human beings and paid accordingly, receive basic health protection and decent housing conditions. The Peñarroya strike empowered immigrant workers, but instead of being a sign of integration within the working class, this conflict laid bare persisting differences between the proletarian conditions of these immigrant workers and an increasingly gentrifying French-born working class.

The *Cahiers de Mai* (1968–74), a group of militant film-makers and film technicians formed in the aftermath of May 1968, brought their support to these immigrant workers. Unhappy with the theoretical dogmatism characterising most factions in the radical left of the time (Maoists, Marxist-Leninists, the French Communist Party), this small group of militants, gathered around Daniel Anselme, promoted more innovative forms of actions in workers' struggles, including a greater emphasis upon action committees and militant *enquêtes*.[73] In 1972, Dominique Dubosc, who had joined the *Cahiers de Mai* a few years earlier, collaborated with the workers of Peñarroya and helped them produce *Dossier Peñarroya: les deux images du trust* (1972), a scathing exposé of the company's treatment of their immigrant labour. The film garnered the workers on strike wide-ranging support from local populations, artists and, most importantly, medical professionals, whose involvement had a decisive impact on the positive outcome of the strike. In the late 1990s, Jérémy Gravayat, then assistant to Dubosc, discovered unused footage of this film, which he then included in *Les hommes debout*.

Gravayat's attachment to long-term, immersive residence projects within localised communities reprises, to some extent, some of the guiding principles of the militant tactics mentioned in the previous paragraph, even if his methodology remains devoid of the strict political agenda that informed early 1970s experiments. The recent publication in 2015 of *Atlas*, which Gravayat describes as a *livre-journal*, bears a resemblance to the primary function of the *enquête* – 'initiate or sustain the process of self-formation of the group [in this case, unrecognised residents or inhabitants of La Courneuve near Paris], reinforcing the group's consciousness of its existence as a group'.[74] If the films Gravayat produces in residence are not meant to be 'instruments of propaganda and agitation', he still sees them as 'instruments of liaison', social cohesion and integration.[75]

Though *Les hommes debout* engages more indirectly in what dwelling and inhabiting a place means, one can see how Gravayat invests the vanishing workplace with a clear metonymic function. What interests the film-maker in the evolution of Gerland as a neighbourhood and as an industrial wasteland is less the political consciousness that occurs with work exploitation than the difficult inhabitability and the precarious living that become the everyday condition of immigrants and migrants mobilised by the need to work. About 10–12 minutes into the film, we meet with Amor in front of the old Peñarroya factory. The entire sequence unfolds in black and white. The retired worker guides the camera through what used to be his workplace. In the scene, viewers are subject to several sensory interpellations, repeatedly provoked to move beyond their passive position.

First, before Amor enters the warehouse in ruins, Gravayat de-synchronises the audio and visual tracks: as we watch Amor standing in front of the building (at a slight distance from us, filmed in a medium shot), his voice and footsteps slightly echo, as if he were speaking from inside an empty space:

> Ah, such a good time, yep, it was such a good time! A lot happened, a lot … (*inaudible*). Unfortunately, we were up to our neck in shit! Lead poisoning, everywhere, but I will never forget how much fun we had. Especially with all the friends, we had a lot of fun. We were united, strong, and because of that, we got things done! (*sound of footsteps on the gravel*) (15"05–15"34).[76]

Memories of horrid conditions overlap with more positive recollections of solidarity and friendship.

Shortly after, Amor walks through one of the building's entrances, covered with a plastic strip curtain; once he disappears from our view, a series of several chiaroscuro shots of the inside of the warehouse ensues. This montage unfolds without a voice-over commentary, almost in silence – we can hear a faint background roar when listening carefully. These images, followed by a shaky, low-angle point of view shot of the old metallic roof structure, convey a subjective, quasi-impressionistic view of the inside of the factory: it is as if we saw it through Amor's eyes. The stark chiaroscuro lighting of this montage sequence, which contrasts with the light grey scale of previous scenes, introduces a more cinematic, neorealist aesthetics and places us in a somewhat indeterminate temporality that blends the present state of degradation in which Amor finds Peñarroya (debris, broken windows and glimpses of graffiti suggest this is current time) and the resurfacing of memories of his past work environment. We are quickly submerged in this virtual past when the 13-minutes-long rearranged montage of Dubosc's unused images summons the political rupture achieved by Amor and his fellow workers in 1972 back into the present of the film.

As the film's editing switches to this archival footage, Daniel Anselme's original voice-over commentary gives a factual presentation of the dangerous conditions faced by the Peñarroya workforce. A series of mobile long takes guides the spectators through different rooms, shops and corners of the industrial site. Suddenly, after having listed several cases of work-caused injuries, the commentary stops, letting the spectator read through newspaper clippings, all pieces of evidence of deaths recorded on various sites belonging to the Peñarroya global trust. A letter issued by the CFDT trade union at the time signals that, in response to Peñarroya's carelessness, workers started to organise. Close-up and medium shots document this double process of collective political consciousness and self-affirmation as rightful individuals and workers.

At this point, past and present conjoin again as a voice reads aloud the text that Amor and his colleagues wrote in 1972.[77] The end credits later identify that it belongs to the actor playing the young squatter in present-day Gerland, a delayed clarification that further reinforces this long sequence's symbolic function. This disembodied voice connects the documentary bodies of the past with the precarious voices lacking representation in the present into an endlessly repeating cycle of exploitation, demolition, re/construction. But the sequence does not end here on this audio-visual suturing of past and present and acts of political subjectivation. More archival footage images, commented in Arabic this time, situate the grievances raised by this group of workers within the larger context of the neighbourhood. Scenes shot on the streets surrounding the factory, in local cafés and overcrowded housing, reveal a community consisting exclusively, at least from what we can see, of men of immigrant origins, many of whom had more likely left their families behind hoping to find better opportunities in France. This footage conjures up the neighbourhood as it used to be, inhabited by bodies who were nevertheless already spectralised in the socio-economic context of the time in which these images were recorded.

In the last few rushes gleaned from the past, we can see the collaborative process previously described as the *enquête* and Dominique Dubosc working with Amor and the other workers to edit their *film inséré* (an inserted film). For Dubosc, a militant film is first and foremost political but rarely artistic. *Films insérés*, in particular, reflect the efficient craft of those who make them with a very specific objective in mind:

> [M]ilitant films [...] have little to do with cinema as an art form. On the other hand, I believe they are fundamentally political, meaning they must be rigorously inserted into political actions [...] This is how I define militant filmmaking [...] these films are not the work of an auteur [...] they are made by craftsmen and skilled technicians, who can deliver in time commissioned tools and weapons needed for such and such movement, or strike, for instance [...] As you can see, it has nothing to do with revolutionary rhetoric or some sort of 'big concept'.[78]

Dubosc's distinction between militant film-making and cinema is quite interesting in the light of younger film-makers' reluctance to use the term *militant* to describe contemporary social documentaries. Though not *auteur* films per se, in the way we would describe a film by Alain Resnais or Agnès Varda, recent social documentary films nevertheless display clear aesthetic ambitions. These, as I show and will continue to show throughout this book, are, in fact, crucial to the formulation of political aesthetics of precariousness from the 1990s onwards. In the credits, a second *film inséré* released by Dubosc in 1973, *Peñarroya: comment se mettre d'accord*, is referenced. It documented the preparation and development of the strike, betraying its retrospective editing intervention. Whereas the beginning of the sequence is clearly to be associated with materials shot for *Dossier Peñarroya: les deux visages du trust*, it seems that the rest of the footage comes from the later film.

Figure 9. The gutted factory. *Les hommes debout* (2010)
© Courtesy Jérémy Gravayat.

The sequence ends with slightly more damaged rushes, shown in slow motion, filmed during the strikes by the workers. Images have been resynchronised with a recording of another chanted narration, in Arabic: 'Le Chant des grévistes de Peñarroya Gerland', written and performed by Miloud Amrani and Amor Boughanmi (the same Amor that Gravayat films) in 1972. As the chant ends, a long take, shot from within a car driving around Peñarroya, guides us out, leaving us on a back street. As we switch back from old to new materials – once again signalled by a series of rough cuts and white screens – we find ourselves facing the present construction site (see Fig. 9). Amor was right: 'There is nothing left of Peñarroya!

The aesthetic construction of this extended sequence is exemplary of Jérémy Gravayat's rejection of a synchronic approach to social structures and power relations, which, as we can still see, largely dominate the engagement of social documentary film-makers against inequalities and injustice in the neoliberal context. What is evidenced here, in comparison, is a successful attempt to open up the space of the factory to 'a multiplicity of trajectories and voices' and reimagine what has become a symbol of 'static contemporaneity' into a productive heterotopia.[79] As a space simultaneously reclaimed by the Other (immigrants, migrants, outcasts) and, like so many converted industrial spaces, now almost unrecognisable, Peñarroya is quintessentially heterotopic. If 'multiple transient events [and transient characters] and different temporal narratives' coexist in this memorial heterotopia, they are never romanticised.[80] Here, industrial ruins are not aestheticised; on the contrary, Gravayat insists on this space's 'relational dimension'.[81] The vanishing Peñarroya is displaced and replaced on a peripheral axis where marginalised group memories acquire a universal dimension. The act of remembrance occurs at multiple levels throughout this sequence: personal, collective, lived and cinematically constructed. Yet, its aesthetic impact is first and foremost the result of a phenomenological event: 'the past acts by inserting itself into a present sensation [that felt by Amor during his visit to the dilapidated Peñarroya] from which it borrows the vitality' to resurface and anchor otherwise dislocated experiences and bodies from the present within a 'unifying framework of collective consciousness'.[82] In other words, rather than being a fixed *lieu de mémoire*, the vanishing factory as mobilised in *Les hommes debout* becomes the vector of an active or reactivated memory that is at once specific and universal.

Most importantly, the vanishing factory becomes another space altogether. Peñarroya symbolises the connective tensions between a centralising discourse in the history of working-class militancy and militant/social cinema and a plurality of marginalised voices, particularly those of immigrant workers. Through the constant intermeshing of trajectories resisting complete identification, this film instates the possibility of filiations that are not defined by a common identity to recover but are rather generative precisely because they are a priori disjunctive. Thus *Les hommes debout* is not about reparations and excavating marginalised memories. More ambitiously, this film restores what Kristin Ross saw as the sacrificed spirit of May 1968 in the aftermath of the events: 'a disjunction [...] between political subjectivity and the social group, thus a shattering of social identity that allowed politics to take place'.[83] In *May '68 and its Afterlives*, she is particularly critical of the overemphasis placed on questions of 'religious', 'ethnic and regional' identity in post-war discourses to the detriment of a renewed engagement with 'politics or collective political agency'.[84] Gravayat's film offers one possible answer to Kristin Ross's dismay at post-war 'prevailing theories of social memory and forgetting', though without a renewed investment in 'collective political agency' in traditional working-class politics.

The cinematic interrelations of these three singular journeys forge an 'impure filiation' between 'old immigrant workers' and contemporary 'figures of young homeless vagabonds', and between squatters and undocumented migrants.[85] For Nico Baumbach, impurity and even more so documentary's impurity – as 'the documentary condition of all fictions and the fictional condition of all documentaries' – is one of how a film/a documentary can be political.[86] Here, Baumbach channels Jacques Rancière's position on the relation between cinema and politics: 'the politics of cinema is played out in the relation between the "documentary" principle – observation of autonomous bodies – and the fictional principle of rearrangement of spaces.'[87] In the film, space – especially the spatiality of the vanishing workplace – is produced anew through the diligent work of (cinematic) memory. As it anchors itself in and around the continuously morphing Peñarroya industrial/construction site, *Les hommes debout* introduces a third element in this political dialectic: time.

The politics of cinema as formulated by Jérémy Gravayat is therefore palpable through the aesthetic tensions that are continuously impelled between Amor's 'autonomous body' and the constant rearrangements of spaces and time(s) that the two fictional characters perform and embody. Relentlessly defying generic identification, interlocking documentary and fiction, and folding the essence of militant film-making into experimental visual poetry, Gravayat's careful visual and narrative orchestration of these three characters invites the viewer to reflect on the principles of film politics. The film reclaims the vanishing workplace anew from the perspective of workers displaced or disowned, and presents it as a vast canvas across which the two fictional characters trace a complex network of invisible tracks and routes, revealing new memorial genealogies. Because of that, it acquires a political value that exceeds the limits of the workplace and strictly work-based struggles.

For Dominique Belkis and Michel Peroni, the unusual reliance on fictional devices in *Les hommes debout* is crucial to the film-maker's successful articulation of a critical politics of memory.[88] It is through the presence in the film of 'present-day spectral bodies', they argue, that 'the memory of what took place [in and around Peñarroya]', a memory that has either been forgotten or been consistently erased in the last decades, is simultaneously embodied and freed from restrictive identifications.[89] Once supported by the spectral bodies of the young squatter and the young Algerian migrant, what was once a highly localised and historicised memory is successfully 'disidentified' from a specific context and community (the immigrant workers on strike in 1972) and 'dislocated' from the active industrial workplace. According to Belkis and Peroni, Gravayat brings this about thanks to several 'disidentifying' devices: first, Amor and the young migrant share the same Arabic voice-over, a symbol of the convergence of their nonetheless distinct migratory experiences; second, the task of transmitting collective memory falls onto pariahs, disenfranchised fictional characters (squatters, vagrants, undocumented migrants) rather than legitimised subjects (immigrant workers); and third, the film accentuates gaps, lacks and lapses, meaning that continuity is never a given and needs to be constituted, embodied and reconciled.[90] This faith in the interval as what weaves together the political fabric of the film directly points to Jacques Rancière's definition of cinema as 'a system of differences' and 'intervals', a system that is profoundly aware of its limitations.[91]

In *Les hommes debout*, this contradictory, yet necessary, pull between emancipation, on the one hand, and dissolution, on the other, comes out in the last sequence. As we have seen already, the film turns the working-class narrative around by rebuilding the vanishing workplace as a contradictory place, a trespassed 'home' from the mobile, peripheral vantage points of migrants. This reorientation ends with a direct address made in Arabic by the young vagabond to the audience: 'Toujours la même histoire ... nous rêvons pour vous' (Always the same story ... we dream for you). One could read these last words as some ironic nose-thumbing gesture (particularly given that they are uttered by a fictional character) pointing out the systematic marginalisation of immigrant and migrant voices in dominant working-class narratives. But we could also choose to hear them as an expression of Gravayat's reflective nostalgia, which draws upon immigrants' experiences to 'create a global diasporic solidarity' in place of 'economic globalism'.[92] Belkis and Peroni consider that this dreamer incarnate intervenes here in the quality of a counterfactual agent or subject: his words 'poeticise' more than they 'criticise', 'accuse' or 'demand'; they act as a performative call to reclaim the/our capacity to dream where we are expected to survive.[93]

Heard over a black screen, this last sentence offers a virtual answer to the dissolution of the factory and the working-class collective that ended *Rêve d'usine*. In this last confrontation between the young migrant and the spectator, which creates interdependency between the two, Gravayat's visual strategy 'humanises' a 'we' that has come to identify those typically 'excluded from the perceptual experience of the viewer' in the course of the film.[94] Paradoxically, their humanity is affirmed in a final act of effacement – the screen goes black as we hear the second part of the sentence '*nous rêvons pour vous.*' What ends up being erased is only the fictional representation/embodied personification of a universal migratory trajectory. Fittingly incongruous, these fictional bodies roaming around the construction site and peripheral wastelands could not capture the transient presence of such characters in the vanishing workplace and the social landscape any better. This virtual bridge is contingent upon the film's internal logic, and its full materialisation lies outside. Uttered by a fictional presence, from the fictional present, this sentence, this virtual connection through common dreams, can only suggest a heterotopian encounter between different spectres, those of the past and those from the future, modernity's working class and postmodernity's migrants, displaced labour and gentrifiers, the spectators and actors of social change.

Instead of bringing any resolution, his last words cause even greater uncertainty and ambiguity regarding the viewer's position in the narrative and the remapped territory of Gerland. If *Rêve d'usine* and *Les hommes debout* refer to an intangible dreamscape, they both also leave us pondering on a double disjunction: the unresolvable gap separating and holding together identification and difference, we and you. Gravayat's documentary ethic is not concerned with 'truth' in the most ordinary sense of the word; rather, it posits the precariousness of memory as that upon which the possibility for future, counterfactual political communities unbounded by identity in time and space rests. Like Luc Decaster, he reaffirms documentary cinema's aesthetic commitment to *'justice* (involving representations of conflict, suffering, injustice) and *justesse* (the precise and subtle calibrations of its arrangements of space and bodies)'.[95] As a documentary, *Les hommes debout* fulfils 'the fictional capacity of documentary': 'allow[ing] for new kinds of histories to be told that create new common worlds heterogeneous to official narratives marked by inequality'.[96] Jérémy Gravayat's documentary 'fiction' grounds itself in the constant mobilisation of memory – to be understood here in the most literal sense of the term, namely, setting into physical motion.

Roughly about the same time as Jérémy Gravayat was filming around Gerland, Denis Gheerbrant travelled his camera around Marseille for *La République Marseille* (2009), which I will consider more thoroughly in chapter 5. Adjusted to a slightly broader scale, this multi-part project films the residents of the *cité phocéenne* who have been pushed further into its folds: dock workers, immigrants, former working-class militants, drug addicts, Marseillais of immigrant origins. Nathalie Rachlin views *La République Marseille* as an excellent example of what she calls 'post-global cinema', a cinema no longer bound by neoliberalism and its critique. Instead, she goes on, 'post-global cinema can be defined […] as a cinema that helps us – or perhaps dares us – to look beyond that horizon, inviting us to seize the term "global" from the neoliberal *doxa* [a doxa grounded in a threefold ideology, depoliticisation, individualisation and privatisation] and to redefine it for ourselves.'[97] 'The "proletarian Marseille"' that Denis Gheerbrant produces through his film is 'impossible' and 'a pure product of cinema', Rachlin concludes. Because no actual identification is possible between this new 'we' created and the viewers, the film effectively opens up a space from which vantage point the 'new "proletarian" Marseillais' can speak and become visible.[98] Something similar takes place in *Les hommes debout*, but if Gravayat ends with an impossible identification, he also refuses to let his viewers off the hook. If 'we' are not these two fictional characters introduced in the film, we cannot escape our interdependency and our shared precariousness – which is, like Gheerbrant's newly uncovered/recovered 'proletarian' Marseille, purely cinematic. In Gravayat's project of heterotopic precariousness, Peñarroya is not just another vanishing factory; it is already and has always been a post-global cinematic site. The film constructs a cinematic Peñarroya that transcends all existing referential frameworks typically used to situate ourselves in time and space. Therefore, it can only exist in the (im)possibility of their intervals.

## Conclusion

Rejecting didacticism, Gravayat seeks to make his spectators feel something, to destabilise them and push them out of their comfort zone.[99] To that effect, the viewer is continuously confronted with the ambiguity of the cinematic image and the duality of cinematic bodies. *Les hommes debout* confronts the viewer with a hybrid cinematic narrative that relentlessly outlines centrifugal trajectories, looking outward towards inequalities and heterogeneities. It reclaims energy from the margins of this virtual topography. Instability, precariousness and ambiguity dominate our viewing experience. In *Rêve d'usine*, the precarity of this interface lies in the anachronistic effect of the spectralisation of the workers' presence and the disjunctive non-reciprocity of the gaze between the workers on the screen and the spectators looking through them. Spectrality acts differently in *Les hommes debout*, where it enables the film-maker to weave a cinematic memory that 'accords everyone [in this case migrants and nomadic bodies] the dignity of fiction'.[100] There might not be anything left in Peñarroya, as Amor exclaims, but Gravayat substitutes this material nothingness with documentary fictions that activate a new aesthetic regime of the precarious.

The industrial workplace of political cinema has always been, at least partially, an aesthetic construct – as evidenced by films as varied as *Sortie des usines Lumière* (Louis and Auguste Lumière, 1895), *Strike* (Sergei Eisenstein, 1925), *Modern Times* (Charlie Chaplin, 1936), *Les*

*Bâtisseurs* (Jean Epstein, 1938), *Classe de lutte* (Groupe Medvekine-Besançon, 1969) and, more recently, *Dancer in the Dark* (Lars von Trier, 2000), *Ce vieux rêve qui bouge* (Alain Guiraudie, 2001) and *The Nothing Factory* (Pedro Pinho, 2017). The gradual disappearance of the industrial workplace places militant cinema practices into a sudden state of precariousness. The lasting entwinement of cinematic social and political imaginaries and industrial work explains why film-makers rushed to closing manufacturing sites in the late 1990s. *Rêve d'usine*, *Silence dans la vallée* and *Les hommes debout* offer a different take on factory closures. They question the possible role(s) a film practice, historically defined by its activism in and around sites that are gradually disappearing, can play in the future. These factories transcend their mere physicality, simultaneously becoming allegory and metonymy.

The 'fictional' dimension of documentary cinema has never been more productive than today. As workers and factories disappear from our sight, effaced from society by an irrepressible economic teleology – or so we are told – documentary film-makers film absent/ed subjects. Do Luc Decaster's white dissolve at the end of *Rêve d'usine*, and Marcel Trillat's opening aerial view of the Ardennes valley, imprint a lasting memory of the working class in the viewer's mind? Or do such visual tricks question the social and economic processes that produce their invisibility? Which fiction(s) do we need? Tragic fictions, which, as Mariette suggests, turn the defeated workers into 'characters'?[101] Or documentary fictions, as Jacques Rancière understands them, new 'cartographies' of the social world?[102] *Les hommes debout* almost literally sets into motion this last work, while *Rêve d'usine* disrupts representational logics and the landscapes in *Silence dans la vallée*, memory and deferred justice. A vestige of a lost modernity, the scene of the dislocation of working-class political teleology, the vanishing factory also manifests the original precariousness of the working class. The promise of new filiations, new solidarities and new politics can be found and held in its vacuity.

## Chapter 2
# Global precarity, local struggles

Chapter 2 picks up where chapter 1 ended, with the urgency for both labour struggles and political cinema to 'reinvent a new theatricality', as the workplace becomes an abstract and diffuse reality for an increasingly large number of workers.[1] As I have demonstrated in great detail in the opening chapter, the resurgence of social documentary film-making in France in the late 1990s coincided with a wave of industrial relocations abroad and drastic transformations of employment. The normalisation of interim, subcontracting and short-term contracts, combined with a growing reliance of industrial and service sectors on foreign nationals, has made employees' identifications with a given workplace and the cohesion of co-workers into collective social bodies impossible. With the workplace no longer the site where social conflict between the workforce, represented by its unions, and business leaders, can effectively take place, *la lutte* (class struggle) has become invisible. Additionally, the rapid globalisation of the labour market from the 1990s onwards intensified resentment among the French workforce and public opinion against foreign workers from China, South-East Asia and Eastern Europe recruited by third-party contractors at a low cost.[2] However, Sophie Béroud and Paul Bouffartigue warn that the 'practical consent of migrant workers' to their situation should not be confused with their 'adhesion' to systemic exploitation. Such analysis suggests that what André Gorz and Robert Castel described as a 'non-class of surplus workers' could take a prominent role in reimagining collective actions and labour solidarity in the future.[3]

Sociologists have not been the only ones paying close attention to the globalisation of the French workforce on French soil and its disruptive effects on union activism and the protection of labour rights. Film-makers have been instrumental in uncovering practices that resemble modern forms of enslavement while using cinema to foster new ways to conceive solidarity. The last twenty years have, as a result, seen sociology and cinema become more enmeshed with each other's social and political preoccupations. In France, these shared concerns have resulted in various cross-disciplinary initiatives, such as the creation in 2009 of *Filmer le Travail*, a partnership between the University of Poitiers, l'Espace Mendès-France and the ARACT (Regional Organisation for the Improvement of Labour Conditions). Since 2008, the organisation has hosted an annual film festival featuring documentary films from all over the world on subjects pertaining to labour conditions and rights, struggles and social experiences related to work. Its mission statement insists on three principal objectives, translated here at length into English: (1) *Filmic*, introduce larger audiences to the vast film production dedicated to the question of work, its crucial contributions to documentary creativity and the endless reinvention of its relationship with fiction; (2) *Scientific*, connect this production to ongoing research in the social sciences and their expanding use of film and video as part of scientific inquiry; (3) *Civic*, promote civic engagement and active discussions among the general public about work, its transformations and its future.[4] As chapters 1 and 4 also demonstrate quite specifically, shared concerns for the direct impact of work on our social lives and psychological well-being have invited cross-pollinations between the social sciences and cinema, fostering more complex depictions and understandings of work's political and ethical underpinnings.

Focusing on two economic sectors, shipbuilding and cleaning service industries, this second chapter addresses the aesthetic, political and ethical challenges that French documentary film-makers face as they seek both to document how precarious the reality of such de-territorialised globalised worksites is and present a labour force actively resisting and fighting for justice and recognition. Between 2000 and 2005, three films, *Le dernier navire/The Last Ship* (Moutout, 2000), *Les prolos/The Proletarians* (Trillat, 2002) and *Un monde moderne/A Modern World* (Malek and Soulier, 2005), were filmed at two major shipyards in the north-western French cities of Saint-Nazaire and Le Havre. They reveal an extremely fragmented workplace, with different laws and rules dividing the workforce and allowing shady third-party subcontracting companies to take advantage of migrant workers lacking basic social protections. They also highlight opportunities for a reinvigoration of labour-based politics: we see local union representatives, better informed about French legalities and accustomed to negotiations, and disenfranchised workers from India and Romania forging tactical alliances that successfully get the latter the payments they had been denied for months. Contemporary to films focused on factory closures – a subgenre examined in detail in chapter 1 – *Le dernier navire*, *Les prolos* and *Un monde moderne* offer insightful portraits of a manufacturing sector precariously adapting to address the urgent need for a more dynamic, creative and international labour activism.

Since the early 2000s, the multiplication of small-scale local actions led by undocumented and legal immigrant workers in the cleaning industry around the Paris metro area have raised similar questions. *Remue-ménage dans la sous-traitance/ Upheavals in Subcontracting* (Ivora Cusack, 2002–11), *On est là!* (Luc Decaster, 2012) and *On a grévé* (Denis Gheerbrant, 2014), in particular, have brought attention to these strikes of a new kind. They follow small groups of employees who decide to stand up for their rights, often in concert with local union chapters, despite the precarity of their employment and, for some, immigration status. As such, they provide a good contrast with the militant cinema of the late 1960s. In the cinema of May 1968, immigrant workers mostly appeared as speechless figures.[5] Olivier Barlet considers that the limited visibility of immigrant figures, at the time, 'serve[d] a cause'; they 'embodi[ed] a slogan, "French and immigrant workers, united!" – a slogan repeatedly written on posters and graffiti and sung in every single protest at the time'.[6] Even in the early 1970s, films such as *Etranges étrangers/ Strange Strangers* (Frédéric Variot and Marcel Trillat, 1970), *La grève des ouvriers à Margoline/ Margoline workers' strike* (Cinélutte,1973) and *Jusqu'au bout/ To the end* (Cinélutte, 1975), directly committed to making the living and working conditions of immigrant workers known, failed to convey these men's political agency. Tangui Perron notes that, while voicing their experiences at work and the indignities they suffered, 'immigrants are first seen as victims (of housing conditions and institutionalised racism), then as (exploited) workers and, finally, as aspiring fighters'.[7] In some regard, *Un monde moderne* only slightly shifts this point of view: the migrant workers Malek and Soulier meet in Saint-Nazaire are, first, presented as being caught in the crevices of a global system that extorts their labour and gives them very little in exchange. Second, we see them constrained to live in overcrowded accommodation away from the urban centres where they are brought to work. Third, the film sketches new forms of transversal collective organisation they and local union activists devise together. In *Remue-ménage dans la sous-traitance, On a grévé* and *On vient pour la visite/Coming for a Visit* (Lucie Tourette, 2009) examined in the second half of this chapter, the camera more forcefully bears witness to the empowerment of workers as they become self-sufficient activists.

## Tactics and resilience in the shipyards, a global workplace

Due to their relative synchronicity and thematic continuity, *Le dernier navire, Les prolos* and *Un monde moderne* form a coherent, albeit fortuitous, corpus that deserves to be examined as such. In the spatial confinement of the Atlantic shipyards, local, national and global scales continually blur into each other while maintaining their distinct realities. The focus on shipbuilding is significant, not least because the shipyards have been relatively absent in cinematic representation, despite the mythic status generally assigned to the dockers, especially since the strikes of the late 1940s. Cinema has focused its attention on other manufacturing sectors, particularly automobile and steel production, which combine the dramaturgy of occupation strikes with the possibility for a more pointed critique of the alienating assembly line.[8] Noël Burch and Allan Sekula view 'the sea [as] "the forgotten space" of our modernization', an omission they aimed to correct with their essay film, *The Forgotten Space* (2010).[9] 'The sea remains the crucial space of globalization', they write, adding, 'nowhere else is the disorientation, violence, and alienation of contemporary capitalism more manifest.'[10] Burch and Sekula's film deconstructs the cargo economy, 'the global production-distribution system' that millions of containers, 'mobile and anonymous', '"coffins of remote labor-power" carrying goods manufactured somewhere else, by invisible workers on the other side of the globe', materialise on the sea horizon and in ports around the world.

In *Le dernier navire*, *Les prolos* and *Un monde moderne*, the ACH-Graville and Atlantic shipyards stand as the epitome of the global workplace. As an industry, the shipyard sits right on the limit separating the national from the international. Ports have long been points of entry and transit for migrants and immigrants. The films establish the shipyard as an ad hoc transnational political stage where structural fragmentation (of the shipyards and global labour more generally) forces migrant, temp workers and union representatives to be reactive, creative and tactical in their actions. Such depictions empower migrants and interim workers, whose experiences have traditionally been marginalised on and off screens, as potential agents of social change in the global workplace. In these films, the shipyard functions as a metonymic space, contiguous and imbricated with both the cargo economy tracked by Burch and Sekula at sea and the broader dismemberment of collective solidarities and labour's spectral social and political body on land. Shipbuilding also offers a singular historical and sociological vantage point from which to address the erosion of sociality in the workplace. Established five hundred years ago, its activities have served military needs, commercial enterprises and service industries, adapting in parallel with the transformations of capitalism.

Concerns about the brutality of work relations run through French film-maker Jean-Marc Moutout's filmography, from his early shorts to the few critically acclaimed fictions that he directed after *Le dernier navire*, his first and only documentary to date.[11] *Le dernier navire* was shot in 1998–9 and released in theatres in 2000. Admittedly, the emphasis it places on the imminent closure/ bankruptcy of the shipbuilding site, ACH-Graville in Le Havre, the threats of layoffs and the predictability of a social conflict that opposes trade unions and employees to invisible executive leaders recalls many documentaries made in the late 1990s. It brought more pointed attention to the strategic dismantlement of the working class by employers, however, documenting the drastically downsized contingents of full-time, permanent employees (many of whom had spent their entire career working for the same company) and their swift replacement with fixed-term contracts. When the former protest against layoffs, going on strike, management brings in external labour, subcontracted either from abroad or through local temp hiring agencies, to finish the job and undermine the impact of such actions. Spanning an entire year, Moutout's film highlights the disintegration of shipbuilding as a corporate body and how traditional forms of collective solidarity are rendered ineffective by the managerial instrumentalisation of low-paid, low-skilled, fixed-term and migrant labourers to this end.

In contrast, *Les prolos* and *Un monde moderne* offer a slightly more optimistic view of the role this extremely precarious workforce may play in struggles to come. In *Les prolos*, shot just a couple of years later, in 2002, Marcel Trillat, who later authored *Silence dans la vallée*, examined in chapter 1, sets out to deliver a comprehensive portrait of the French working class(es) in this early new century. The businesses introduced in the film – of different sizes and operating according to varying management models – reveal a broad spectrum of social identities and economic realities. In this changing landscape, industrial manufacturers cinematically stand alongside custodians, the new proletarians of the twenty-first century. The fifth segment takes Trillat back to Saint-Nazaire, where, in 1967, he and his collaborator Hubert Knapp documented a historic shipyard workers' strike that lasted two months and rallied the whole town behind them. The widespread solidarity apparent in the footage struck a nerve with the Ministry of Information, a censorship agency created in 1962. *Le 1er mai à Saint-Nazaire*, a 24-minute-long film, was never broadcast on French television.[12] Returning to Saint-Nazaire in 2002, more than thirty years later, Trillat finds its shipyards, among the most renowned worldwide, still in activity, albeit with a few changes. They are now a branch of Alstom-Marine, a multinational company partly owned by international investors. Subcontracting has become ubiquitous on the site, even if these men are hard to film as they disappear daily inside the gigantic carcass in the middle of the shipyard to do the dirty work. *Les prolos* was among the first French documentaries to address the legality of cascade subcontracting, a practice also referred to as 'exotic montage', filming clandestinely, without authorisation, in the ships' holds.

Sabrina Malek and Arnaud Soulier's *Un monde moderne*, released in 2005, prolongs the work already done by their peers.[13] Like *Le dernier navire*, *Un monde moderne* adopts a dual narrative structure. Denied access to the Atlantic shipyards in Saint-Nazaire, the film-makers were forced to adapt and modify their approach: interviews are conducted off-site, locally, in public spaces (cafés, the streets of Saint-Nazaire), union facilities and in the hotel rooms where migrant workers stay. Incidentally, this relocation of the filmic space outside the worksite encourages both temporary and migrant workers to speak more freely about their working conditions. In the background, the construction of the Queen Mary 2 unfolds, without any interruption, even when migrants start protesting to demand payment of their wages. Critics have remarked that the film-makers successfully turned what could have been a major hindrance to the project into effective aesthetic and political interventions.[14] A feature-length examination of the global shipyard, like *Le dernier navire*, *Un monde moderne* emphasises the discrepancies emerging between labour protection laws inherited from the twentieth century and the twenty-first-century reality of labour on a site like this one. For one, national regulations fail to regulate multinational corporate entities. *Un monde moderne*, however, expands on the relatively short sequence in *Les prolos* dedicated to the Atlantic shipyards (approximately twenty minutes) by presenting subcontracting as a model that may, in time, spur renewed solidarities.

Subcontracting, like temporary work and fixed-term contracts, appeared as early as the late 1970s, long before companies started recruiting abroad *en masse*. The practice covers a wide range of personal, professional and sociological experiences. As *Un monde moderne* suggests, these are reasons why it should, or could, become ground for transversal alliances between all workers affected by it, across generations, genders and nationalities.

Labour geographer Andrew Herod describes capitalism and by extension workers' struggles in this context as fundamentally spatial systems of action: 'Both space and place are actively built and created as sites of engagement where social interaction takes place, thus providing both opportunities and constraints for workers wanting to organize collectively.'[15] In *Le dernier navire*, *Les prolos* and *Un monde moderne*, the shipyard space precludes social interactions between workers more than it promotes opportunities to meet and organise. The segmentation of the global workplace, both actual and symbolic, is perfectly encapsulated in the ship's map hanging on the wall in the Indian workers' hotel room. The ship's body is reproduced on the diagram, divided into several zones and small compartments along vertical and horizontal axes, a partitioning that the editing strategies adopted in all three films echo. *Un monde moderne*, for instance, alternates partial views of various ship zones with the narration of social conflicts and personal testimonies. Only a few shots reveal the ship in its entirety, towering over an anthill of up to 15,000 workers strategically assigned to separate zones, clearly delineated. These shots, often static and held for a while, draw attention to the constant presence of human labour, night and day, in the workplace, and to shipbuilding as an uninterrupted race to completion – oblivious of the protests organised by the workers. The soundtrack, which is particularly notable in *Un monde moderne,* is dominated by drilling, banging and other metallic noises.[16]

Upon his arrival in *Les prolos*, Marcel Trillat notes that long-term Alstom-Marine employees wear light blue overalls, whereas contractual labour is in darker shades. He also remarks that these colours gather more visibly in pre-assigned locations on the worksite. Light blue uniforms are typically seen 'in the central boatyard [...] docked onto the ship' while darker blue vests, 'most welders, metal carpenters, electricians and painters, employed by third-party contractors, get back every morning to the steerage and the holds of the ship under construction'.[17] Such colour-coded social citizenship comes into view above ground. Helmets similarly introduce another taxonomy: dozens of logos identify as many third-party subcontractors involved in the construction process. Few of them are in business more than a few months or a few years, at best. Working conditions are also subject to different regulations: permanent Alstom-Marine employees can enjoy a 40-minute lunch break while subcontracted labour is only allowed 20 minutes. The former eat in the cafeteria at a lesser cost, while the latter cluster in non-heated prefab facilities to avoid paying twice as much for a hot

caméra cachée

Avec un respirateur ça va.

Figure 10. Clandestine images aboard Queen Mary 2, *Les prolos* (Marcel Trillat, 2002) © Courtesy of Marcel Trillat and Jean Bigot – VLR Production.

meal and a seat in the restaurant. Additionally, we witness groups of migrant workers arriving and leaving the site in shuttle buses. Regular employees, in contrast, drive and park their cars on lots situated close to their workstations.

Even starker troubling signs of inequality between both groups appear in the hidden parts of the worksite. Both *Le dernier navire* and *Les prolos* resort to clandestine filming devices to document the atrocious conditions to which some of these men are subjected. Young welders explain to Jean-Marc Moutout that the air is unbearably thick in the 'underbelly' of the ship. In *Les prolos*, Julien Trillat's hidden camera records an equally toxic work environment. Confined for hours at a time to ill-ventilated areas with restricted access, or none at all, to sanitation, they face conditions that recall another century (see Fig. 10).

Furthermore, several workers testify that they often lack essential tools, the result of drastic cost-saving measures adopted by third-party companies walking a thin line between legality and illegality.

They add that subcontractors, their employers, encourage stealing. One man, masked to protect his identity, shares the information that he knows of a local third-party subcontractor that hires people on their easy ability to steal equipment, not on their professional skills. In many instances, such behaviour is the only way they can finish job assignments in time. The normalisation of such practices seriously impacts the quality of their work and undeniably undermines the safety of the workers and these ships' future passengers. On 15 November 2003, one of the gangways on the Queen Mary 2 collapsed during the ship's inauguration, killing several people and injuring many others. More generally, this lawlessness intensifies divisions among the workforce, as full-time employees mistrust their fixed-term counterparts. By superimposing cascade subcontracting onto the Taylorist assembly line model – meaning one third-party subcontractor handles each stage of the manufacturing process – labour becomes its own self-regulator. Work can only be delivered in time if every subgroup finishes according to their deadlines. When work cannot be done – for lack of equipment, inadequate labour supply or failure to pass quality control checks – the entire line is at risk of being fired, causing frictions among the labour force. When unemployment is on everybody's mind, all means become acceptable, even illegal ones, to keep a job.

In a place like the shipyards, the atomisation of the workplace and the workforce operates as a mode of control that weakens trade unions' leadership and class solidarity. Across the three films, several testimonies stress the impact that the growing presence of fixed-term contracts has on collective organisation. Permanent employees blame their contracted colleagues for not getting involved. Young temp workers admit having no personal stakes in the grievances that union members voice; it does not reflect their experience. *Le dernier navire* contrasts the affective connection most long-term employees have to the shipyards with the motivations of younger employees, typically on fixed-term contracts. They need a payslip, small as it is. One scene introduces several family members; the father, who is retired, explains that everyone in their family has worked for the shipyards (brothers, father, uncles, wife and now his son). For a very long time, they were the region's principal employer, building loyalty and solidarity. Union membership reflected these values and the workers' shared identity. Things have changed. His son, who also works for the shipyards, has no idea whether he will still have a job come Friday. He sees no point whatsoever in being a union member. He is not a shipyard worker; it is not how he identifies himself. Instead, the shipyard is a place where he has found a job for the time being.

In an economic context where industrial workers have been forced into inactivity, from one generation to the next, the increasing reliance on subcontracting has further degraded the sense of security people used to have in the workplace. It has also profoundly corrupted working-class sociability.[18] The challenge for 'imagining a politics of the precariat', Patrick Cingolani contends, lies in 'com[ing] down to understanding this plurality of conditions and to looking for the cultural and intellectual means that can foster convergences and solidarities'.[19] As a whole, the corpus resists seeing subcontracting as the sole cause for the decline of trade unionism. What visible antagonisms we see in *Le dernier navire* have been reimagined slightly more positively by the end of *Un monde moderne*. Initially portrayed as unskilled, uncommitted and largely disengaged professionally and socially, subcontracted labour gradually becomes the voice of a renewed resistance to global exploitation and social pride. How the shipyards can function as a site of political engagement remains an open question. However, *Un monde moderne* suggests that, in the short term, collective organisation mainly happens through ad hoc tactical alliances between the migrant workers, who are the most disenfranchised, and local union representatives. Glimpses of trans-sectorial and transnational solidarities can occasionally be caught in the films. For instance, at the end of *Un monde moderne*, we see an Indian welder discuss his working conditions with a fellow Indian waiter, who will soon be a service staff member on the Queen Mary 2. On other occasions, the films suggest connections between local unemployed individuals checking in every day at various temp agencies and Greek, Romanian or Polish migrants, many in their forties and fifties.

According to Jean-Emmanuel Ray, the very notion of social conflict is now synonymous with 'social regulation' and 'reproduction':

Throughout social history and theory, conflicts were closely tied to the notion of social change. Conflicts triggered social transformations that, at times, could be radical [...] Nowadays, work-related conflicts are incapable of producing subversive practices globally and of transforming society in depth. Moreover, collective actions (new or not) are also failing. The reason for this is that conflicts have become essential tools to regulate and reproduce social structures.[20]

Indeed, business leaders argue that wage rises hinder the company's competitiveness and force them to close worksites. Similar arguments can be heard in *Rêve d'usine*, *Ex-Moulinex: Mon travail, c'est capital* (1997) and another of Trillat's films, *300 jours de colère* (2002), among many examples. In many instances, workers have become defensive; they want to save their jobs, at all costs for them. Subcontracted labour, local temp workers and migrant workers, by contrast, can mobilise more offensively, having nothing to lose.

In *Un monde moderne*, the conflict lies in the formation of a collective, and thinking through the obstacles built into the existing system to block solidarity. The fragmented nature of the global workplace and the mass recourse to subcontracting forces workers and unions to improvise new uses of a space that business executives and management have reclaimed. First, struggles need to demonstrate tactical nimbleness to address the wide range of legal situations and social positions on the ground. Furthermore, the precarious workforce of the early twenty-first century comes with varying degrees of training when it comes to organising effectively. Michel de Certeau's distinction between strategies and tactics of resistance offers a productive critical framework for understanding the redistribution of power in the workplace. More still, it makes us attuned to the promises that ad hoc labour movements bring forth while encouraging us to reconsider the roles film-makers and cameras can play in this process.[21]

For Certeau, strategies reflect 'the calculation (or manipulation) of power relationships that becomes possible as soon as a subject with will and power can be isolated'.[22] In contrast, tactics consist of 'calculated action[s] determined by the absence of proper locus'. For this reason, tactics are the 'purview of the non-powerful', forced to adapt to a new environment. In contrast, strategies presuppose an 'in-group' and are enacted per shared principles and values.[23] Twentieth-century trade unionism and militant cinema strategically enforced the dramaturgy of a unified working class (the in-group) actively fighting the business class over what they saw as the rightful appropriation of the factory. Yet, 'the calculation (or manipulation) of power relationships' was historically deferred to trade union organisations. If successful, these strategies were thought to lead to economic emancipation. Jean-Emmanuel Ray compares the politics of class struggles to the Aristotelian three-unities model.

> Labour laws are fundamentally theatrical in their assertion of a three-unities rule: time unity (bells punctuate the working day at the beginning and the end of the day), space unity (the factory, the mine), and action unity (the assembly line). This triptych was perfectly in line with the interests defended by the three main social actors of the time. Trade unions needed a collective body to exist. Employers' priority was to maintain the workers' discipline. The government was also a winner since it could easily keep the working class gathered in one location under control.[24]

In the globalised workplace, a growing number of workers do not identify with the in-group, however. There is no single theatricality: different groups operate on different schedules, and the unity of space is only purely circumstantial and temporary. Not only is there no more single collective body, but there are also multiple employers with varying concerns about the workers' discipline. To a large extent, the dispersion of the workplace has been neoliberal management's strategic response, or its counter-attack, to trade unionism. As a consequence, labour has lost the capacity to develop strategies.

In 'the absence of proper locus', precarious migrant and temp workers can only address the injustices they face through 'tactical' actions. To begin with, union representatives and film-makers must map out different spatial and temporal practices of the *workplace*. What is underscored in the films is that union representation of migrant workers is often, in and of itself, tactical. It is done locally;

there are no national guidelines or frameworks for the few delegates taking on this time-consuming project to follow. But, as René Fadda explains to Marcel Trillat in *Les prolos*, hiring practices are evolving faster than the legislation, giving third-party contractors a head start. Patrick Cingolani describes the emergence of precarious labour in France as the product of the slow and steady introduction of new forms of employment, compared with other European countries, where it is often connected to alternative economies, such as the black market or crime. For this reason, economists, sociologists and legal experts typically identify them as they start appearing in job postings.[25]

The surreal car chase that Fadda and Marcel Trillat embark on in the film is a perfect metaphor for the interstitial nature of a system that benefits business interests at the expense of workers forced to operate without any safety net. In the sequence, he is trying to locate the housing quarters of a group of migrant workers to identify their hiring subcontractor. By the time they arrive, the building has been vacated. He tells the film-maker that this group came to Saint-Nazaire under a new scheme, called 'exotic montage', which consists of hiring 'cheap, skilled labour' abroad, in 'Morocco, the Ukraine, Portugal, the United Arab Emirates', to curb Alstom-Marine's overall production costs. A team of sociologists, who studied subcontracting practices in the petrochemical industry, shipbuilding and automotive parts manufacturing, see the work of local union delegates like René Fadda as an individualised form of activism.[26] Similarly, increasingly denied access to work sites, film-makers are forced to approach their subjects differently.

Refused access to Alstom's shipbuilding site, a space strategically stratified, divided and regimented, Malek and Soulier choose to emphasise time as the migrant workers experience it. With the camera aimlessly meandering the space that it intends to penetrate, in vain, *Un Monde moderne* effectively stops short of producing a new theatricality and a new collective body – the precariat, made up of interim and migrant workers, French and foreign.[27] Instead, I argue, the film achieves a much more impactful tactical coup. It lets us view the global workplace from the vantage point of the 'non-powerful' while dramatising the protracted temporality of legal procedures that renders them invisible. Unable to 'view the adversary as a whole within a distinct, visible and objectifiable space', they decided to select fragments taken from the vast ensemble of this production system to compose new stories with them.[28] The valuable insights these Indian workers give trace 'tactical' pathways that invite us to re-envisage the shipyards differently. The film skilfully mobilises Certeau's connection between tactics and time: 'tactics are procedures that gain validity in relation to the pertinence they lend to time [...] on a clever utilization of time, of the opportunities it presents and also of the play it introduces into the foundation of power.'[29] The globalised Atlantic shipyard, a free zone, is protected by restricted access policies. Regardless, Sabrina Malek and Arnaud Soulier unveil its invisible structures, only to bring out those voices, experiences and stories that have been silenced at its very core. Herod's grounding of social engagement and interactions in space leaves out the question of time spent in the workspace and place, which is, in fact, of crucial importance to the political and aesthetic intervention of Malek and Soulier and to their ability to regain control of their narrative.

The ships' massive structures become symbolic of the entire neoliberal production system. Omnipresent and unstoppable, they are like an ogre that insatiably swallows its human labour until it runs out of resources. This image is used by one of the Indian workers. In the opening minute of the film, he tells us the following story in a voice-over narration edited over images of the town filmed from the film-makers' car.

Once upon a time, one evil (*translated as 'ogre' in the subtitles*) stayed in one forest. One day, that evil declared: 'I want two children daily for my food'. All mothers, all parents daily bring two children to that evil. But, one day, that place finished all children. Then, that evil declared to parents: 'Ok, I want daily two women for my food'. Then, all the women are finished. After this, there are only men left. These men also, daily, were given food like the women and the children. Then, after this, this evil is alone; he don't have food, there don't have nothing there, it left him dead.[30]

In *Les prolos* and *Un monde moderne*, the shipyard and the ship act as direct metaphors for a global system of exploitation that *consumes* its most vital resource, human labour. In his analysis of Marcel Trillat's *Etranges étrangers*, Tangui Perron describes Aubervilliers, the town where several African men were found dead on New Year's Eve 1969 in comparable terms.

> At the bottom of French society, a shadowy people, immigrants, live in shantytowns, humid cellars and slums, and survives in unrighteous conditions. At the top, a witty and cynical businessman preens seats in his office comfortably as Marcel Trillat seeks to destabilise him with impertinent questions and his customary nonchalance. In between these two radically opposed worlds, the French population, the Communist mayor of an emblematic town and union militants fail to shatter this implicit social hierarchy.[31]

In their films about Saint-Nazaire, Marcel Trillat, Sabrina Malek and Arnaud Soulier relocate this 'social hierarchy' from Paris's red belt, home to various industries and the working classes since the early twentieth century, to the shipyards. Standing in its centre, the ship, Queen Mary 2, visually imprints for us this vertical stratification of the global economy on the screen. By 2005, business leaders have entirely disappeared, industrial sites are in the hands of abstract entities, international hedge funds and international joint ventures. At the bottom, migrant workers continue to do the dirty jobs nobody else wants to do. In the middle, we find the dwindling body of full-time Alstom employees, union militants and Saint-Nazaire residents worried about the decline of the local economy.

Such racial stratification is not limited to the sea economy. These past twenty years, more attention has been paid to the imbrication of the globalisation of the labour market and domestic economies – understood here in the most literal sense of the word. Etymologically, economy means the management of a house or household, which evokes, in particular, the labour involved in cleaning, serving and caring for children.[32] Since the early 2000s, several local strikes have erupted in the service industries – fast food, cleaning services, and, more recently, food delivery services and other activities of the gig economy – where many employees are underpaid, subcontracted and denied fundamental social rights. Films like *Remue-ménage dans la sous-traitance*, *On a grévé* and *On vient pour la visite* provide rare insights into struggles that do not benefit from the same labour political infrastructure and media visibility as traditional industries.

## Tumult in the lobby

In 2002, a group of housekeepers employed by Arcade, a subcontractor of the hotel chain Accor, went on strike to protest against the conditions imposed by their employer. Several prominent French union organisations, including Sud, CGT and CNT, supported them. They fought for over a year before Accor finally gave in to their demands: a lower number of rooms to clean in an hour, each employee should not be expected to work more than 130 hours a month and have the guarantee to receive a monthly minimum wage of 4,000€. They also requested that all employees who had previously been laid off for their involvement in the strike actions and sued for damages to property, verbally assaulting managers and other offences be rehired, and legal suits against them abandoned. Many of these women were born in African countries, primarily in Mali, Mauritania and Senegal. They moved to France to join their husbands, living and working in the country for decades while barely speaking or reading French, which made them particularly vulnerable to unscrupulous employers.

Ivora Cusack first came across these women's strikes in 2002 when Boris Perrin, another member of the community channel Zalea TV and later co-founder of the digital cooperative Les Mutins de Pangée, asked her to stand in for him on one action he was to cover.[33] Fascinated by the energy and determination of these women, she continued to film them for four more years. By 2005, Cusack co-created, with Agathe Dreyfus and Christine Gabory, a collective named 360° et Plus, based in Marseille. *Remue-ménage dans la sous-traitance* perfectly illustrates their shared artistic vision and activism:

Our cinema is directly engaged in the world. We value as much the process of filming as the film as a finished product. We mainly work with persons who are made invisible and inaudible in a world where, most of the time, only cisgender heterosexual rich abled adult white men are visible and audible. Because of this reality, our cinema is de facto feminist, even if we do not necessarily enunciate it in such terms.[34]

Cusack and Dreyfus released the DVD *Remue-ménage dans la sous-traitance* after almost five years working part-time on editing the film, and went on a 'national tour' with it, working with a few independent theatres.

When watching this film, one is struck by the soundtrack. Cusack is a sound engineer and editor, concerned with the silencing of racialised, gendered and economically marginalised voices. The film opens with conventional interviews with several of the women involved in the 2002 strike. It later becomes clear that these were recorded in 2004 after Faty Mayante, a leading figure of the movement, was laid off for allegedly spending too much time of her work time on union responsibilities. The second half of the film focuses on Faty's second strike that she conducted with the support of a *Comité de soutien* – activists devoting themselves to the cause, with the know-how and the determination to see a struggle through.

The women we meet are all black and African-born, except for one young Martiniquaise; all have lived in France for over twenty years. Immediately after these introductions, during which they describe their career paths, almost exclusively spent cleaning hotel rooms and office buildings, we are thrown outside on the street, with the protesters, many wearing traditional dresses and making much noise. The juxtaposition of these two radically aural atmospheres – their relatively quiet domestic life and the loud, cacophonous eruption of their bodies and voices in the public space – suggests a social and political catharsis for these women. We see, and hear, them banging on rubbish bins, singing, dancing and, for Faty and a few others, speak up about their poor working conditions, meagre wages and variable hours. These explosive tactics seem to be working. Cusack uses local news archival footage to point out both the sudden visibility of women otherwise unseen and persistent racial stereotyping: 'These Malian women, who, for the longest time, were docile and workable, are now striking', the female journalist's voice-over in the TV reportage states (05"11–06"30).'[35]

For Faty, their spokesperson, the strike is obviously about demands for substantial changes at work, but it is, most importantly, about being treated humanely, not like animals. In other films, like *On vient pour la visite*, undocumented workers, also on strike, refuse to be treated like children ('*On n'est pas des enfants!*'). Invisibility, audibility and dignity are, therefore, real stakes of these struggles and decisive factors for the success of the actions undertaken by these women. Hence, the music, the noise and the irruption in places where they can be seen, where their fight can be visible and where they will also be heard, to the great displeasure of hotel managers and some customers. These employees, who do not even have a staff room to take a quick lunch break, can only grab public attention by occupying the hotel lobbies where their presence is most out of line ('*ça fait désordre*').

A central hub in any hotel, the equivalent of a store's window, the lobby is where they are, in normal circumstances, the most invisible. They come and go through back service doors, they may be seen in hallways on the floor, in their uniforms, but they never appear in the lobby. The film thus enables us to see various ways in which they and their support committee appropriate hallways, plastering walls with stickers and flyers, and disrupt the peace of hotel personnel and guests. In the second half of the film, focused on Faty's specific case, someone on the *comité de soutien* thought one aggravating yet significant tactic would be to have a picnic lunch on the floor of a different hotel lobby every Friday. It worked indeed, since, in 2006, a year after she went on strike for the second time, Accor presented Faty with a severance payment. Three years after she led her co-workers to their first victory, Faty accepted the terms of the agreement. She first joined a union in 2001, three years after witnessing one of her co-workers in a previous job being laid off because of her union activities. Five years later, she is the victim of the same injustice; yet, unlike her co-worker, her fight has not been in vain, and, most importantly, there are audio-visual records of its impacts.

Documentary cinema becomes complicit with this active politics that consists of seizing visibility (*mise en visibilité*) while being careful not to exoticise the festive physicality of these women's appropriation of the strike. This delicate balance tactfully permeates Denis Gheerbrant's film *On a grévé*. In 2011, a union acquaintance let the film-maker know of a group of house cleaners getting ready to strike in front of a Parisian hotel. Interested in these women's experiences, he stayed with them for the duration of their action, on the pavement, with his camera. Like *Remue-ménage dans la sous-traitance*, dance, songs and music are central to these women's existence as political subjects in the public sphere, even more pronounced as they recur throughout the film. It is their way of '*faire corps*' (to be in solidarity with one another), writes Olivier Barlet in his film review.[36] Still, one must add: '*faire corps*' differently, in ways that thwart economies and politics that have subjected these bodies, objectified and erased them from the public space. Wearing red baseball caps and jackets with the CGT logo over traditional dresses or a veil, chanting in languages other than French while handing out tracts, they come to exist simultaneously as a different political body and as bodies that are actively engaged in a politics of the everyday.

Both Cusack and Gheerbrant describe their role in these struggles as an act of bearing witness that actively 'supports the actions' as they unfold. They are an active witness whose role is simply to be present, in the space, *with* these women.[37] Whereas Cusack speaks of the moment in which the film is produced, the cumulative and aggregative effect that these films have, as a corpus, is equally significant, insofar as they create a living archive that evidences the visibility of these precarious workers as political subjects. Jean-Michel Denis considers this process all the more critical, given that cleaning services are 'a major blind spot of all representations, social, political, unions and sociological'.[38]

In 2009, Lucie Tourette also decided to take her camera to bear witness to what is now described as a historic mobilisation: more than 6,000 undocumented workers in different sectors went on a strike that lasted about a year, among them over 1,000 undocumented temp workers. She stayed with one group for several months, filming their transformation from striking employees into seasoned union delegates and militants, capable of organising and keeping the course. The opening sequence of *On vient pour la visite/Coming for a Visit* takes place in 2010 at Randstad, one of France's largest temping agencies. A group of men rapidly walks up the service stairs of a building, talking vividly among each other: 'We'll talk later! Let's reach the last office, and then we will talk.' The camera throws us in their midst as credits appear on the screen in bold red letters. When the title, *On vient pour la visite/Coming for a Visit*, imprints across the frame, we have finally entered a floor lined with offices. 'We must occupy the whole building', exclaims one of the men, while others are already taking up places in between desks where employees still work. The police arrive, ready to evacuate the strikers. There ensues a respectful dialogue between two police officers and the small group of men assembled on the floor. The latter explain that they want to pressure this employer since they have thus far refused to sign labour contracts, 'CERFA', that undocumented employees need to apply for legal immigration status.[39] The scene unfolds calmly, the two policemen listening carefully to what the men explain about their motivations and reasons for wanting to occupy this particular building.

Meanwhile, in the main lobby downstairs, the situation is more strained and about to turn violent between a larger group of strikers and more police forces. Shortly after the film moves downstairs, a few CGT union delegates from the company walk into the developing action. They try to calm everyone and restore some order among the strikers, who do not appreciate being asked to step outside. One of the men, who has seized the loudspeaker, exhorts the others, in another language than French, to 'occupy all rooms'. 'The union representative wants us to leave', he keeps repeating, 'but we shouldn't go out, we must occupy all rooms' (3"50–5"29). These strikers are mainly undocumented workers, who, for several months, have tried to pressure many temping agencies into signing their 'CERFA'.

Lucie Tourette, the director, stayed close to this movement for several months, filming their meetings, street protests and collective actions in temp agencies:

This film is a raw testimony, a direct immersion at the core of a movement [...] Because trust had been established, we could circulate freely during the shooting phase [...] When we accompanied strikers for negotiations with their employers, we always filmed openly. Businesses and police officers accepted our presence to varying degrees. At times the camera turned into a stake in power relations: strikers mentioned its continued presence as a precondition for negotiating. Backing away on this would have meant displaying weakness. The strikers never asked us to stop filming.[40]

A journalist by training, Tourette joined a group of sociologists working together under the acronym ASPLAN in 2008. That year, small groups of undocumented workers started to strike in the food industry and cleaning services before spreading more widely among temp workers in 2009.[41]

*On vient pour la visite* served a dual purpose. First, as a research tool, the film was intended to document emerging forms of collective mobilisation and organisation. Second, in its final, edited version, it serves as evidence of a sociological praxis committed to blurring the line between research and activism. Avoiding editorial effects, Tourette provides minimal contextual background, which can be disconcerting to viewers. This choice defines the film's intervention; it sends its subjects back to their political achievements while putting them in a position where they can now be in charge of transmitting this knowledge. French white union delegates are only present in the first few sequences, disappearing in the background to encourage the workers to take the lead, a point Maurice Amzallag, an experienced union delegate in the temp workers' section of CGT, makes clear in one of the meetings (19"13–19"52):

Gradually, YOU are the union activists. At first, you didn't think you could discuss with employers. Today, some comrades negotiate daily, and bosses discuss seriously with them. Most of the 'cerfas' we have were obtained by strikers [...] In the future, when you go back to work, you'll be the unionists. Start training yourself now!

From that point on, the film presents us with a movement that is organised, led and, most importantly, carried by these men.

Tourette's narrative highlights the radical empowerment of a category presumably blocked from the political sphere because of its highly precarious position in the labour economy, their illegal residency status in France and their de facto political inexistence. Considered side by side with the migrant workers of *Un monde moderne*, *On vient pour la visite* provides a stronger argument in favour of politics of precariousness to come. Contrary to positions according to which 'NGOs and unions that support, guide and organise precarious workers inevitably fall into a sort of transactional relationship with them and prevent them from making their own decisions', *On vient pour la visite* shows us men who are acting on their own and defending their rights not only to work in France but to live and stay in France.[42] I am referring to their slogan, '*On bosse ici, on vit ici, on reste ici!*'[43]

## Conclusion

Sociology and documentary film-making concur that, despite the essential heterogeneity of these highly localised struggles, temp work, undocumented and subcontracted labour have laid the foundations for a renewal of trade unionism in the early twenty-first century. Most importantly, traditional structures of labour organisation have been forced to acknowledge the potentially productive effects of transnational mobility to that end, as these workers have been more responsive to the necessity to organise and fight collectively than their French-born counterparts. Film-makers have also found in these ad hoc, tactical modes of action, where different cultures blend, opportunities to reimagine their activism anew. Generally speaking, they have implicated themselves in the temporality of struggles fought for months at a time in many instances, investing public spaces – hotel lobbies, streets, temp agencies – with them. The sum of these films, produced in the last fifteen years, now bears witness to the gradual visibility, within the political sphere, of bodies otherwise forced into the interstitial economy and, therefore, condemned to social inexistence.

The living archive that these films produce is vital for these men and women, in the most elemental sense of the word. Carine Eff remarks that, too often, the support of traditional union structures for the most marginalised among the contemporary labour force is 'ambiguous, counter-productive sometimes'.[44] These 'punk strikes' – as she offers to name these actions of a different kind – short-circuit the system in its core, drawing their strength from the 'radical equality' embraced by those involved. The solidarities at work in these struggles, less institutional, more individualised, raise different political and ethical stakes than class-based strikes. In considering the ethics of political action, especially when it brings together individuals who 'have a part' and others 'who have no part' in the social order, Todd May posits that solidarity results from the 'weaving together of cognitive and affective elements around the presupposition of equality', in other words 'sharing (*partage*) and trust (*confiance*)'.[45]

May's argument illuminates the political and ethical stakes of the documentary films presented in this chapter, but it also reverberates more widely, returning us to *Fragments sur la misère*, for instance, or anticipating a film like *Mon diplôme, c'est mon corps*, analysed in chapter 4. The documentary encounter rests on the production of precarious solidarity between the film-makers, the subjects they film and the viewers who willingly join this temporary community held together by a desire to share and trust each other to maintain the radical equality of all involved. Nevertheless,

> the ethical character of political action [the documentary encounter] is not the same for those engaged in the action as it is among those confronted by it. In the latter case, a contradiction of principles is central to the ethics of politics; in the former case, the principles at play are at times grasped cognitively, at times affectively, and at times both.[46]

Solidarity in these films is therefore different from empathy, insofar as it unsettles the viewers as it binds them to another (political) subject.

# Chapter 3
# Precarious filiations

Je me souviens d'une région moribonde [...] Je me souviens d'avoir voulu partir, partir vite, partir loin, partir pour toujours ... Pour toujours? En l'an 2000, je suis pourtant revenu. Je suis revenu parce que la fuite laisse un goût amer, un sentiment d'inachevé, l'impression obsédante que quittant la région précipitamment, j'y ai laissé une partie de moi-même...à reconquérir peut-être par le biais d'un film.

    – Laurent Hasse (*Sur les cendres du vieux monde*, 2002).[1]

J'avais honte de mon milieu. Je voulais ressembler à ceux que j'avais rejoints dans le haut de la ville: les fils d'ingénieurs, de médecins, de pharmaciens avec qui je partageais mon lycée. J'ai quitté Forbach il y a plus de trente ans. Mais Forbach ne m'a jamais quitté. Et je reviens avec le souvenir de ces sentiments qu'on ne dit pas.

    – Régis Sauder (*Retour à Forbach*, 2017).[2]

Oui, je suis un fils de Lip qui croit encore que c'est possible.

    – Thomas Faverjon (*Fils de Lip*, 2007).[3]

Chapter 3 returns to the post-industrial territorialities already trodden in chapter 1, moving further into communities shaped by industrial activity and hollowed out by its decline in recent decades. It tracks how Laurent Hasse, Régis Sauder and Thomas

Faverjon enact and reformulate familial, social, regional and cinematic filiations in their films, respectively *Sur les cendres du vieux monde*, *Retour à Forbach/Return to Forbach* and *Fils de Lip*. Each film-maker returns home, a camera in hand, years or decades after moving away. By personally implicating themselves with(in) these familiar territorialities and histories, they draw attention to the changing economic, social and political landscapes of post-industrial France in ways that are personal, cathartic and generative. *Sur les cendres du vieux monde* grapples with the loss of economic vitality and the rapid social come-down of steelworkers, their sons and grandsons – stories that have also been addressed in recent publications, including Nicolas Mathieu's novel, *Leurs enfants après eux*, recipient of the 2018 Prix Goncourt, and Benoît Coquart's sociological investigation, *Ceux qui restent: Faire sa vie dans les campagnes en déclin* (2019).[4] *Retour à Forbach* and *Fils de Lip* stress the political urgency to mediate reconciliation processes with the past. While Sauder turns this work onto himself, Faverjon's documentary labour facilitates his mother's recovery of her ability to voice deep-seated feelings and betrayals.

Most importantly, I argue that, across these three films, documentary cinema is affirmed as a shared practice, that is premised on reciprocity, between the film-makers and their subjects. Admittedly, the film-maker-as-heir acts at times as a *passeur*, at others as an anchor, for voices, stories and subjectivities that have lost, or are gradually losing, their capacity to be heard as a result of the 'ongoing activity of precariousness in the present' – to borrow from Lauren Berlant.[5] Not speaking for the subjects they film, these film-makers use their position to allow the latter to speak through them instead. In doing so, they redefine documentary film-making as a 'narrative mould' where individuals subjected to social disregard and scorn can, as Guillaume Le Blanc proposes, safely voice their experiences and emotions to an implicated Other, the film-maker himself.[6] Through this shared (documentary) practice, the filmed subjects actively reclaim a place in the social fabric, if only by sharing their experiences and feelings directly in front of a camera. Thomas Faverjon's task is at once extremely specific and consequential for cinema at large. His exploration of Lip's local and national archives not only recovers his mother's past, it also reactivates the silenced contributions of women to social *History*.

## Shame, responsibility, healing: inheritance at work

In *Specters of Marx* (1993), Jacques Derrida asserts that 'we *are* insofar as we *inherit'*, that 'the *being* of what we are *is* first of all inheritance'.[7] Indeed, identity, heritage and indebtedness are inextricably enmeshed in *Sur les cendres du vieux monde*, *Fils de Lip* and *Retour à Forbach*, and in how their authors describe their relationship with the places and histories they film. For Derrida, being heir to something or someone implies engaging this legacy or inheritance critically: 'reaffirm[ing] what comes "before us" [...] means not merely accepting this heritage but relaunching it otherwise and keeping it alive.'[8] In *Derrida and the Inheritance of Democracy*, Samir Haddad considers some of the political implications of such a project. Of particular relevance to the present study is the suggestion that, in Derrida's writings, not only is 'democracy [...] inherited', but 'inheritance itself can be a democratic action'.[9] Furthermore, Haddad contends that Derrida's critical work of inheritance towards Western conceptions of democracy, friendship and fraternity effectively deconstructs the 'particular masculine economy' upon which this philosophical lineage was built and has perpetuated itself. Derrida's reluctance to include any woman in his philosophical corpus fails to correct this heritage.[10] Nevertheless, Derrida's conception of critical inheritance provides for a model that productively engages these three films' interventions.

As early as 1999, *Sur les cendres du vieux monde* committed itself to the urgency of recording the 'crisis ordinary' that renders post-industrial subjects precarious, while allowing them to voice this reality as they have internalised it.[11] *Retour à Forbach* and *Fils de Lip* are much more deliberate in their intentions to 'reaffirm' socio-political heritages as inherently heterogeneous and discordant. *Retour à Forbach* sees in the shared – not similar –

precariousness of post-industrial working-class, post-colonial and immigrant subjects a fertile ground for affiliations and new processes of identifications.[12] *Fils de Lip* rewrites Lip's political legacy from the perspectives of those who, like his mother, were left out of this famous social struggle's triumphant narrative. In doing so, the film successfully weaves back into Lip's legacy affects and statements that conflict with its collective memory, powerfully reconducting its significance into the future.

In *Vies ordinaires, vies précaires*, Guillaume Le Blanc explains that when individuals and communities find themselves socially disqualified, discredited and reclassified as precarious subjects they lose the social, political and, ultimately, ontological attachments that are crucial to their subjective being.[13] Documentary cinema, in Marion Froger's view, exceeds its most immediate sociological and ideological contributions. Most significantly, it must be understood as a relational practice whose force is eminently poetic – and, as argued in this book, ethical.

> The question of (documentary) enunciation duly records the heteronomy of artistic gestures; it seeks to rejoin creative activity not with a social imaginary but with the assertion that a 'we' comes into being through an 'I'. This 'we', however, eludes the power relations that govern social roles.[14]

Froger's comments speak more specifically to Québécois cinema's distinctive political and social claims in the 1960s and 1970s, but they are nonetheless relevant to this analysis of *Sur les cendres du vieux monde*, *Retour à Forbach* and *Fils de Lip*. By physically and emotionally implicating themselves in the territoriality and social histories they film, the three filmmakers advance a documentary practice that melts their 'I' into a precarious 'we' to regenerate the latter's social constitution.

## Social anchors in *Sur les cendres du vieux monde* and *Retour à Forbach*

Born in 1970, Laurent Hasse and Régis Sauder are of the same generation, grew up in the same region, Lorraine, and feel the same responsibility to tell the story of their region before it is too late. In 1999, Laurent Hasse comes back, ten years after 'running away' from the Fensch valley. *Sur les cendres du vieux monde* examines the local economic, political and social devastation caused by the idling of Lorraine's steel industry. With this first feature, the film-maker also faces his feelings of guilt and betrayal. Starting with footage from old home movies, Hasse explains that 'when you were from Lorraine, you were a steelworker!' The opening credit sequence, a compilation of archival footage, then reconstructs over half a century of the region's social history, from the golden age of the 1930s–1950s to the workers' struggles of the 1960s and the increasingly violent labour disputes that marked local industries' final decline in the 1970s and 1980s. The film's first live images land us in a small dive bar in Hayange, a town centrally located in the valley, home to a large mill. It is 31 December 1999. A handful of patrons celebrate as joyfully as they can the beginning of a new year and a new millennium.

Channelling the pessimistic 'discourse of the end' that dominated the 1990s, *Sur les cendres du vieux monde* presents a region left lifeless, hurriedly 'wiped off the map', to quote Hasse's introductory voice-over narration. In reality, Hasse's hometown, Moyeuvre-Grande, lost 41 per cent of its population in the last thirty years of the twentieth century.[15] Local rates of unemployment, averaging 25 per cent by the turn of the century, leave those still living there with few options and increasingly fragmented and uncertain career paths that often take them across the border, into nearby Luxemburg and Germany. As a result, local businesses struggle to stay open, ultimately turning commercial centres into ghost towns. Resentment, resignation and pessimism are the dominant feelings we get watching this film. With each election, far-right candidates assert their presence more strongly, gladly taking advantage of the region's

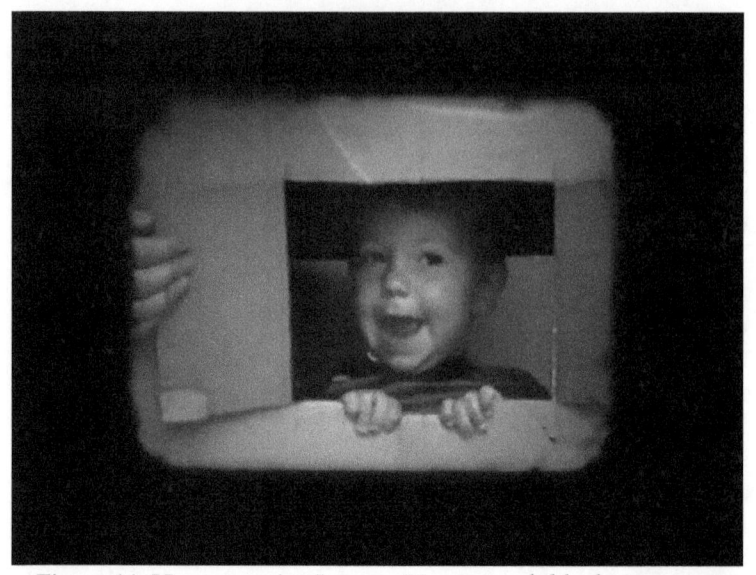

Figure 11. Home movies: Laurent Hasse as a child, playing movies,
at the end of *Sur les cendres du vieux monde* © Laurent Hasse/Iskra –
Sombrero – Tarantula – CVB – Arte - RTBF.

disarray. In 2017, the two candidates leading the presidential race
locally after the first round of elections were Marine Le Pen
(Front National on the far right, now known as Rassemblement
National), and Jean-Luc Mélenchon (La France Insoumise on
the far left).[16] If the film ends with a montage sequence showing
a series of steel mills collapsing to the soundtrack of Kat Onoma's
song 'Le déluge', its purpose is not to indict a system.[17] Instead,
as remarked in a review, Laurent Hasse 'intimately question[s]
local pains without pathos' through casual conversations with
relatives, old friends and new acquaintances.[18]

    The desire to record a living memory of local affects, beyond
anger, seems to be the determining factor in his first feature film.
Bookending this bleak portrayal of his native region with footage
from old home movies starring his young self, the film-maker
assigns a double meaning to *Sur les cendres du vieux monde* (see
Fig. 11). On the one hand, the film contributes to the region's
collective memory a debt that local children may no longer meet

in the future; it ends with the question: 'Who will tell us about History's next chapter, now that there is no maternity ward left in the area?'[19] On the other hand, Hasse reclaims this film as part of his private collection of home movies, now archived as a reminder that he could recover that missing piece of himself by filming these brief moments shared with friends and relatives. This final gesture also emphasises that he was able to return with the tools to tell this chapter of his region's history precisely because he left the region to pursue his childhood dreams to be a film-maker.

*Retour à Forbach*, Régis Sauder's third feature-length documentary to be released in French theatres, starts with a series of static shots revealing rooms turned upside down, drawers left wide open and personal effects thrown around all over the floor. In 2015, Sauder's parents were the victims of a burglary; nothing was stolen. At the time, the film-maker was in town, with his camera. In 2014, shortly after the Front National declared victory in Forbach's local elections, Sauder decided to return and film what had become of his hometown, an old coal-mining town sitting on the border with Germany in north-eastern France. Thirty years earlier, he had left to pursue a degree in neurosciences in Paris. He later found his true vocation was film-making, releasing *Nous, Princesses de Clèves* (2011) and *Etre là* (2014) to critical acclaim. Both films were shot in Marseille, where he lives.

With these images of the burglary early on, Sauder dramatises the sustained imbrication of the social and the personal throughout the film. In fact, the forced entry shatters the film's chronology and the dramaturgy he had initially envisaged. Watching his parents' belongings 'scattered around the floor', Sauder is reminded of every little thing that made him 'ashamed of [his] social background' as a teenager (1"36–3"27) and what this film is about.

> I wanted to be like the sons of engineers, doctors and pharmacists with whom I went to school uptown. I left Forbach thirty years ago. Forbach never left me. Today, I come back, reminiscing about feelings we don't say.

Everything that I unjustly despised for a long time is now scattered around the floor, in front of me. My family's memories have been thrown into disorder. Even my father's brain scans have been removed from their envelopes. Because of his disease, Alzheimer's dementia, he cannot remember a single thing at this point. A condition that seems so intricately connected with this region's history. In Forbach, nobody talks about things. Memory is not preserved. Everything that my father doesn't tell me today will forever fall into oblivion. Nobody seeks to remember things. It seems to be better to forget than to think – our century's dis-ease. As for me, I film to remember. But how can I show History when I don't have access to archives or accounts from the past, when everyone suffers from collective amnesia.[20]

This 'subjective topography' – a project perfectly encapsulated in the design of film's poster (see Fig. 12) – tracks Forbach's transformation and its residents' mix of anger and resilience. Also at stake is the film-maker's reconciliation with the social milieu he fled as a young man. *Retour à Forbach*, whose title is an obvious nod to Didier Eribon's and Annie Ernaux's memoirs *Retour à Reims/Returning to Rheims* (2009) and *Retour à Yvetot* (2013), two books that inspired his journey back, is Sauder's most personal film to date. It expands on themes and questions that were already latent in his film school project *Libérez Régis* – a short he never got to shoot, probably for the best in his opinion, as it was a bit too 'narcissistic'.[21]

Shortly before he started filming in 2014, Sauder penned a scathing op-ed in the French daily *Libération*.[22] In this piece, he takes responsibility for 'betraying' his social heritage, preferring to leave instead of facing his hometown's gradual 'economic, intellectual, affective and poetic' impoverishment. He also claims understanding why people make such decisions in the current context:

While I hate some individuals and despise those who vote FN, I can also understand what collectively drives people into such an impasse. Because they do not have my life.

Figure 12. *Retour à Forbach's* film poster reveals Régis Sauder's face,
as a child, imprinted over an aerial view of Forbach
© Régis Sauder.

They are sometimes unemployed, poor. They have no
library or real cinema to go to, no real prospects. In other
words, they lack what allows us to build our lives with an
agency, to stand tall; hate is all they have to affirm
themselves. I understand what is happening, and I feel
responsible as someone who contributed to this situation.
Forbach has betrayed its history and memory because we
betrayed and abandoned Forbach to free ourselves.[23]

In a way, *Retour à Forbach* answers this personal call to take actions
against the rise of xenophobia, shame and hate. As he meets old
acquaintances and friends who stayed, listens to them and sees
what they do in their everyday lives, Sauder reconciles himself
with his social and regional origins. Once shameful, this heritage
appears to him anew as a vital force that can (re)connect people
when everything seems poised to divide them and reignite
solidarity as an alternative to violence. *Retour à Forbach* thus uses
its visual economy and the conversations we, as viewers, partake
in to uncover latent filiations and connections in the post-
industrial topography of his hometown.

No longer living in Lorraine, Laurent Hasse and Régis Sauder
acknowledge the ambivalence of their position. While natives
of the regions they film, they are also outsiders, protected from
the 'virus' of precarity that affects both the territory and the
people who live in it.[24] In the following analysis, I contend that
this social in-betweenness is what confers on their interventions
greater effectiveness. In an interview with the magazine *Vacarme*
published in 2002, Laurent Hasse made clear that 'the force of
documentary is precisely its subjectivity, meaning the place and
status that film-makers occupy in the stories they tell'.[25] Had he
shot in a different region, he went on, the result would have been
nothing more than a gallery of portraits. Moreover, he did not
include any interviews recorded with local officials and business
people because they sounded like stand-ins for institutional
discourses, not actual people talking to him. They had, therefore,
no place in the film.

Régis Sauder shares this concern for a documentary practice
cultivating human and social relations and fostering reciprocity

between all involved, different subjects in the film, the film-maker and the viewer. Hasse's and Sauder's implications in and with their subjects are not about self-performativity; their presence is rather to be seen as an embodied mediation for these cinematic encounters. Both film-makers grant importance to the quality of the voices we hear in their films; they consider documentary film-making an art of enabling an absolute truth of enunciation. While they use voice-over comments as personal ruminations to reflect on the state of their regions, their films primarily revolve around casual conversations that broach a variety of topics: the legacy of trade unionism, immigration, the rise of far-right populism and racism, individual and collective resignation, the structural degradation of miners' houses following the closures of coal mines and the broader destructive effects of financial capitalism on these communities and individual lives. In the specific post-industrial contexts they depict, their approach is also invested in enacting connections and spontaneous filiations grounded in shared precariousness between the white industrial workers, who face social demotion, and their neighbours, the post-colonial and immigrant 'others' they blame.

In both films, the camera appears to be accepted quite quickly. Anchoring these friendly, informal conversations in a common ground – *we* from Forbach or *we* from the Fensch – Sauder and Hasse provide crucial points of attachment for their interlocutors' social subjectivity. The use of *tu* – a more casual, personal address than the formal *vous* in French – reinforces familiarity while creating equity in the exchanges. In a sequence filmed with local teenagers, one of Sauder's childhood friends becomes a surrogate for him. Just as he mediates the viewers' encounters with Forbach's local population, she mediates his encounter with the teenagers and the residents of the housing estate, engaging them on the delicate issue of racism. Guillaume Le Blanc discusses the importance of the *tu* address to support precarious subjects' ability to reclaim social visibility and audibility. For him, and I paraphrase, the relation of a *je*/I to a *you*/*tu* presupposes a *we*/*nous* that rests in the net of social protection. He elaborates, saying that it is only from this *we*/*nous* that *you*/*tu* can act as an address for a *I/je*.[26] The following excerpt from *Retour à Forbach* clearly illustrates this multidirectional interplay of *je* and *tu*. In this case, Sauder is addressed by Flavia, another childhood friend, who grew up poor, the granddaughter of an Italian miner. Now, she is the director of a local elementary school, standing right across from the field where her childhood home, a housing estate, used to be.

> —You do not betray your social heritage, Régis. Look at what you do. You came back. You are back here. You want to talk, you have things to say. The rise of the Front National in Forbach angers you. I mean, you can't bear it since you decided to come back. And you want to do something, say something, so that it doesn't win. See Régis. You didn't altogether leave. We are from somewhere Régis. See, me, I am from Forbach, and a girl from Konelberg. I mean, I am not proud of it, but it seems to me, it doesn't seem to be as hard as it used to. You see, because I believe that what I have become, what I am today, well, it made me who I am. I can also take a step back about all this. Some people used to tell me I was taking French people's bread and butter, you know. Like I told you earlier, I was the daughter of Italian immigrants; I suffered from that too. In the end, well, I want to think there is always an explication. I can understand the fears the Front National manipulates. (31"00)[27]

For Le Blanc, a *je/I* without the possibility of a reciprocal address and 'the reversibility of pronouns' is an act of enunciation, not self-enunciation.[28] Knowing that the *tu* she addresses is Régis Sauder, this statement legitimises Flavia's voice as a pure voice – we hear it as a voice-over interpellation as we watch the snow falling over Forbach. Sauder's and Hasse's embodied implications produce conditions that help restore interpersonal sociality within the film encounter as a space created between two subjects. However, the actuality of a broader communal *we/nous* remains in question in both films.

*Sur les cendres du vieux monde* grapples with the degradation of economic vitality, the erosion of social life and the general resignation taking hold in everyone's minds. The dislocation of working-class culture as well as regional and sectorial identities prevents a collective identity from being fully enacted and enunciated. Hasse introduces recurring subjects in his personal cartography of the Fensch valley's precarious territoriality. Didier is a forty-year-old interim steelworker; Hamid and Djamel, both sons of Algerian immigrants, never left, even though they never worked for the mill, unlike their fathers. Omar is a disillusioned twenty-eight-year-old whose immigrant status has kept him unemployed and dependent on his mother's support. The film-maker also meets again with his father, who retired early after spending a career as a mid-level manager at several local steel mills, and two childhood friends. 'James Dean', who recently returned to the region after spending years in Australia, unloads cargo planes at Luxemburg airport. Rachel, whose grandfather was a coal miner, works in finance in Luxemburg city.

Employment, or rather its lack, structures the film. The town, nestled in the heart of the valley, is home to a large mill, one of the few still active in the region. Echoing Djamel, who early on describes this mill as 'the heart and the brain' of Uckange, the editing consistently reminds us of its centrality in the region's economic and social topography. The metallic carcass finds its way in the background of almost every sequence throughout the film. Once this heart and brain have stopped for good, the town will face its finality like a human body. Images of empty streets, old mining neighbourhoods slowly engulfed by underground waters seeping in the coal basin and apartment buildings scheduled for demolition, and the final announcement that the only maternity ward has closed, all attest to a region abandoned to a programmed fate.

The old paternalist social assistance system, which prevailed and structured industrial working-class and coal miners' communities through the late 1960s, is evoked on several occasions in the films. Hasse reminisces with Hamid and Djamel when, as children of steelworkers, they would all receive a Christmas present – the same present – from the mill. Growing up, the Fensch was home to a diverse community: the children of Italian, North African, Portuguese immigrants played together, as friends, with the sons of French-born families. Workers' families could buy coal directly from the mill to heat their houses at a discounted price through the winter. These conversations remind us that it was in the interest of industrial capitalists to keep their workforce healthy and loyal in this old model. To that end, various 'social protection techniques and institutions' were set up in the twentieth century 'to reduce social insecurity and keep the risk of unemployment, illness, accident and social exclusion calculable for an increasing number of the national population', as Isabell Lorey points out.[29] Still, working at the mills meant facing harsh conditions and the possibility of tragic deaths. If these social protections were politically motivated – 'tam[ing] the virus of social vulnerability' warded off 'the potentiality for revolt', as Robert Castel posits – they nevertheless granted the workers and their families the ability to 'plan for the future'.[30] For instance, this system allowed coal miners to buy out their houses from the mines' managing companies, after years of sacrifices, providing them with the security of a home for the rest of their lives – or so they thought. Today, old miners face expropriation from houses that have become inhabitable.

For the predominantly male subjects that we encounter in *Sur les cendres du vieux monde,* 'this plan for the future' no longer seems realistic and achievable. Didier's professional history is particularly representative of this new status quo. When we first meet him, he has been on and off temporary jobs for ten years and spent three years unemployed. The benefits he collected during that time allowed his wife to open a small sewing business. Throughout the film, which covers a whole year, Didier goes through five different jobs. Coming off several short-term contracts, extended with unkept promises of full-time employment in steel mills, he was forced to accept various temp gigs. In Luxemburg, he worked as a forklift driver. Later, in Germany, he weighed large pieces of meat in a slaughterhouse before returning to Luxemburg. Because of this discontinuous professional trajectory, Didier's dream of owning his own house with a small private yard for his dog while his wife's sewing business continues to thrive have all evaporated. He and his wife have lost faith in the system, collective solidarity and trade unions; now, they just 'live this way', one day at a time.

In 1988, Claudine Offredi distinguished between the territoriality/space of poverty and that of precarity.[31] Poverty, she claimed, is typically marked by stigmas and symbols that affirm poverty as an individual and collective identity. Stasis defines the space of poverty. Precarious subjects, in contrast, find themselves stuck in the endless mobility and discontinuity of their situation, a tension *Sur les cendres du vieux monde* makes clear. Because of that, their identity ends up being paradoxically built on provisional markers. Solitude, difference and invisibility characterise precarious social territoriality.

Many of the people Hasse interviews respond to the indeterminacy of their future by clinging to an ambiguous local identity as if to reclaim some sense of groundedness amid forced mobility, uncertainty and insecurity. Asked why he never left Hayange, especially now that the only jobs available to him seem to be in Luxemburg and Germany, Didier retorts that he has travelled. Still, his life remains here with his family, his house, his roots. Everything is here for him. 'We are from Lorraine, period! I can't explain it!', he states. Being from Lorraine also means identifying with the post-industrial downturn. This attachment may grant him stability in a state of permanent ambiguity, in-betweenness and invisibility. Nonetheless, it further entraps him into this precarious space and the precariousness of his future.

Didier's longing for his Lorraine recalls what Le Blanc describes as the 'social melancholy' of the precarious subject: a 'stubborn attachment to loss, as the sole available mode of response'.[32] While Offredi distinguished poverty from precarity in spatial terms, Le Blanc introduces subjective, psycho-social aspects.

[P]recarity [...] is first and foremost subjective, as the precarious subjects feel useless. [...] Precarious subjects are always in surplus in the specific social site in which they live [...] Precarious subjects are thus both inside and outside the social community [...] Precarious subjects still wish to participate in the disqualifying game of social norms, to continue to feel like 'someone' who has not entirely fallen out of sight, who strives to keep head above water.[33]

These tensions are palpable in Didier's frustrations, his repeated assertions that he cannot stay inactive, and his rejection of trade unionism. Employed, he still maintains the fiction of being someone somewhat normal. While 'excluded' from the stability and security of permanent employment, he still feels included in the social game. This determination may explain his disenchantment with trade unions and his decision to vote Front National at the end of the film. Others also insist on the connection between the willingness to share responsibility and social change; yet, they cannot foresee any successful collective action crystallising in the region, or more broadly, in the current system of work. Hamid and others appeal to the force of collective solidarity: if people started taking actions together, *we/nous* could stop this system, he proclaims. An old ideal, collective solidarity has ceased to be a (realistic) aspiration. Resignation and cynicism thus predominate.

Rachel, who seems to have protected herself from her region's destiny by working in the financial sector in Luxemburg, is under no illusions and offers no comfort. Towards the end of the film, she calls out her old school friend, now film-maker Laurent Hasse, as they discuss Didier's situation:

> Rachel: There is no solution. But he didn't lose his job because Luxemburg, a global financial hub, is only a few miles away.
> Hasse: No, he did because precarity is now integral to the contemporary workplace so that people can be laid off more easily.
> Rachel: And it's the law of profitability [...] But I don't personally pull the world's strings. I have no say in this. I have my opinion; I know it's despicable. I also know some day someone will thank me before they fire me.

Hasse: You do think this will happen?
Rachel: Of course! It will happen to everyone.
Everyone gets shown the way out someday, don't you
think? I do […] What should I do? What do you do?
Well, you film him, and I pity him. (55"12–56"25)

Here, Rachel questions the utility of her friend's work, as Hasse
remarks in a follow-up voice-over narration: 'Rachel pities yet
another unemployed man, and I film him. In her mind, my work
is useless. I might as well believe in Santa Claus and film his
cousin from Lorraine, Saint Nicolas' (56"28–56"39). These
comments touch upon the stake of films like *Sur les cendres du
vieux monde* and *Retour à Forbach*: how to film so as not to
generate pity? What does/can cinema do? What is the intended
intervention of these films?

Insecurity is equally central to Régis Sauder's *Retour à Forbach*,
as rising xenophobia and fear aggravate Forbach's residents'
precarious social reality. However, this second film is less directly
invested in the transformations of employment, focusing more
on the social and political effects of the town's economic decline.
Several sequences echo what Judith Butler describes as 'the social
and economic organization of needs and, more particularly, the
production of "insecurity" for the purpose of extending excessive
security policies', or 'precarization as a process that produces not
only subjects but also "insecurity" as the central preoccupation
of the subject'.[34]

Concerns about economic and social insecurity are
particularly pronounced in two interviews with two natives of
Forbach, both sons of Algerian immigrants, working in local
factories. One used to live in the same coal-mining
neighbourhood (now an empty lot) where Sauder's friend, Flavia,
spent her childhood; the other in the now infamous Cité du
Wiesberg, a housing project that continues to house a large
immigrant population. In a sequence that connects their two
testimonies, they describe the increasingly violent nature of the
workplace. Discouraged and fearful of losing their jobs, workers
are increasingly resigned to accepting conditions that leave them
financially vulnerable, they say. Common threats of relocations

allow management to curtail demands for higher salaries. Like many of his colleagues, the first man admits he has grown accustomed to these everyday aggressions in the workplace. Sadly, such hostility deters individual workers from engaging in collective action. Instead, everyone feels lucky to hold a permanent contract (CDI), like him, and chooses self-protection: 'I try to save my job, it's not like saving my life, because it has not become a question of life and death yet, but you feel socially steamrolled. Hence you just hold on to everything you can to not get completely crushed' (58"34–58"46). Shortly after, the second interviewee confirms the decline of collective solidarity in the workplace. Social vulnerability no longer entices people to revolt. Quite the opposite, precarity has become a tool to keep people in check, the man adds:

> — It's not my world; I don't belong in our present reality. Today, we live in a world where employment has become scarce, a situation that profits business owners. Today, when you complain, your boss replies: 'if you're not happy, you can just leave; fifteen people are waiting for this job.' What can we do? We have become lackeys. Let's face it: we are scared of losing our jobs, we have a mortgage, so we just accept everything, we are resigned, we shut up! (59"02–59"49)

Editing intermeshes these testimonies with static portrait shots of Forbach residents of different backgrounds, ages and ethnicities standing, facing the camera as if to draw the viewers' attention to their existence.

Both *Retour à Forbach* and *Sur les cendres du vieux monde* remind viewers that immigration has been integral to Lorraine's industrial social history and local cultural sedimentation. Families of French, Italian, Algerian, Moroccan or German descent have long cohabited in these mining and steel workers' neighbourhoods. This diversity defined both film-makers' childhoods and their social relations. Hasse recalls that, growing up, his friends' last names would be Schiltz, Del Vecchio, Cartéri, Benara, Taîbi or Bonfils. It only mattered that they could all play together. Sauder's memories evoke a more complex understanding of who he was, positioning him as a link between different communities. Returning to the grounds of his former middle school, he bluntly addresses in a voice-over monologue the social violence that surrounds children and teenagers when they are most vulnerable, still unsure of who they are independently of how others see and define them:

> Shame is like a second skin. Everyone is ashamed of something. The shame we don't talk about. I was a young boy who liked to dream and read and who didn't like to play soccer. I am afraid of the ball, which causes suspicion about me. I am like a girl since I am scared of balls. So, I am the victim of insults. In middle school, dickheads have their moment of glory. *[Sauder lists a series of slurs commonly heard in school].* I carry a supplemental defect: I speak with hardly any of the local accent. I am like a bastard child, the son of a *pied-noir* mother and a Lorraine-born father, a daddy's boy, the schoolteacher's son. I am well-mannered, and I speak like the uptown's bourgeois, the French language that they speak in France's heartland. In German classes, pure Lorraine kids are assigned to groups who speak the local dialect. I am moved into the Francophone group with immigrants. Because of that, my friends are girls and Arabs who live in the housing estate. (24"19–26"51)

Throughout *Retour à Forbach*, various interlocutors reflect on these social and ethnic lines inherited from childhood. The question of identity is much more pronounced and painful in *Retour à Forbach* than in *Sur les cendres du vieux monde*, where it is hardly emphasised as such. In *Retour à Forbach*, Front National votes and xenophobia are explicitly debated, 'understood', defended even, by people whose parents immigrated to France decades ago. In contrast, Didier's decision to join a FN electoral list at the end of *Sur les cendres du vieux monde* is met with criticism. Some friends ask whether he is 'stupid' or 'naive'. These two different sets of reactions are sobering reminders of

Figure 13. Noah waving at the camera, from his new bedroom's
window, in *Retour à Forbach* © Régis Sauder.

the Front National's steady rise and strengthening influence in France since the early 2000s. Class and ethnicity intersect throughout Régis Sauder's self-labelled 'subjective cartography' of Forbach. In acknowledging that his social ambiguity led to his malaise as a child, the film-maker leverages his personal history to intercede in encouraging different communities to find common ground.

Intergenerational dialogues are crucial in the film's impulsion to generate hope and mobilise new filiations. The best illustration for this project comes at the very end of the film. By that time, Régis Sauder's father has passed away and the family's house has been for sale. The sequence superimposes the soundtrack from the closing onto images of this house where the film-maker grew up (1'15"09–1'16"02). As soon as the sound of Régis Sauder's pen signing the contract stops, a close-up shot of what was once his bedroom's window introduces Noah, the son of the new owners, waving at Sauder's camera (see Fig. 13). This transition dramatises a symbolic handover between Régis Sauder and Noah, two native sons of Forbach – the former, the son of a *pied-noir* mother and a French-born father, the latter, the son of Moroccan immigrants.

Other connections, less symbolic, occur that reinforce the impact that small actions may yield against racism and xenophobia. If, by the end of *Sur les cendres du vieux monde*, Rachel wondered what she could do, *Retour à Forbach* highlights the small roles that some in the community choose to play. Flavia tells her friend: 'Every day, I feel like I am right. Emotionally, it is not an easy profession, even if it's a beautiful profession. I have to face human needs. Every day, I go back to work, and I have the sentiment, not that I head for battle, but that I simply do something good, positive.' Similarly, we see a local history professor teach French literacy to recently arrived immigrant families and women. Despite Sauder's bleak emphasis on the economic desolation creeping up around the town, *Retour à Forbach* strives to scrape for and uncover Forbach's residual sociality. In that regard, it is overall more optimistic than *Sur les cendres du vieux monde*.

### *Fils de Lip* – Troubling the archive, finding justice

Moving away from post-industrial Lorraine, *Fils de Lip* takes the viewer to Besançon, a mid-size city about two hundred miles south of Lorraine, famously known for being the home of Lip, France's leading watch manufacturer from the late nineteenth century onwards. In the 1970s, the name Lip became a symbol of workers' empowerment after the factory employees united against executive attempts to lay off a large number of them. Following a first successful strike in 1973–4, *les Lip* resumed their fight in 1976. However, the resolution of this second conflict failed to receive the same public attention and critical scrutiny that helped perpetuate the epic and glorious memory of *les Lip*'s victory in 1974. Faverjon's parents, Liliane and André, both took part in these strikes; he was a mechanic, and she worked as a clerk. Born in 1972, Thomas Faverjon spent much of his early childhood inside the Lip factory located in the Palente neighbourhood, where he and his parents lived. In 1979, the movement's leaders prioritised the French government's official recognition of Lip as an Industrial Cooperative in their determination to turn into reality the long-lasting goal of workers' struggles: self-management. Because of that, they agreed to the state's conditions, and most contentiously to the laying off of 108 of them, just under a third of *les Lip*.[35] Liliane Faverjon was among those sacrificed; André, her husband, stayed as a mechanic in the newly established Industrial Cooperative until it went bankrupt in 1987.[36] Liliane and the dozens of others sidelined felt betrayed. For many, like her, a long cycle of unemployment began. At some point in the film, she reminds her son that shortly after that layoff, she started taking care of children for a living, as she was unable to find another long-term job elsewhere.

Faverjon first got the idea for *Fils de Lip* in the late 1990s; then, a film student at the Fémis in Paris, he had seen *Reprise* (1996), Hervé Le Roux's three-hour-long investigation of the history of the Wonder factory in Saint-Ouen. In this documentary, Le Roux searches for the nameless young woman who, on 10 June 1968, unintentionally became the heroine of the short militant film *Reprise du travail aux usines Wonder*. Walking by the gates of the Wonder factory as workers were returning to work after being on strike for weeks, two IDHEC film students started recording the commotion. The long take sequence features a group of men – two union leaders, a local politician and a young student – surrounding a young woman. The film ends before we get a chance to know whether she goes back inside the factory or not. Fascinated by this woman, Le Roux decided to find her to allow her to share her perspective on what happened that day and whether or not she gave in.

Unaware of the real reasons for his mother's decades-long silence about Lip, Thomas Faverjon wanted to do the same: to give her a chance to share her experience with *les Lip* and reconcile with this glorious legacy she had contributed to, despite her present disaffection with it. Le Roux was unable to find his heroine. Faverjon faced a slightly different obstacle: his parents refused to answer his questions. Far from being discouraged, he started investigating on his own, interviewing other Lip militants; he realised that every interview pointed him back to the first strikes, 1973–4. Even the many militant films that were shot at the time, found in the Fémis's archives, focused on the first three years: Dominique Dubosc's *Lip 73, ou le goût du collectif* (1976), Chris Marker and Roger Louis's *Puisqu'on vous dit que c'est possible/We Maintain It's Possible* (1973), Carole Roussopoulos's six-part video series (1973–6). He could hardly find anything about the second strikes, let alone what would emerge as their contentious denouement. While researching for the film, back home in Besançon, Thomas Faverjon found a newspaper article written the day after the vote that took place in 1979. His mother had kept it all these years, hidden in the back of her bedroom closet. The discovery re-energised Faverjon's determination to make the film and gave *Fils de Lip* a new meaning. Intended as an act of transmission between legacies inherited from the past and new stories to come in the future, his documentary labour morphed into a healing practice, despite his mother's initial reluctance to participate.

*Fils de Lip* mixes archival footage from old militant films with present-day footage to provide a rare glimpse into one of France's most emblematic workers' struggles. In his recent book, *Opening the Gates: The Lip Affair, 1968–1981,* Donald Reid recalls that the Lip labour disputes of the 1970s indeed were 'an *affaire* in the French sense of the term [...] a political and social conflict that preoccupied and divided France'.[37] Just a few years after May '68 failed to bring about radical changes, the Lip strikes forced the French to 'question a number of fundamental principles of capitalist market society'.[38] The movement unfolded in two stages, 1973–4 and 1976–9. Both times, *les Lip* united to protect their jobs and oppose the demands of global capitalism. While engaging in this process, they unveiled new possibilities for themselves and other struggles. From the outside, the tactics deployed to put pressure on industrial interests in 1973 were fulfilling the ideals that May '68 had failed to deliver. Internally, Lip opened new doors for women's activism that previous workers' struggles, such as the one recorded in Saint-Ouen in front of the Wonder factory on 10 June 1968, had carefully kept shut. Much of the public and cinematic attention that the strikes received in the mid-1970s celebrated their embodiment of solidarity, community and democracy in the workplace.

To this day, this movement is collectively remembered as a 'positive, glorious, epic' chapter in French modern social history. However, most forget that, in 1979, *les Lip*, the ideal community that this narrative celebrates, ceased to exist.[39] To secure the legal status of the Industrial Cooperative, the movement's union leaders agreed to the French government's conditions that 108 Lips be laid off. This decision disproportionately affected the most vulnerable members of the community, many unskilled and older women. It also signalled the beginning of a new politics of labour in France that would see the government and unions siding with business interest at the expense of the workers' social protection. In his conclusion to *Opening the Gates*, Donald Reid remarks:

> As the Lip conflict becomes history, there has developed a national memory of the conflict of 1973, rooted less in the individual lives of Lip workers than in what those throughout France who participated with them took from the struggle. Although this memory draws on what the supporters knew and experienced in 1973, it is presented now by leaders of the conflict themselves, whose story it is as well, in new forms of the national tours that galvanized the nation at the time.[40]

This approach is clearly at work in Christian Rouaud's feature-length documentary, *Les Lip: L'imagination au pouvoir*, which opened in 300 French theatres in 2007 and was nominated for a César for Best Documentary in 2008. Released the same year, these two films could not be more different.

Faverjon's medium-length film – it is 47 minutes long – did not reach mainstream audiences like *Les Lip: L'imagination au pouvoir* did. Still, it received several accolades in festivals, including the Etats-Généraux du Documentaire in Lussas and the Ecrans du Réel in Le Mans, where it received a prize for Best First Documentary. Intrigued by his parents' refusal to condone the official narrative, Faverjon focused on the later years of the Lip strikes' history to understand the reasons behind his parents' disaffection and his mother's resentment. His decision to take the counterpoint to the prevailing narrative earned him some rare praises, most notably from Chris Marker, who praised *Fils de Lip* as the 'most spirited, most just, and most necessary' film ever made on the struggles.[41] The renowned film-maker noted Faverjon's 'privileged position in the family tree of this struggle' as one possible reason to explain the singularity of this film.[42] I propose, going even further than Marker, that being the son of Lip workers, the young film-maker had 'to know [...] what [came] before [him]'.[43] The resolution taken in 1979 directly impacted the social and political heritage his parents had passed down, or chosen not to.[44] Therefore, making *Fils de Lip* was 'necessary' inasmuch as it honoured his mother's silenced legacy, and 'just' because it enabled her to reclaim her part in this history. Only then could he fully claim to be the son of Lip workers/militants. The film thus stands apart in the existing cinematic corpus dedicated to the Lip strikes of the 1970s. Importantly, it successfully 'reaffirm[s]' Lip's political legacy in ways that Rouaud's film simply does not and cannot.

Intimately rooted in the impact Lip's denouement had on individual lives, particularly his mother's, *Fils de Lip* rewrites Lip's social history and the present legacy of this emblematic struggle from the perspective of discordant voices that were ignored, silenced and sacrificed to the delayed fulfilment of May '68's promises. Bookended with two sequences featuring two widely known *militantes* of that struggle, Fatima (Demougeot) at the beginning and Monique (Piton) at the end, *Fils de Lip* revolves around the recollections and testimonies of a few witnesses – Jacky (Burtz), François (Laurent), Colette and Françoise. Both women, like Liliane, were laid off in 1980. While Colette would do it all over again, Françoise shares Liliane's deception. Jacky and François were among those who denounced the decision made in 1979, and proposed a counter-motion that refused the layoffs and supported continuing the fight as one, indivisible community.[45] Introduced solely by their first names, all are brought on an equal footing as members of the Lip collective, not as leaders or representatives of specific union lines. Resting upon conventional storytelling devices – interviews, a compilation of archival footage and first-person narration – *Fils*

Figure 14. Faverjon family portrait, *Fils de Lip* (2007)
© Thomas Faverjon.

*de Lip* introduces the viewers to new accounts and new voices,
ultimately bringing us to reconsider Lip's history from the
perspective of new (matrilineal) filiations. Most significantly,
Faverjon effectively reopens the Lip archives from the vantage
point of a specific date, 3 October 1979, the day leaders struck
the mortal blow that ended *les Lip.*

By separating 'the Lip experience' from the mainly male
'historical figures' who appear in *Les Lip: L'imagination au pouvoir,*
Faverjon reclaims it as 'central to [his] identity and draw[s]
meaning and inspiration from it'.[46] Crucially, this 'Lip experience'
now reflects the complex affectivity that these struggles
generated for those who lived and shaped it, and not a national
political mythology that remained embedded in the continuing
demise of the Left's ideals in following decades. At the end of
the film, it is this experience and this memory that Thomas
Faverjon performs when posing alongside his parents for a final
portrait, to the sound of his voice-over declaring: 'Yes, I am the
son of Lip [workers/militants] who still believes that it is possible'
(see Fig. 14).[47] This concluding statement recovers the 'positive,

glorious, epic' achievements that *les Lip* realised in the mid-1970s and the political legacy left by/in the (women's) voices that incomplete official accounts unjustly erased, despite their being perfect embodiments of *les Lip*'s most fundamental values at the onset of their strikes in 1973.

Privileging individual recollections that gradually aggregate into a counter-memory, Thomas Faverjon echoes Joëlle Beurier's views in 'La mémoire Lip ou la fin du mythe autogestionnaire', an essay that postulates the coexistence of two conflicting memory 'circles'.[48] In the 1990s, Beurier, whose father worked as a manager on the machine shop floor at Lip, conducted interviews with former Lip workers for her master's thesis. At the time, she was struck by the disconnect she saw between these individuals' testimonies and what collective memory celebrated. In the latter, the Lip strikes of the 1970s were nothing less than bold, radical accomplishments in the history of workers' political struggles.[49] This view came from the outside, from those who had supported *les Lip*'s actions – the 'second memory circle'.[50] These activists had come from other regions of France, sometimes from abroad, and were fascinated by the Lip workers' successful implementation of self-management in the workplace. Their presence helped give the strikes greater national and international visibility. Additionally, when militant film-makers, including Chris Marker, Dominique Dubosc, Cinélutte and Carole Roussopoulos, arrived in 1976, they witnessed the movement's heyday.[51] As a result, their films consolidated *les Lip* as a symbol of working-class cohesion and radical emancipation. However, by 1978, nobody was there to record the collective body known as *les Lip* fall apart.

For Beurier, the positivity of this 'second circle' largely overshadowed a more nuanced narrative, born of the memories, experiences and feelings of a 'primordial circle', namely the Lip workers themselves. Unlike outsiders, who came and went, the workers stayed from beginning to end. Beautiful and inspiring as the collective energy and solidarity were in the early days, by the end, bitterness and disillusionment marred their memory. In their view, *les Lip* no longer embodied the victorious affirmation of workers in the aftermath of May '68. Instead, their failures signalled the advent of a new economic, political and social order where workers' security would come under the attack of not only capitalist interests but also, and most alarmingly, of the state.[52]

In the light of Beurier's distinctions between these two parallel memories, *Fils de Lip* needs to be seen as a rare attempt to honour the memory carried on by this 'primordial circle'. In comparison, Christian Rouaud's *L'imagination au pouvoir* contributes, as Tangui Perron rightly points out, to the cultural memory work supported by the 'second circle'. Rouaud himself is keen to note his participation in the 1970s and relate different ways in which he and others brought their support to the Lip workers: 'Lip, we all contributed to various extents, we went on supporting strikes, we posted flyers, we handed out *Lip-Unité* on the streets, we sold watches, we took a tour of the factory in Besançon, we demonstrated in the rain with the crowds.'[53] He also stresses the inspirational value of Lip's 'collective dream' for present and future generations.[54] In line with the narrative promoted by the 'second circle', *L'imagination au pouvoir* perfectly encapsulates the enduring currency of this vision in present times. Writing on the genesis of his film, he states that Lip remains a victory in the memory of every person who was politically active in the aftermath of May '68. The focus of *L'imagination au pouvoir* on the first two years (1973–5) and the leaders of the movement supports the consensual narrative promoted by the 'second circle' – a decision that partly explains the film's broad appeal to French audiences and its warm critical reception.[55] In that regard, Fatima Demougeot's presence in both Rouaud's and Faverjon's films is quite striking. In *L'imagination au pouvoir*, her voice joins the chorus of former leaders recollecting the chronology of events that propelled *les Lip* to national headlines. *Fils de Lip* gives her the opportunity to reconsider her actions and those taken by *les Lip* as a community from the more complex vantage point of their end.

If Perron finds *Fils de Lip* to represent, in contrast, the memory of the 'first' circles, I would like to suggest that this film opens up the dichotomy drawn by Beurier. Thomas Faverjon is the son of Lip workers left grappling with a heritage where pride, loss and deception cannot be fully disentangled from one another. In that sense, he embodies a third circle, whose perspective has been shaped by both memories; subsequently, his response is to actively rework Lip's (hi)story by recognising and reaffirming *les Lip* as a fundamentally disparate community.[56] By the time it reaches its conclusion, *Fils de Lip* has acknowledged the complexity of this legacy, restored justice to voices and feelings that have been left out, and its title can successfully invoke the multiple filiations that converge, without merging, in the name Lip.

As a collective incarnation, the movement harboured a variety of experiences, commitments, outcomes and affects – male, female, professional, militant, union leaders, old, young, radical, moderate, managers, unskilled workers, skilled workers, and so forth. Considering Liliane Faverjon's central role in *Fils de Lip*, much consideration must go to the affective toll the conflict's resolution had on unskilled female workers. To that end, the film successfully imbricates an intimate familial narrative with a broader social history. As he recalled in an interview recorded in 2007, Faverjon had no idea, as a child, that his parents were involved in the most emblematic workers' struggles since May '68.

> In 1978, I was six years old, and my mother was working at Lip. She had not explained to me that, for a few years, she had been on strike, nor that Lip was not an ordinary factory. The fact that workers would take turn watching the site on Sundays seemed utterly normal to me, so did the presence of a childcare centre and the fact that everyone knew everyone.[57]

In 1976, the women in the movement set up the childcare facility – three years after the idea had been proposed. 'Half of the Lip workers and office personnel were women', Donald Reid explains in the opening chapter of his *Opening the Gates*.[58] But, most importantly, 'close to half of them were single, widowed, divorced, or unmarried mothers', he adds. A concern for working women long before the strikes, childcare became a vital issue for those who joined in the strikes.

Faverjon's recollection of a childcare centre inside the factory is, therefore, not as anecdotal as it may seem. While the union leadership saw job protection and self-management as their primary goals, women's activism gradually emphasised the need to combat pervasive and systemic forms of gender bias at work, at home and in union culture. In 1975, the Women's Group made more specific demands to remedy gender inequality within *les Lip* and at Lip: first, in *Lip au féminin*, a publication introduced in 1973 to offer a female perspective on the movement; second, through a list of demands extended to both union leaders and Lip's executive director.[59] In the years that followed, the predominantly male union leadership started restricting the Women's Group's activities, even though the issues they raised were gaining national momentum.

*Fils de Lip* effectively demystifies Lip's official *His*tory while reaffirming the (film) archive as a site of radical heterogeneity. Indeed, the effects of dissonance linger well beyond their immediate occurrence in any given instance to reverberate across the film, altering the viewers' reading of other sequences and the story of Lip more broadly. Visual and editing effects, such as slow motion, freeze frames and audio-visual dissonance, repeatedly trouble the official emphasis predominantly placed on collective pride and solidarity in the collective memory of the Lip struggles of the 1970s. Liliane and André Faverjon's resistance to being documentary subjects, and their persisting hard-to-break silence, forced the film-maker to imagine creative ways to recount their story. Among them, two montage sequences initiate a critical interrogation of film and print archival materials. The first of these comes early in the film (4"40–12"01) and provides viewers with a handy chronological overview of the critical moments and events that took place between 1973 and 1979. While the voice-over accompanying this assembled footage follows a fairly traditional pattern, it nonetheless begins the film's sustained and meticulous deconstruction of Lip's official narrative. This voice-over narration relates what Faverjon's father *could have said* had he been more willing to answer his son's questions. Left to his own words, Faverjon is forced to stage an imagined dialogue with his father, cued with these words: 'It's up to me to figure it out, and tell the story? You feel no pride in the six years you spent fighting for your jobs? Nothing? Father, you could tell me.' The cheerful tone and music that run through the montage betray Faverjon's ironic rehashing of the 'positive, glorious, epic' legacy of the strikes.

Faverjon's *troubling* of the archive becomes more pointed a few minutes later, when he repeats the trick, focusing this time on his mother's recollections. His voice-over recalls how the movement took a turn after efforts to get the Industrial Cooperative legally authorised were initiated. In particular, he points to the growing tensions that arose within the community over the decision to comply with the French government's request to divide *les Lip* into three groups, A, B and C. As we hear these explanations, archival footage shows the massive demonstration that took place in Besançon in 1976 despite the rain. The voice-over narration mentions the rebellion of a few leaders from the Action Committee against such deliberate divisions. Fatima, Jacky and François, the leaders in question, are all interviewed in *Fils de Lip* (21"58–22"17; 22"36–23"20). These clips prominently feature the famous slogan 'Lip Vivra/Lip will Live', causing ironic dissonance between the images and the narration. Moreover, just before we see the crowd gathered behind the banner, the footage undergoes a slow-motion effect, and the screen splits in three unequal vertical bands, symbolising the fragmentation of this collective force into three groups. The split screen, combined with a black fade-out, visually captures the violence that *les Lip* exerted upon themselves and, more directly 108 among them, when they cut them off from the group and *les Lip*'s political legacy (22"40–22"55) (see Figs 15–16).[60] Seconds later, a shrinking iris closes in on Liliane Faverjon, lost in this massive crowd gathered for the 1976 demonstration. Faverjon ventriloquises his mother's imagined voice-over conclusion for the sequence: 'June 1980, I am sent back to square one, and on my own to figure it out.'[61]

On 3 October 1979, the General Assembly voted and approved the plan backed by CFDT leaders to accept the two conditions set by the French government for L.I.P. Cooperative to be finally legalised. This vote changed Liliane Faverjon's life.

Figures 15–16. The split screen used to represent the three groups that resulted in the layoffs of 108 members of the Lip community © Thomas Faverjon.

One demand required that workers be divided into three groups, as already mentioned. While groups A and B would be rehired quickly or employed in one of the Workshop Councils set up to operate in parallel with the manufacturing activities, the future of the 108 employees included in group C had yet to be determined.[62] Almost six years to the day, the General Assembly renounced its commitment to protecting 'a community whose identity was rooted in the memory of the vote of October 1973' when it unanimously rejected the government mediator's plan to lay off 159 workers.[63] The resignation of the CFDT leaders to save the cooperative at the expense of the community deeply fractured the cohesion of *les Lip*, many of whom condemned this sacrifice of the most vulnerable among them. This decision contradicted the 'powerful language of social justice' that had cemented the movement from its beginning and, most symbolically, Charles Piaget's opposition to 'mass layoffs from enterprises that workers had made as "a regulator inherent in the capitalist regime, but [...] absolutely not necessary in an economy made for man"'.[64] The 1979 vote disproportionately affected 'female OS, particularly older women, including many who had put body and soul into the conflict', leaving them vulnerable to a rapidly rising unemployment rate.[65]

Leading into this second montage of archival footage, Faverjon includes a series of shots filmed inside his parents' apartments. We follow the film-maker into their bedroom, making our way through empty rooms, closed and opened doors, and dark corridors. There, buried deep in her closet, he finds the newspaper article (see Figs 17–18) that his mother had kept and preserved since 3 October 1979.

This piece of yellowed paper materialises Lip's lasting emotional burden on her life. Returning to Derrida, I suggest that, by keeping this article, Liliane actively 'repress[ed] the archive' while bearing witness to repression as a form of embodied and affected archiving.[66] This imbrication of the political, the familial and the cinematic marks a pivotal turn for the film. Had Liliane not kept this article, Faverjon's documentary investigation might not have led him to elucidate the status of the C list and to uncover the political and affective

Figures 17–18. Article published on 3 October 1979, featuring
Liliane Faverjon that Thomas Faverjon, found buried in his mother's closet
© Thomas Faverjon.

significance of the 3 October 1979 vote. Stumbling upon this article buried in his mother's private belongings turns out to be the key that unlocks her secret. It also allows the film to become the 'most spirited, most just, and most necessary' film ever made on the Lip affair, as Chris Marker put it. Extracted from the repressed archives, this piece of paper becomes, from that point on, tinder for an alternative story to be told, one that reflects *les Lip* as a more complex, heterogeneous and troubled community.

Thomas Faverjon has anecdotally compared the making of *Fils de Lip* to undergoing psychoanalysis. The statement finds validation in the cinematic imbrication, at this central point of the film, of Faverjon's political intervention in Lip's memory and his deep personal commitment to his mother's well-being. Here, these two sequences are not just juxtaposed. It is as if two separate threads were suddenly collapsing into one another – a movement enhanced by the inclusion of brief shots revealing his mother sitting alone in her living room. She reappears in that same position shortly before the film's end when her son *gifts* her the words and testimonies left by others also placed on the C list. The healing happens in this reading session when Liliane can finally align her affects with others' who, like her, found themselves disowned by their community. In this intimate scene, Faverjon sits down with his mother in her living room but stays off the frame while the camera remains focused on her as she sits quietly, her dog by her side, to listen to her son. As he keeps reading, the initial medium shot turns into a close shot, bringing the viewers closer to her attentive face. Her son reads her various statements written by other C listees. His mother listens carefully, acquiescing and nodding when she hears words and sentences that describe her sentiments:

— To be on the C list. Since they divided us, something has been broken. When I told my husband that I was on the C list, he did not believe me. We feel like a burden that needs to be chucked out. What will happen to us? [...]

— It's true!

— We feel bitter, rejected. We finally accept it, we swallow

the pill, but it leaves an enormous deception. We always worked, we always fought, and in the end, they threw us out. They treated us like dirt.
— Exactly. Beautifully said. Beautifully written.
— [...] All we want is work like before. We do not care about the struggle or those who stay. We have so many questions. We are on list C, with a capital C. They fooled us, that's all! (*Liliane smiles, but not without emotions in her eyes*). (43"51–45"31)

This sequence ends with a close-up of Liliane Faverjon, smiling, seemingly content.

In the last minutes of his film, not only does Faverjon bring some relief to his mother, but he also frees Monique (Piton) from her iconic status within Lip's official *history*. Monique's visibility as a leader of the movement was primarily enhanced by her appearances in the videos *Lip I: Monique* (1973) and *Lip V: Christiane et Monique* (1976) in the series feminist film-maker Carole Roussopoulos made to highlight women's radical roles in the Lip struggles. As a single mother, a militant and a writer, Piton was quickly recognised as an unwilling leader of the movement. Most significantly, she voiced the aspirations of a mainly unskilled female workforce, hoping to redefine through their engagement within *les Lip* their roles and status as women in the (industrial) workplace, at home and in society at large.[67] In 1975, Piton appropriated Lip's slogan, *c'est possible!/it is possible!*, as the title of her memoirs of the struggle, published by Editions des Femmes. This commitment to the ideals of solidarity, sorority and equality is what Thomas Faverjon honours in his film's epilogue.

Introducing Monique as one of the many others not featured in the film allows her a meaningful *reprise*. While Monique appears to us as a cinematic figure – Faverjon chooses footage from Carole Roussopoulos's 1973 video *Lip I: Monique* – her image suddenly congeals into a freeze-frame. Faverjon's voice-over then invites Monique to correct what would otherwise be an incomplete history. A discernibly older voice starts reading a letter that Monique Piton had written in 1978, in which she explained why she was leaving *les Lip*. Meanwhile, the cinematic image reveals a concerned look on her face that, a few seconds ago, had appeared to us joyful. Whereas Le Roux's editing highlighted a cry of revolt, Faverjon's dissociation of image and sound underscores Monique's thoughtful critical distance and reflection. Affects come later, painfully revealing the enduring truth and deception captured in words written in 1978, thirty years later: 'Lip was a stain on the history of workers' struggles' (48"12–48"14). At this point, Thomas Faverjon *reprend* (takes over) Monique's reading.

The significance of this moment lies in the stress placed on failure, on deception and the enduring pain that the ideological compromises of twentieth-century workers' struggles have left in their wake. In *Fils de Lip*, the need to pass down past failures to the next generations is presented as vital. In this symbolic handover between Monique's and Faverjon's voices, and the intertwining of three temporalities – 1973, 1978 and the early 2000s – *Fils de Lip* replaces the fixed image of the past with a living voice, and allegorical stasis with human vulnerability and affectivity. In this moving sequence, Faverjon enacts a second act of transmission between himself and Carole Roussopoulos as two film-makers committed to social and political justice for all.

*Fils de Lip* engages in a reflection on cinema's intervention in history and collective memory and social documentary cinema's internal conflict between its support of communal politics and its recognition of individual justice. Thomas Faverjon's work with the Lip archives exceeds the mere goal of 'remembering' what has been forgotten or left out.[68] *Fils de Lip* restores a sense of justice for these Lip workers who were betrayed by their own, bringing legitimacy to the 'embodied affectivity' that is both foundational and residual to any social struggle. Martin O'Shaughnessy uses this phrase in his analysis of Hervé Le Roux's *Reprise* (1996). He contrasts 'the *langue* of political and institutional mediation' – used by trade unions, politicians and leftist militants – and 'the *parole* of embodied affectivity' of the young female OS worker who, in 1968, refused to comply with political and union authority's order to resume work at the Wonder factory in Saint-Ouen.[69] Both *Reprise* and *Fils de Lip* address the *langue/parole* and institutional/affective dialectics, underscored by O'Shaughnessy, with very different results. In *Reprise*, Le Roux's failure to find the mysterious woman in the Saint-Ouen of the 1990s leaves her for ever fixed as a celluloid allegory of 'insubordination'.[70] In contrast, Faverjon's dual implication in his film, as the son of a female Lip worker, laid off because of an ideological and political agenda, and as a film-maker, successfully delivers on his ambition to offer his mother, and other Lip workers, a chance to speak again. *Reprise*'s allegory of women's insubordination in 1968 foreclosed their political horizon for the future.[71] In contrast, *Fils de Lip* encourages us to trust that cross-generational transmission has political effects.

By the end of *Fils de Lip*, when Faverjon finally states, 'yes, I am the son of Lip (workers/militants) who still believes it is possible', he invokes numerous filiations at once: his mother's, his father's, *les Lip*'s, female militants', as well as the many disenchanted individuals left out of Lip's collective memory. He then reclaims a heritage that is fundamentally plural, contentious, simultaneously empowering and unjust. From this dual assertion of both strength and vulnerability, for *les Lip* as a collective body and for the movement itself, *Fils de Lip* stands out as a unique, 'just' and 'necessary' film in the corpus devoted to the significance of the Lip strikes.[72] Forsaking visions that are either too idealistic or victimising, Thomas Faverjon invites his viewers to see *les Lip* as the embodiment of painful contradictions between emancipatory politics and the pursuit of a political ethos defined by solidarity and care for one another.

This film remains committed to freeing his mother from a world in which she has been 'incarcerated' all those years, feeling abandoned and betrayed; for this reason, its intervention resonates widely.[73] Like Liliane, tens of thousands of employees continue to be laid off regularly, often on false premises, joining millions of individuals already unemployed. Inviting us to reconsider Lip's emblematic strikes from this perspective, *Fils de Lip* indirectly engages in more recent intersections of precarity and politics. In *State of Insecurity*, Isabell Lorey defines precarity as 'naturalized relations of domination, through which belonging to a group is attributed or denied to individuals'.[74]

According to Donald Reid, 'les Lip brought the values and practices of 1968 to their confrontation with business mergers and industrial downsizing in a new era of globalization' by 'defending the enterprise [...] as a geographically situated space [...] where employees could build communities, contest the untrammelled mobility of capital and labor'.[75] In contrast, Faverjon leaves the 'geographically situated space' of Lip's factory and industrial cooperative off-frame to focus instead on *les Lip's* failures to see that the 'enterprise' that they needed to defend as their main political accomplishment was, in fact, the social community (*les Lip*) it had successfully created, not the factory. Faverjon's inheritance from Lip is, therefore, a commitment to politics as the recognition of disparate voices.

> Lip leaves me with a question, democracy. It was clearly underscored by the vote that took place on 3 October 1979. Until then, none of the articles published in *Lip Unité* was signed. Following the rupture that caused the vote within the community, everyone made their positions clear, and names started to appear. An interesting debate about democracy unfolded among the leaders of the movements, with essays by Fatima, Jacky, and Charles Piaget. They each started speaking as individuals and diverged on how to practise democracy within the cooperatives. These texts were so fascinating that I thought about making something about it. I would like to revisit the question of democracy and its practical challenges for social struggles and movements and all of us in society. How can we organise without any entity seizing power over others? This question fascinates me.[76]

While *Fils de Lip* is committed to bringing closure to the Faverjons, mother and son, the film-maker's words redirect Lip's legacy outward and forward. *Les Lip* becomes a precursor for more recent radical social experiments in France such as Nuit Debout, Notre-Dame-des-Landes or the *Gilets Jaunes* as well as others conducted abroad, from Occupy to Podemos; it no longer stands solely as a follow-up to May '68. These movements have all explored and struggled with the challenge of practising radical equality and collective organisation. They also exceed the geographical confines of a specific worksite.

## Conclusion

In *Sur les cendres du vieux monde, Fils de Lip* and *Retour à Forbach*, film-making is endowed with the task of counteracting amnesia – as a cognitive process and as a politically and socially motivated project. As I have already argued in chapter 1, (re)affirming the value of a heritage inherited from the past and (re)claiming specific filiations do not necessarily stem from a nostalgic impulse to restore what once was. Quite the opposite, as they reckon with various forms of inheritances, these three films reveal new filiations, 'relaunching [through these] the past otherwise and keeping it [and its legacy] alive' for the future.[77] The precariousness of white male industrial workers' lives and the social exclusion of immigrant populations become contiguous experiences. Furthermore, *Fils de Lip* lets us hear an alternative story of *les Lip*, one which reconnects indignation and silent resignation into one single chorus of women's voices, sacrificed in the affirmation of *les Lip* as the living legacy of May '68. On a more personal level, *Fils de Lip* 'keeps' the film-maker's mother's legacy 'alive' – expressing gratitude to those, like her, whose actions were ultimately erased from the social and political heritage left by Lip.

# Chapter 4
# No pain, no gain: the ordinary brutality of (the) work(place)

Capitalism cannibalises us.

– Sophie Bruneau.[1]

Peut-on attendre que la masse extraordinaire de souffrance que produit un tel régime politico-économique soit un jour à l'origine d'un mouvement capable d'arrêter la course à l'abîme? [...] Le passage au 'libéralisme' s'accomplit de manière insensible, donc imperceptible, comme la dérive des continents, cachant ainsi aux regards ses effets les plus terribles à long terme.

– Pierre Bourdieu.[2]

Late September 2019, on a Saturday morning, just a few weeks into a new school year, Christine Renon, the highly respected director of an elementary school in Pantin, a northern suburb of Paris, took her own life on school grounds. Before doing so, she had mailed a letter to fellow school directors and regional administrators; she detailed her profound 'exhaustion' and utter hopelessness before the soul-crushing bureaucratic reality of her profession and the lack of resources available to her and her teaching staff.[3] The tragic event rattled the French education community. Gathered in front of the school to honour her memory a few days later, colleagues, parents, children and residents of the neighbourhood mourned a 'devoted', 'committed', 'caring' and 'human' teacher, mentor and friend.[4] For Marie Pezé, the founder of the first *Santé et Travail* (Health and Work) medical consultation at the public hospital in Nanterre in 1997, and author of *Ils ne mouraient pas tous mais tous étaient frappés: Journal de la consultation Souffrance et Travail 1997–2008* (2010), Renon's suicide is as eminently 'political' as those committed by the employees of France-Télécom (renamed Orange) and PSA Peugeot-Citroën back in 2007–9.[5]

> [Christine Renon] was simply someone who had her heart set on doing her work well, she had the sense of duty, like many civil servants, and she valued the very notion of public service [...] This suicide is signed, her message was political, and the Department of Education must answer to it.[6]

Clusters of suicides taking place in several French high-profile work sites during the second half of the 2000s intensified then-emerging debates about the correlation between work and many psychosomatic disorders. Sarah Waters, who has studied France's early twenty-first-century 'suicide epidemic', points out that France 'has the second-highest rate of workplace suicides in the world after Japan', with 'a 70 per cent increase in recorded cases since 2000'.[7]

Many sociologists, psychologists and labour historians have attributed these chilling statistics to a 'French paradox'.[8] Compared with other Europeans, French people 'expect more from work in terms of self-fulfilment and quality'.[9] As a result, they are more likely to express disappointment as regards their professional activity.[10] Dominique Méda, a prominent French sociologist of work, has long argued for a much shorter working week, positing it as a revolution that could simultaneously address the social and ecological crises French society continues to face.[11] Psychologist Yves Clot and psychoanalyst Christophe Dejours have, on the contrary, affirmed the centrality of work in the construction of human subjectivity and as a factor of well-being.[12] The main issue for them is not working per se but how work is currently organised. For this reason, they do not agree with the proponents of the 'end of work', a position that started gaining in popularity among radical economists, sociologists and political scientists in the late 1990s and early 2000s.[13] Together, however, these critiques promote a comprehensive review of work, as an economic and political system and a subjective and affective experience in the early twenty-first century. Historically, the question of work had been posed in terms of social in/justice, alienation and emancipation. Individuals' affective investment in their work had not drawn much scrutiny to date.

Documentary film-makers were already attuned to this correlation between work and suffering before news media started paying attention to the French epidemic of workplace suicides in 2008–9. Directly referencing Christophe Dejours's best-selling book *Souffrances en France. La banalisation de l'injustice sociale* (1998) as an inspiration in the opening sequence of their film *Ils ne mouraient pas tous mais tous étaient frappés/They didn't all die but all were hit* (2005), Sophie Bruneau and Marc-Antoine Roudil were the first to bring 'the very term of suffering […] at work or suffering caused by work' to the screen.[14] Within a few years, two more films followed, also done in collaboration with Christophe Dejours, Marie Pezé and a few other occupational therapists: *J'ai (très) mal au travail* (Jean-Michel Carré, 2007), and the three-part series co-produced by France Télévision, *La mise à mort du travail* (Jean-Robert Viallet, 2009). Against all odds, the unexpected attention these films garnered from a wide range of audiences, in theatres, on television and at various festivals, contributed to bringing public awareness to the growing *malaise* in the French workforce. Most significantly, these films successfully redirected already well-established discussions of the 'new post-Fordist, globalized and finance-driven [economic] order' towards public awareness about the much less debated affective impact of such 'profound changes in the nature of work'.[15] Well received by critics, these films helped audiences see experiences of burn-out, work-induced depression and suicidal thoughts as symptoms of 'broad structural changes in the economy' rather than individual disorders and a person's inability to cope with the demands of life.[16]

In this chapter, I concentrate on Sophie Bruneau's (and Marc-Antoine Roudil's) singular approach to the effects and affects of the transformed workplace and the resulting systemic degradation of work. My focus on Sophie Bruneau's films is motivated by her sustained cinematic interest in the subject over the years. In 2017, twelve years after *Ils ne mouraient pas tous mais tous étaient frappés* came out, she released *Rêver sous le capitalisme/Dreaming Under Capitalism*, a one-hour-long solo project, which she shot in her native Belgium.[17] An anthropologist by training, in these films Sophie Bruneau probes the reality of the contemporary workplace, focusing her viewers' attention on the pains that bodies, voices and dreams both internalise and manifest. Deeply influenced by Frederick Wiseman's work, she seeks, like the American film-maker, to produce films that 'make the ordinary visible and intelligible, that instil distance and make us see things as less familiar', and therefore more obvious.[18]

The focus on bodies, voices and how, together, they release meaningful social drama is evident in the three films that this chapter examines. Through minimalistic and suspensive cinematography, Bruneau's films draw out, for the viewers' attention, what Kathleen Stewart calls *ordinary affects*.[19] According to Stewart, the labels 'neoliberalism, advanced capitalism, and globalisation' that are commonly used to denounce the various economic, social and political systemic pressures exerted on individual lives fail to grasp fully 'the situation we find ourselves in'.[20] Instead, she urges us to consider 'the way [these forces] pick up density and texture as they move through bodies, dreams, dramas, and social worldings of all kinds'.[21]

Keeping Stewart's attentiveness to the embodied and internalised social dramas we each carry inside ourselves, I read Sophie Bruneau's documentary treatment of suffering in the workplace and from work as a practice of ordinary affectivity. As various *corps-parole* (embodied voices or speaking bodies) incarnate themselves before our eyes and ears, they return to being whole subject(ivitie)s again. The cinematic recording of the therapeutic process opens the private, confidential space and time of the 'Santé et Travail' consultations outward, bringing it into the public sphere. Through their work, Roudil and Bruneau interrogate documentary cinema's ability 'to affect and be [an] affected [...] mode of attention, attachment, and agency', in other words, the extent to which it can mediate an act of care.[22] To this end, my analysis cannot be limited to the two documentary features already mentioned. It must include

*Mon diplôme, c'est mon corps* (*My body is my degree*), an unfortunately overlooked eighteen-minute short that is included on the DVD of *Ils ne mouraient pas tous mais tous étaient frappés*.

These three films bind together reflections on the changing workplace, understood as a metonymy for society at large, and work as a practice of (health)care. In this specific context, ordinary affects simultaneously signal individual and collective dis-eases and surging capacities to react and reclaim agency and subjective autonomy. Bruneau's engagement with work, the workplace and the (non-)working subject is positioned across this chapter as a practice that intersects with, on the one hand, sociological, political and ideological critiques of neoliberalism focused on its destructive impact on individual subjectivities and collective solidarities, and, on the other hand, ethical considerations that posit care as an act of resistance and a condition for the protection and renewal of sociality.

## Facing, listening and providing care

Broadening sociological accounts that predominantly emphasised unemployment, social exclusion and precarity, Bruneau and Roudil shift focus from work to the workplace. Their cinematic representation of the workplace as a metonymy for the entire social structure of democracy – or its programmed weakening – profoundly challenges historical assumptions about work, alienation and politics in the workplace. It is no longer limited to the alienating factory that was the last century's dominant trope. When they started filming *Ils ne mouraient pas tous mais tous étaient frappés*, France had just passed a law that legally recognised the damaging effects of harassment in the workplace – or, in layman's terms, workplace bullying – on employees' well-being.[23] The first charges of systemic moral harassment were officially pressed in France in July 2019 against three former France-Télécom executives. On 21 December 2019, they were convicted of 'implementing a general strategy of bullying' that, ten years earlier, had pushed over thirty of their employees to suicide and caused many more to suffer from severe depression.[24]

Christophe Dejours's 'Psychodynamics' of work most significantly introduced a distinction, rarely explored in previous debates on class and social alienation, between *work* and *working*.[25] For Dejours, work 'is not, as it is often thought, limited to the actual physical time spent on the shop floor or in the office. Work exceeds any limit assigned to working hours and mobilises the whole person.'[26] When human intelligence, individual and collective, is recognised and encouraged, work, and the inherent suffering of working understood as 'affective resistance' to the 'material and social constraints' of the workplace, is a transformative experience and 'an opportunity for subjectivity to test or [...] fulfil itself'.[27] What becomes a cause for dis-ease, in Dejours's view, is the fact that the workplace and work are increasingly organised in such ways that they leave no room for human intelligence and solidarity. 'New forms of suffering and pathology', he declares, 'reflect the defeat of thought in the face of the contemporary prophecies that assert that everything in this world is quantifiable and should be quantified, while triumphantly announcing that work is a value in the process of disappearing.'[28] The introduction of standard technologies of management in every workplace, from the 1980s onwards, made work fundamentally abusive.

For Yves Clot, professor emeritus of work psychology at the CNAM (Centre National des Arts et Métiers), the problem lies in how individuals are expected to perform at work and what working has been reduced to:

The question is that workers can no longer feel proud about what they do at work, which leads to a greater need for recognition. Leadership, whether in government or the workplace, only provides fake/false forms of recognition. They say: 'your life is difficult, the world is a hard place to be in, there is a market, we are all under pressure, we understand it hurts, but we recognise your efforts.' It just does not add up [...] What is at the heart of human work's anthropological and psychological functions [... is] that it be useful and done according to specific standards. Otherwise, rightly or wrongly, it makes us sick.[29]

Clot's focus rests upon the fact that, even when the quality of their work is hindered, people still desire to keep on working, leading them to accept compromises that are damaging for their physical and psychological well-being. What is certain for him is that individuals' capacity to work well is now significantly impaired. However, people are not sickened by work; they are sickened because they cannot accomplish good work. Quality is held up by productivity, and employees' care for a 'job well done' is systematically denied. It is, therefore, urgent to change work by reintroducing quality and care as fundamental values of the workplace and society as a whole. Clot's notions of *qualité empêchée* (hindered work quality) and *travail soigné* (conscientious work) offer a productive bridge between the question of suffering in the workplace and the greater attention given in France from the mid-2000s to the notion of care as a more encompassing multifarious ethic of social and ecological relations.

The concept of care appeared in the United States in 1982, championed by Carol Gilligan, a psychologist, in her book *In A Different Voice*. A decade later, Joan Tronto, a political scientist, expanded on it in her book *Moral Boundaries: A Political Argument for an Ethic of Care* (1993).[30] In France, care surfaced in scholarly and public discourses in the early 2000s, thanks mainly to the interventions of a multidisciplinary community of scholars (philosophers, sociologists, political scientists, psychologists).[31] The French ethic of care has built upon Gilligan's aspirations to (1) replace vulnerability as a cornerstone of human experience while (2) calling out the blind spots of universalistic definitions of social justice to restore the moral (and political) value of voices marginalised by dominant masculinist ethics.[32] 'These are not only the voices of women', as Sandra Laugier explains; 'they are the voices of all the categories of people that are socially, ethnically, and racially disadvantaged.'[33] These voices have historically been (dis)regarded as insignificant in the public sphere because they relate experiences and affects that counter or fall outside the 'masculine' ethos – the measure of 'what is good, bad, valuable or despicable' as well as what constitutes strength or weakness.[34]

The ethic of care sets out to deconstruct the current global organisation of social relations in the world, bringing light to the indissociable interdependency of autonomy with vulnerability. Its focus on uncovering critical blind spots of contemporary Feminist and Marxist politics is particularly effective at drawing out the vulnerability of marginalised bodies and voices in the workplace and their difficulties in getting their suffering heard and seen. Therefore, it is not surprising that, when applied to work practices, these ethical pursuits have primarily focused on professions grounded in acts of care, such as healthcare, education, cleaning and care for the elderly or persons with disabilities. Though more clearly committed to sociological critique and political action, the ethic of care shares Dejours's and Clot's ambitions to elucidate the connections between work, subjectivity and identity. Pascale Molinier's scholarship, in particular, bridges the specific considerations brought up by the Psychodynamic of work, Yves Clot's plea for a revaluation of careful work (*le travail soigné*) and the promotion of care as a more equitable foundation for our social ethos.[35]

*Ils ne mouraient pas tous mais tous étaient frappés* was one of the first few films to address the question of (psychosomatic) suffering and moral harassment in the workplace. It was also the first to draw attention to the activism that occupational doctors, psychologists and ergonomists initiated in the 1990s, mainly by implementing a new clinical approach grounded in the act of listening.[36] Twelve years later, Bruneau used cinema, once again, to impact public discussions and policies, making listening to strangers' accounts of their work stories/dreams the primary material of *Rêver sous le capitalisme*. Asked why she decided to shoot this film in Belgium, she explains that the phenomenon of workplace suicides, though publicly debated in France, was still taboo in her country. Her second film on the subject of work-induced emotional pain allowed people to speak more openly about work's violence.[37] *Ils ne mouraient pas tous mais tous étaient frappés* and *Rêver sous le capitalisme* reveal the contemporary workplace's emprise on individuals as an internalised force. They concentrate the viewers' attention onto bodies, suffering bodies, and dreams, dreams of confined and damaged bodies. Initially inspired by Christophe Dejours's 'pessimistic vision of contemporary work practices', Sophie Bruneau's cinematic treatment of the ordinary brutality of (the) work(place) had grown much more explicitly political by the time she shot *Rêver sous le capitalisme*. Influenced by Charlotte Beradt's work in 1930s Germany, which collected dozens of dreams made by friends, relatives and fellow citizens as Hitler was strengthening his political power, this film aligns with scholars for whom 'workplaces [...] are a central learning place of democracy'.[38] But let us consider *Ils ne mouraient pas tous mais tous étaient frappés* in greater detail first.

This feature-length documentary takes viewers inside three Health and Work medical consultations at the hospitals in Garches, Nanterre and Créteil in the Paris metro area, headed by Dr Marie-Christine Soula, Dr Marie Pezé and Dr Nicolas Sandret, also collaborators of Christophe Dejours. During the film, we are introduced to four patients working in four different professional sectors – an industrial worker, a retail store manager, a nursing home custodial employee and an insurance company's senior executive: three women and a man. When we meet them, most have been on medical leaves for an extended time. The Health and Work consultations, recommended by their family physician or an occupational health doctor, are the last resorts for their health recovery. Though their circumstances differ, their stories lead back to comparable breaking points in their relationship to work: a physical injury, a layoff followed by depression or a dramatic nervous breakdown in the workplace. As we watch, and most importantly, listen to these people recount the reasons for their medical leave, describe what it was like working and share their present feelings, patterns emerge. The workplace is increasingly synonymous with (1) isolation, (2) the fear of being constantly under scrutiny, subjected to continuous performance evaluations, (3) the meaninglessness of professional activities that are measured in terms of quantity, increased productivity and cost reductions rather than quality and, for some, (4) undue humiliations and violence. *Ils ne mouraient pas tous mais tous étaient frappés* lays bare the overall degradation of work as a social activity while carefully making visible the range of circumstances that make work unbearable for many people.

Hired as a cleaner in a nursing home, a woman recalls repeated forms of harassment from her manager after she injured her back while working (see Fig. 20).

— That's where it all started [*she started giving me trouble*] because it was an accident at work.

— Did you declare it as a work accident?

— Yes, I did. I shouldn't have done it [...] When I went to get my documents, the declaration for the accident, I was alone with her in her office; she told me I was lazy and useless (*her face, grimaces and voice reveal raw emotions*).

— Did she give you your documents?

— She threw them at me while saying I did it on purpose and that there were [*of course*] no witnesses. I said I wasn't going to take fifty people with me to help someone get up.

— And you feel it all started then ...

— It's not a feeling. It really did start then. She told me to go back to the cleaning!

— OK, reprisals ... back to the cleaning. You were gently told that ... you couldn't do that work anymore [which was not your work in the first place].

— I wasn't allowed to do it. I wasn't allowed to take care of the old people anymore. I was even told not to approach them or talk to them.

— How is that possible? If you're cleaning, you're –

— I wasn't allowed to go near them, to say hello or to shake hands.

— When you were told that, were there some witnesses?

— Yes, my colleagues (*her face grins, showing the humiliation endured by such public interdiction*)

— [...] Then your sleeping problems started, tell me about it. (31"57–34"18)[39]

Mentioning she went from working at a gas station to cleaning in the nursing home suggests she did not see herself qualified to do anything else than cleaning in this establishment. She was nevertheless assigned responsibilities that involved taking care of elderly residents – against her better judgement. The exploitation, repeated humiliations and violence that her superior subjected her to made her feel used, rather than useless, and infantilised.

Another patient of the Health and Work consultation, a mid-level executive manager (see Fig. 19), found himself unable to reconcile his managerial ethic – 'motivating people through relationships' – and 'the brilliant yet diabolical system' he was expected to implement.

> — A few years ago, they set up a brilliant yet diabolical system.
> — Tell me about it.
> They set up standards: this action takes that much time, this other one takes that much time [...] It's an analytical time and motion system [...] The problem was that everything was measured. It's a problem and an advantage; let's not be too negative. [...] Little by little, the figures went                                                  down [...] I consider that my crew doesn't have to undergo the same pressure as I did. This is how my motivation worked. I might not be right, but I prefer acting humanly instead of being authoritarian [...] I can't see the interest in stressing people in such a negative way. (22"30–26"30)

The man's repeated comments about his philosophy, his managerial style and his preferred methods to motivate his team suggest a need for validation of what he sees as positive values, something to feel good about. This personal ethic may precisely be the reason why he broke down.

For Christophe Dejours, recognition is a crucial mode of validation that can remedy the suffering and ethical alienation that many people currently feel in their workplace. Building on this notion, Pascale Molinier distinguishes between 'recognition deficit' and 'denied recognition'.[40]

> Denied recognition occurs in work situations when the work performed is disavowed by hierarchy, during a performance evaluation, for instance, and when work, though recognised, is not compensated with pay increases, a promotion or other forms of social mobility.[41]

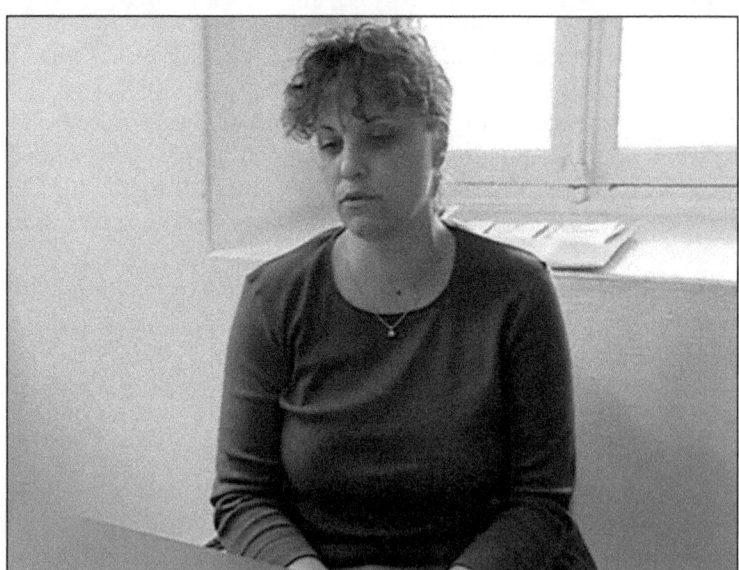

Figures 19–20. Patients in Dr Marie-Christine Soula's Health and Work consultation in Garches, *Ils ne mouraient pas tous mais tous étaient frappés* © Sophie Bruneau/alter ego films.

Even when recognition rewards the employee financially or socially, suffering can still occur, as is evidenced by the increasing rate of white-collar employees consulting for depression, burn-out or other work-related pathologies. This phenomenon has to do with the fact that recognition is exclusively granted by the employers and based on expectations that are quantified (productivity, profits, revenues). According to Molinier, individuals work less for recognition than to be recognised, based on criteria and values *they* set for themselves as they commit their time and mobilise their intelligence to perform their work.[42] Crucial, this last point by Molinier echoes with Yves Clot's understanding that when people cannot recognise themselves in their work and are denied the possibility to find value, meaning and moral validation in professional tasks, they suffer. This seems to have been the case for this man. The new system may have been 'brilliant' in terms of financial results and productivity. Still, it was 'diabolical' in its negation of human qualities and limitations.

Filming mostly first visits, with the exception of the fourth and last patient, the film-makers can rely on the narrative economy of these introductory sessions between patients and doctors to introduce the viewers to the confidential space of the consultation and the origins of these patients' intimate pains. For Bruneau and Roudil, 'the suffering would not be visible in the workplace', hence the need to find 'locations where individuals could speak about their pain freely, unambiguously'.[43] This decision caused lengthy delays since trust needed to be established with the therapists, hospital managers and the patients who were granted the right to withdraw from the film at any point during shooting and editing.

Using a simple cinematic approach, Bruneau and Roudil focus the viewers' attention on the patients' voices and their doctors' (see Figs 19–20). The long, fixed shots allow speech – *la parole* – to flow on its own terms, slowly releasing revealing information for the discerning practitioner. Closed off from the outside, the confidential space of the consultation nonetheless includes the film-makers and the viewers. This inclusion comes with an important responsibility emphasised by the stripped-down cinematography: we are only expected to do one thing, listen attentively, not passively, to what is being said and how it is said. As the consultation unfolds, the medical professionals intervene as little as possible, letting their patients describe any physical pains they have been experiencing and voice their feelings and emotions. On occasions, they invite the patient to provide further details about an incident at work, highlight the choice of a word or note a particular voice inflexion or the appearance of a bodily twitch. They never make a diagnosis, however. In these sessions, the doctors' main task is to 'be attentive to what these people have to say' and 'search for solutions with them'.[44]

The film thus stages an encounter with 'affected-beings', a term used in the Psychodynamics of work to describe the embodied dis-ease experienced by individuals such as those we see in the film.

> The Psychodynamics of work aims at understanding what the subject experiences through work [...] The emphasis is placed upon making sense of the situation, shielding oneself from suffering and dis-ease by calling upon one's human intelligence and character, as well as cooperation and collective solidarity [...] With this in mind, human beings are *affected-beings*, their bodies, a corporeality, and suffering, an affect. Suffering refers to a dimension of psychological experience that is inherently subjective, in contradistinction to neurological descriptions of specific mental states that may comport with them but are in no way indicative of what we feel and even less of what we think we feel.[45]

Bruneau and Roudil introduce us to the question of suffering in the workplace by confronting us with similarly embodied *récits de soi* (personal narratives), a raw material that collapses recollections and emotions and can point us to the source of the affliction and its physical and psychological scars. They also direct our attention to ordinary incidents, routine expectations and anecdotal remarks that shape everyone's working experience.[46] The film, like the consultation, is reimagined as a caring and careful inter-subjective experience, focused on the patient's/subject's affectivity. Their voices acquire corporeality; they are textured, their grain and cadence altered by the patient's physical and psychological pains.

The clinicians who see patients in their Health and Work consultations weekly describe their work as one that consists of practising '*l'écoute risquée*' ('risky listening'). The term signals that, in order not just to listen carefully to these people but to do so with care, they must put aside their own professional identity and expert assumptions. While sitting across from them, they must be present and available as another person these patients can address and to whom they relate their experience and feelings, not as someone who knows better than them. For Carol Gilligan, 'the act of listening is eminently political', particularly when it means we listen to voices that have been suppressed or ignored because they did not align with the dominant masculine ethos.[47] The four patients repeatedly allude to the fact that any physical pain, injury or the difficulty of keeping up with the pressure to produce more with less and in shorter times would be ignored, dismissed and lead to humiliations and retaliations.

Patient 1:
> — You're competent, and you're productive. So, they reduce the number of workers. And when you say, 'I can't do it alone' [...] When you ask to slow down the machine, you're put on the side, and controllers come and see you. It's pretty hurtful when you get told, 'So, today you can't make it then ...'
> — How did you feel then?
> Humiliated, I can't go on like that anymore. When you talk to a boss, she can see you feel bad, excuse me [*she stops to look for a tissue to wipe her tears*]. They can see you're not OK. [*Marie Pezé gives her a tissue.*] You explain it to her, but for her, everything is OK. 'Listen, I'm not a robot, I'm a human being' [...] 'I can't do the work of two people', 'Because you don't want to do it'. Then we argue, and when you're in pain, you go crazy [...] When you tell them what you feel, they call the manager who says you're crazy. Then they have the right to talk, and we don't. (9"25–11"55)[48]

Having someone listen to how and why they got to a breaking point and telling them in their own words without being judged or dismissed is therefore essential. It validates their suffering and

Figure 21. Left to right: Marie-Christine Soula (Garches), Christophe Dejours, Marie Pezé (Nanterre), and Nicolas Sandret (Créteil), *Ils ne mouraient pas tous mais tous étaient frappés* © Sophie Bruneau/alter ego films.

their affected response to the demands placed on them. At that moment, they are (affected) subjects.

If one of the film-makers' goals is to make us listen to a few of these embodied narratives, another is to give the physicians who have provided a space to them a platform to showcase the nature and significance of their professional care. The first voice we hear is, in fact, that of Marie-Christine Soula, who, at the time, oversaw the Health and Work consultation at the hospital in Garches. She is on the phone, reviewing a patient's records with a colleague. The camera is positioned across from her as if we were sitting in a patient's chair. This prologue is relatively short, but a more extended sequence, a roundtable discussion entitled *viatique* between the three clinicians met in the film – Marie Pezé, Marie-Christine Soula and Nicolas Sandret – and Christophe Dejours, concludes the film (see Fig. 21).[49]

After they were done editing the film, Bruneau and Roudil decided, in consultation with Dejours, that this final sequence would help put into perspective the raw narratives presented to the spectators throughout the film.[50] Indeed, it provides helpful contextual clarifications, encouraging the viewers to reflect on what they have just seen and heard, and consider their own workplace experiences.

They detail their methodology, *écoute risquée*. Facing individuals who suffer physically, psychologically and morally, and addressing them from the position of an expert who knows how to fix them would not be productive. Instead, they must refrain from making quick assumptions. They need to listen, take notes of everything that may help the patients make sense of the roots of their lasting suffering and why they now feel ethically alienated from work. Weekly, they see recurring patterns that connect the diffuse psychological distress of today's workforce to key structural transformations implemented in the last decades. (1) Work is increasingly fragmented into micromanaged tasks. (2) Employees' performances are subject to constant evaluation, making the workplace, once a cooperative environment, extremely competitive. (3) Employees feel isolated while being expected to do ever more with less. Consequently reduced to its strictly financial value, work has lost its personal, social and existential meaning for these people. When combined with recurring humiliations and moral harassment, the pressure becomes unbearable, and bodies and nerves break down.

Historically, the term *viaticum* had a religious connotation. It was used to refer to the last rites administered by a priest to someone dying. By extension, the word has also been used to describe any remedy or action that effectively appeases pain, crises or social ills. Figuratively, it has also described any agent of support, assistance or help that may bring relief to someone.[51] In the context of *Ils ne mouraient pas tous mais tous étaient frappés*, the word makes perfect sense, despite being an obscure reference at first. The Health and Work consultations and the *écoute risquée* practised by the therapists are *viatica*, or at the very least intended to remedy the menacing social dis-ease plaguing the contemporary workplace.

In his film review, Philippe Roger noted the slight shift in camera placement in this sequence, a decision that, in his view, left the viewers excluded from a closed conversation between peers and undermined, for this reason, the reflexive value of the film.[52] Unlike Roger, I see this shift define more clearly the space of the consultation to which we have been summoned, not only as viewers but also, and most importantly, as 'risky' listeners to another person's suffering and being. We are now released from it, in some way. The conversation that ensues between the four professionals serves different functions. On the one hand, it leaves us with vital keys to make sense of the lengthy sequences and the process we have sat in on. On the other hand, this conversation is the occasion for these (health)care practitioners to state the twofold nature of their intervention, clinical and political.

> Christophe Dejours: Why is this clinic different from any other Industrial Medicare? And what brought you to do that? Because it is not the usual position for an industrial doctor [...] One cannot improvise on this receptive position that implies the shelving of our knowledge [...] What did it mean for you to reach this more modest position?
> Marie Pezé: Does it imply any changes as to your professional identity?
> Marie-Christine Soula: Exactly! I couldn't link the brutality that some patients underwent at work to the clinical diagnosis that I had met before as a doctor. There was a disproportion between what the patient was telling me and the usual diagnosis. I couldn't relate to my usual professional values. So, I started thinking that we had to find other ways of working. We started working with Marie and others. To confront the brutality that the patients were evoking, we had to find other solutions because the actual diagnoses are not valid here. We questioned our own practices; that's how we made some progress.
> Marie Pezé: The extraordinary thing was the cooperation we managed to set up, which was the positive side in relation to the loss of solidarity in society that generates these pathologies. Our consultations are successful because we work together. What I can't do, I can ask you or you ... we also work with lawyers, and Industrial doctors who are now working differently, and some

psychiatrists and therapists. This method is spreading very slowly. We have to be well organised to keep up this clinic that is mainly based on cooperation. If we weren't so strongly related to each other in our work and ethic values, we wouldn't be able to help people through their terrifying situations. (58"42–1'02"24)

The film is, therefore, performative on different levels: for the therapists who put their work on display to sound the alarm about socially induced pathologies and advocate a new ethic of (health)care, and for the spectator who is summoned into acts of 'risky listening'. In that regard, *Ils ne mouraient pas tous mais tous étaient frappés* restores the corporealities of the working subjects/patients and of the medical professionals, resisting a system that continuously erases them despite growing evidence that their work is acutely needed.[53]

## Work's macabre economy

Whether or not work has lost its meaningfulness is a question that structures both *Ils ne mouraient pas tous mais tous étaient frappés* and *Rêver sous le capitalisme*, but it is particularly pregnant in the latter. Sophie Bruneau's readings of Georges Didi-Huberman's *La survivance des Lucioles/Survival of the Fireflies* (2009) and Charlotte Beradt's *The Third Reich of Dreams* (published in 1966, with the help of Hannah Arendt, this book was written in the 1930s) inspired her to probe deeper into affective alienation in the workplace.[54] In 1933, after Hitler had claimed power, Beradt started collecting accounts of dreams made by her fellow German citizens.[55] 'Dream imagery', Beradt writes in her introduction, 'help[s] describe the structure of a reality that was just on the verge of becoming a nightmare.'[56] Dreams are not only reflections of our unconscious, our deepest anxieties and intimate hopes; they are also shaped by shared emotions and affects that broad social and political forces generate in any given society. In 1930s Germany, the dreams she gathered revealed the strong hold Nazi ideology had over minds and people's subconscious. Of course, she was very aware that the 'documentary value [of a dream] is greatest if it is recorded immediately, [because] if it is written down only later, or merely told from memory, more conscious notions creep into its formulation'.[57] Bruneau's project, which aims to reveal the pervasive intrusion of neoliberalism, as an economic and political ethos, into people's lives and their very being, comes with the same caveat. It took her three years to assemble all the materials. In the end, she selected twelve dreamers. She had to record footage for the nine present in the film only through voice-over narrations.

More meditative, less clinical than *Ils ne mouraient pas tous mais tous étaient frappés*, *Rêver sous le capitalisme* is a chilling montage of unmediated voices and long tableaux of work sites, many nocturnal. Bruneau's connection with Dejours's vision is once again apparent in the film's focus on how neoliberal society 'direct[ly] challenges [...] psychic economies'.[58] Jean-Philippe Deranty writes that, as Dejours sees it, 'contemporary society, articulated around a flexibilized, fluidified, individualized organization of work, produces massive amounts of anxiety':[59]

> The affect that arises at work and from work, to subsequently vitiate all social bonds, is fear: the fear of losing one's job; the fear arising from systematically organized competition with other workers both inside and outside the work place; the fear of not being able to achieve ever increasing productivity targets; the fear of not coping when the productivity targets and the work organization are in contradiction; the fear of being caught at fault by the surveillance of management [...] the fear of being able to adapt in the face of the systematic compulsion to introduce rapid and constant changes, and so on. For Dejours, given the constitutive importance of work for subjective identity, those different types of fear all ask of the subjects the same, terrible question: will you be able to cope, and for how long?[60]

In *Ils ne mouraient pas tous mais tous étaient frappés*, the fear of losing one's job forced employees to endure months, years even, of humiliations and harassment from managers, leaving them broken to the point that they could no longer show up at work. In *Rêver sous le capitalisme*, this anxiety translates into a vast repertoire of ghoulish imagery that pervades these people's dreams.

For an hour, we listen to twelve male and female voices take turns recounting work dreams/nightmares. As in *Ils ne mouraient pas tous mais tous étaient frappés*, different professional categories are represented: caregivers, executive managers, cashiers, public administrators, call centre employees and motorway emergency responders. Two themes dominate the scenarios playing out across these twelve dreams: a widespread sentiment of uselessness and the erosion of community. The question 'What is my purpose?' concludes several narratives. In contrast, most of the situations taking place in the dreams reflect upon the loss of collegiality among colleagues and increasingly difficult relationships with office managers. Most striking are the recurring references to zombies, ghosts, mummies, corpses and suicides. The imagery, which turns the workplace into a horror movie, reveals the extent to which 'capitalism cannibalises us' for Bruneau.[61] In some instances, the dreamers are merely witnesses to their colleagues' mutilations and deaths; in others, they catch themselves about to commit atrocious acts or are the victims themselves.

One dream, in particular, stays with viewers. Halfway into the film, a physician nearing retirement recounts an unsettling dream that perfectly encapsulates this idea (see Fig. 22).

> My dream started here, on this chair. It started with a very loud bang, a cracking sound. This sound came from my skull cracking open. A bony piece of my cranium lifted up. After that, a series of little chairs placed themselves around the gaping hole in my head. A whole series of tiny people sat on them, very tiny, with the peculiarity that they each held extremely long spoons, spoons that were five to ten times as tall as they were. Very long and very thin. These people plunged their spoons into my skull and fed on me. That was the end of the dream. It was no longer than that. At first, it was a dream, and later, it became a fixed image. Each time I sat down, here in this chair, to start my consultation, I heard this noise and I saw the image of the people who were eating me. How might we interpret this dream? I think things are

Figure 22. 'Tiny people were feeding into my skull with long, thin spoons', *Dreaming Under Capitalism* (Sophie Bruneau, 2017) © Sophie Bruneau/alter ego films.

pretty clear. All the little chairs correspond to my waiting room, with the people sitting in a circle, waiting. The fact that it involves my skull ... This is essentially an intellectual job, so it's logical that things be situated there. But the most disturbing thing was the length of the spoon, the spoon handles. That suggested people weren't satisfied with just the grey matter in my brain, but that they really wanted to dig much deeper, into my inner being. That's what alarmed me in this dream. (35"01–37"54)[62]

The lingering discomfort that her account produces is enhanced by the fact that she is only one of three people who appear onscreen. As she describes the horrific act of cannibalism to which she is a victim in her dream, her calm voice makes the details we hear even more vivid.

With the exception of these three dreamers who speak directly to the camera, the film consists of a long flow of disembodied voices, seamlessly sutured together over long, fixed shots of quasi-inert *tableaux*-like scenes. This choice produces a suspension – a detachment from the world – which contrasts starkly with the violent images described to us and the sounds that punctuate them. At the beginning of the film, a female voice recollects the intensifying sounds of a cash register permeating her sleep as we scrutinise an empty parking lot, unsettled by the shrieking cries of the seagulls flying around. In the scenes filmed by Bruneau, sounds are amplified, hyperreal, thus abnormally conspicuous: the rain splattering on the street and commuters' umbrellas, the cacophony of conversations filling up a cafeteria during lunch hour or the loud noises of jackhammers coming from a construction site. The film's cinematography and sustained dissonance between sound and images activate our senses in both aggravating and soothing ways.

Furthermore, the oppressive length of Bruneau's fixed shots, most of them filmed at night, demands that the viewers pay attention to what may only become perceptible in the scene when/if they direct their full attention to it, immersing themselves in the depth of the image. Only then do they catch a glimpse of a tiny movement in the background, often a human presence working but invisible – a sweeper, an engineer, a bulldozer driver, a cleaner. The same holds for the many details that mark out the plots of dreams that draw from ordinary events, routine requests and anecdotal interactions – until something shifts.

Beradt's book inspired Bruneau to probe the materiality of work dreams, but it is Didi-Huberman's fascination with the firefly that shaped her cinematic approach. *Survival of the Fireflies* attempts to prove Pasolini and Agamben wrong about the disappearance of fireflies, metaphors for the glimmers of (popular) resistance '*breaking through the horizon* of totalitarian constructions'.[63] For Didi-Huberman, 'firefly-images' survive; what we have lost is our ability to catch them as they flash before our eyes:

> We do not perceive the same things at all: depending on whether we widen our view to the *horizon* that extends beyond us, immense and immobile, or whether we focus our gaze on the *image* that passes by us, tiny and moving, right up close. The image is the *lucciola* of passing intermittences;

> the horizon bathes in the *luce* of definitive states [...] The
> little fireflies give form and glimmer to our fragile
> immanence [...] Giving all our attention to the horizon
> means rendering ourselves incapable of looking at the
> slightest image.[64]

The long, fixed shots that appear throughout *Rêver sous le capitalisme*
similarly play with our visual acuity. When fixing the horizon, all
we can see is stillness, but when focusing our gaze, tiny human
movements suddenly appear in the background or a corner. In his
final chapter, Didi-Huberman mentions Charlotte Beradt's book,
which he describes as an 'intimate "seismography" of the political
history of the Third Reich' unearthed from the hundreds of dreams
she collected: 'We can understand, then, how an *inner experience*,
the most "subjective", the most "obscure" there is, may appear as *a
flash for another*, from the moment that it finds the right form of its
construction, its narration, its transmission.'[65] Following Didi-
Huberman, Bruneau encourages us to see, in the work dreams and
nightmarish visions,'brief, weakly luminous flashes' that she records
and pieces together in her film. The macabre that imbues these
nightly fantasies may be signs 'of openings, of possibilities, of flashes,
*in spite of all*' the fears currently muffling voices of resistance and
discontent.[66] It manifests these people's resistance to a profoundly
unjust system that is dangerously dehumanising to the point that it
risks undermining the social cohesion of the workplace
community.[67] In that regard,'that these people are suffering is quite
reassuring' for Bruneau.[68]

*Ils ne mouraient pas tous mais tous étaient frappés* and *Rêver sous le
capitalisme* weave together feelings, pains and dreams, once thought
to be intimate and individual by those who consent to share them
in front of the camera. Merged into unified voices, they give
individual sufferings political resonance. Emmanuel Renault
considers 'sharing negative social experiences' to be political if it
produces a new subjectivity that is no longer individual but speaks
to shared suffering.[69] Both films are invested in fashioning
'*communautés de souffrance*' (communities bound by shared suffering)
while affirming vulnerability as a crucial safeguard for protecting
civility, sociality and democracy.[70] They encourage the viewers to

understand these people's psychosomatic suffering as a defence mechanism against the degradation of the 'work collective' and social and political life.[71] *Rêver sous le capitalisme* is *stricto sensu* a review of dreams people have in a society increasingly corrupted by the law of capitalism. Grounding itself in such primordial material, it lets us envisage what social life may look like if we become complacent with this 'deleterious' workplace that 'corrode[s] democratic habits', 'strengthen[s] [...] vices: intolerance, voluntary servitude, the acceptance of injustice, and even evil being done to others'.[72]

In 2012, Cécile Mabileau and Marcel Trillat co-directed another film using the verb *rêver* (dreaming) in the title.[73] Featuring interviews with several people from different professional backgrounds, *Rêver le travail* examines people's aspirations for a more fulfilling work life than what they are currently left with. A gardener laments the proliferation of 'soulless gardens'. A nurse explains that reducing care to a series of technical procedures will never account for the time spent by the side of a patient dying. Another man, who has worked in manufacturing for decades, looks unfavourably on the many safety- and efficiency-boosting protocols that have been introduced in recent years. Having to comply with measures designed by technocrats is 'infantilising' and insulting; it ignores the practical knowledge he and his colleagues gained over the years of being on the job. Finally, in the brief epilogue, Yves Clot identifies as a leading cause of suffering in the workplace since the 1980s a widespread negation of empathy, selflessness and human intelligence. His scholarship has argued that any work that we can do with the care that allows us to stay true to our values makes us proud and feeling valuable. Such work is not detrimental to our psychological health, even if we get zero recognition from others.[74] Thus, people need to be able to voice their feelings about the quality of the work they produce and, most importantly, what aspects of their work make it meaningful to them. This position brings us back to the ethic of care and the political implications of 'listening' and 'be attentive to what people have to say' about their values, their conditions and why they may be suffering.

If Dejours's Psychodynamics of Work was influential in Bruneau's interest in these questions, it is clear at this point that her films actively engage with the broad-ranging perspectives that have revitalised how we define work in the early twenty-first century. Before concluding, let us consider *Mon diplôme, c'est mon corps/My Body is my degree*. This short film, presented as a stand-alone film in the DVD of *Ils ne mouraient pas tous mais tous étaient frappés*, effectively captures her and Roudil's understanding of work as a complex nexus of subjective, political and ethical forces.

## An (in)significant body

*Mon diplôme, c'est mon corps* starts with this disclaimer by the film-makers:

> We filmed this short while shooting *Ils ne mouraient pas tous mais tous étaient frappés*. This narrative is, in our view, an independent, self-sufficient film. Indeed, unlike the four situations included in the feature film, this sequence did not directly link the individual suffering observed in the consultations with the introduction of new work management methods in the 1980s. In that sense, 'Mon diplôme c'est mon corps' should not be seen as a sequel to *Ils ne mouraient pas tous mais tous étaient frappés* but as an example of the sufferings that work has long caused to people, in the past as well as today.[75]

Going further than the film-makers, I contend that extracting Madame Khol's sequence from the feature documentary enhances her successful claim to radical presence on screen, as a 'different voice' who brings attention to the essential, yet invisible, contribution of care workers to the good working order of our world.[76] This editorial choice simultaneously underscores the marginality of racialised and socially depreciated voices and endows them with political force.

Bruneau's and Roudil's intervention unconsciously aligns with emerging reformulations of ethics of care in French academic circles. That same year, 2005, Patricia Paperman and Sandra Laugier published *Souci des autres: Ethique et politique du care*. Influenced by

Carol Gilligan and Joan Tronto, the French conception of care as an ethic and a politic initially focused on 'subaltern sufferings' and voices.

> Looking through the lens of care [...] means zooming in on ordinary life and promoting an ethical interrogation of sensitivity: how care is practised and given, what is at stake in relationships of care, what forms compassion and attention take, as well as which situations of dependency include exhaustion, despair and violence. But the perspective of care also zooms out to replace specific conditions in a broad global critique of how social, gender and racial divisions intermesh with the care of others and our shared world. Thus, it makes more salient how unjust the hierarchy of needs and, simultaneously, of people is.[77]

Bruneau and Roudil's cinematic approach effectively scrutinises the neoliberal workplace through the lens of care, maintaining its focus on the ethical stakes of ordinary affectivity. Questions of social, gender and racial hierarchies are only implicitly hinted at across *Ils ne mouraient pas tous mais tous étaient frappés* and *Rêver sous le capitalisme*, mostly through their inclusion of different people. In contrast, *Mon diplôme, c'est mon corps*, brings to the fore the profound inequalities and injustices structuring the global economy of care, embodied here in Madame Khol, a fictitious name.

In *Ils ne mouraient pas tous mais tous étaient frappés*, care refers, first and foremost, to the practice of healthcare, the responsibility of medical professionals. It is a practice whose goal is to enable people's realisation that they are 'not crushed by a story, [but] carry [their] own story' (56"13–56"26).[78] *Mon diplôme, c'est mon corps* brings us to reflect on care as an all-encompassing ethical and political reordering of social relations understood as practices, actions and attitudes that start from the reckoning that vulnerability and dependency are our shared essence as living beings.[79] This short film also stresses how much being allowed to care for what we do is central to individuals' ability to maintain agency and autonomy as subjects, despite one's actual social position. The two features demonstrate the perversity of a workplace that denies this need, or

– worse – hinders it, to echo Corine Pelluchon.[80] In *Mon diplôme, c'est mon corps*, the shift is actualised in the affirmation of Madame Khol as a cinematic and a political body.

When we meet this woman in Marie Pezé's office in Nanterre, she suffers from long-term psychosomatic pains. Unable to diagnose what causes her persistent dis-ease, her doctor referred her to the Health and Work consultation. Born in Morocco, Madame Khol worked for many years as a house cleaner, the only employment available to her since she has no degrees and speaks French with difficulty. One day, she injured her shoulder at work, falling down some stairs. Months later, X-rays can no longer detect signs of a fracture. Nevertheless, she is still experiencing pain – a mystery for conventional medicine. Very similar to the four sequences edited in the feature-length film, *Mon diplôme, c'est mon corps* places the spectator within the confined, confidential space of the consultation. Looking at the encounter from the perspective of few fixed shots, the spectator either faces Marie Pezé, the psychoanalyst, or faces the patient and listens to her speak, adopting the doctor's point of view. Either way, the viewer's focus rests on this woman's speech and her body. Respectful of the principle of '*écoute risquée*', characteristic of her clinical practice, Marie Pezé's interventions are sparse, granting Madame Khol time and space to tell her story in accented French.

> Marie Pezé: What you say also is that if you do your work well, it becomes invisible. When cleaning is done well, people do not notice it.
> Madame Khol: Exactly!
> Marie Pezé: Nobody notices it.
> Madame Khol: No, it's perfectly normal, as expected [… ] But, in the meantime, I have used my body. What have I done? If I walk into a house in the morning, with two bathrooms, two living rooms, an office, three bedrooms, a kitchen […] How do you expect me to clean without moving my body? If I really do my work well, how am I supposed to do it? It's not … I am not a machine. Even the device, you need to move it around. Everything must be clean; everything must be spotless. But in a year, or

two, or three, nobody has ever mentioned that I have cleaned with, with my own hands […] Now, when I say, health does not matter, I mean I work in silence, I am sick in silence, I lose my health in silence … Well, that means, don't speak, be in pain, work, that's all […] I can't think about my health because that's my skill. If I say, I am not healthy, I can't do it, that's it, I can't work anymore. (5"38–7"22)[81]

Madame Khol's distressed body bears the marks of a dominant ethos that promotes (some) womens' autonomy (from the domestic sphere and its moral values). It simultaneously successfully forces recognition of her contributions to fundamentally asymmetrical social relations. She was hired to clean this large house because the people who enjoy its comfort are out, pursuing more rewarding careers financially and socially. Sandra Laugier remarks that achieving social and financial autonomy for many French women meant freeing themselves from everyday domestic expectations and finding a paid job outside. They could only attain emancipation as premised on dominant masculinist values because typically disadvantaged and denigrated immigrant women picked up these tasks considered worthless.[82]

Jean-Louis Comolli highlights Madame Khol's unique appropriation of the consultation space, alternating between sitting and standing postures. The four patients featured in *Ils ne mouraient pas tous mais tous étaient frappés* remain seated. One briefly acknowledges the presence of the film-makers, as he spontaneously turns to them to confirm France's World Cup victory in 1998. In Comolli's view, Madame Khol's standing is very significant because, at that moment, she steps out of the therapeutic relationship and enters a cinematic relationship with the spectators.[83] Comolli does not explain what the sudden eruption of her documentary body in the cinematic encounter enacts. Elaborating upon his reading of the sequence, I propose that Madame Khol be seen as a cinematic figuration of Carol Gilligan's 'different voice'. Her narrative voices an experience historically and systemically depreciated and silenced. Racialised women (less commonly men) have taken care of our world (our homes, our cities, our public amenities) and maintained it, a work that has gone unnoticed and unrecognised. She is this 'different voice' that Carol Gilligan wanted to bring to the fore in the early 1980s to lay the foundations for radical ethics of care.[84]

In Tronto's ethic of care, the person receiving care must not be seen as passive. Instead, caring means that caregiving (an attitude and a role that Bruneau symbolically forces the spectator to adopt in her films) recognises that the person already has specific moral competencies. They may have been deceived into thinking they lack them, but the reality is they do have them. Though inevitably asymmetrical, the relationship between care-giver and care-receiver should stay focused on facilitating this person's journey towards reclaiming their autonomy.[85] So standing, Madame Khol actively resists being confined to the status of a medical patient. Continually relegated to society's off-frame for being a woman, an immigrant, a house cleaner and an employee in pain unable to work, she here asserts her cinematic body, the vector to her re-entry into the broader social frame (see Fig. 23).

The second time she stands up, she refers to her body as the only degree she has ever had, collapsing her capacity to be and her capacity to do.

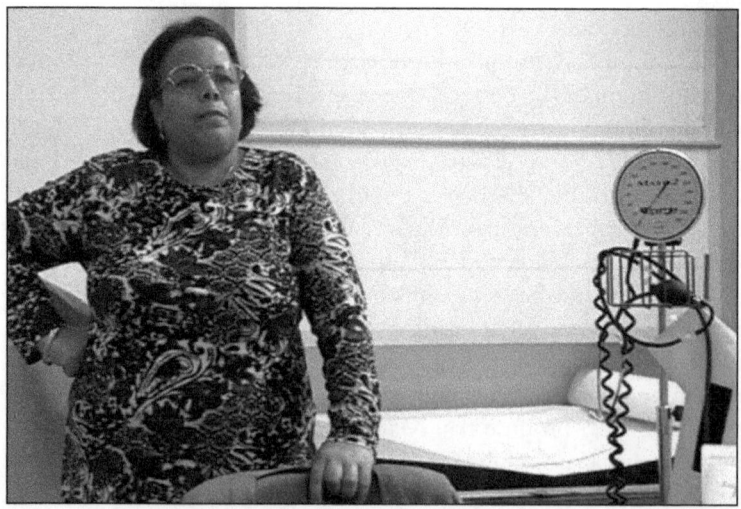

Figure 23. Madame Khol in Dr Marie Pezé's office, *Mon diplôme, c'est mon corps* (2005) © Sophie Bruneau/alter ego films.

Madame Khol: True, I came to France, I needed to work, I could see my marriage was not good. I looked for any qualification I had, what do I have? I can sew, but it is not enough. I didn't have any degree so … I kept looking, and my degree was my body, I could move it, I could bend, I could walk up the stairs. Well, I decided I would use this degree to live. But, usually, degrees do not break, they do not get sick. But my degree broke down, it was not good anymore. So, they told me: 'ok, stay on the side, your degree is not good, you didn't do anything …' That's it (*a long sigh*). (14"47–15"23)[86]

Madame Khol's (in)significant body is thus marginal and supplemental, a position symbolically replicated in the material space occupied by this film in the DVD. They both powerfully stand in excess, a meaningful statement on Bruneau's and Roudil's part.

Sophie Bruneau and Marc-Antoine Roudil never reveal Madame Khol's real name. Before the end credits, they mention that she wrote a book entitled 'Les femmes sont des livres dont le titre est le nom de leurs maris'. In reality, Madame Khol is Fatima Elayoubi, best known as the author of *Prière à la lune* (2006) and the inspiration for Philippe Faucon's award-winning film *Fatima* (2015).[87] A critical and commercial success in France and abroad, the film was generally described as 'a familiar story of immigrants struggling to make something of themselves in an alien culture'.[88] However, few saw in Fatima's character a figuration of the 'subaltern sufferings' rarely addressed in debates about burn-out, workplace bullying and suicides.

In light of Fatima Elayoubi's overall journey, *Mon diplôme, c'est mon corps* marks the beginning of a long healing process that culminates with the publication of *Prière à la lune* in French, another degree resistant to incapacitating injuries. A personal testimony, the book also invokes the invisible community of essential *petites mains* (low-paid workers) who keep our world in order and clean. 'Be proud of the Fatimas who clean the houses of working women', she writes.[89]

## Conclusion

Denouncing the ruthlessness and carelessness of neoliberal managerial ethics, *Ils ne mouraient pas tous mais tous étaient frappés*, *Mon diplôme, c'est mon corps* and *Rêver sous le capitalisme* confront the viewers with the complex affective texture of the workplace. Sophie Bruneau's *mise en scène* meticulously unravels how work, health and care entwine in neoliberal society, productively engaging with critical and cinematographic debates about the changing nature of work and the workplace and these transformations' social, political and ethical stakes. Political critique, clinical care and cinematic commitment ask how human connectivity and sociality can be restored when professional, social and intimate lives are increasingly subjected to the transactional logic that controls the workplace, social relations and our being in the world at large. Across these three films, Sophie Bruneau adheres to Christophe Dejours's pessimistic view of the neoliberal re-engineering of the workplace. Her sustained engagement of this emerging reality for working subjects shares with other critical perspectives an interest in the complexity of work as an affected experience, especially Yves Clot's notions of *qualité empêchée* (hindered work quality) and *travail soigné* (conscientious/careful work) and the ethics of care.

For Bruneau, the cinematic process and its product are intended to counteract the systemic atomisation of subjectivities by (re)creating a sense of collective belonging, social cohesion and connections between individual voices and bodies.[90] Placing the viewers in a position that compels them to be attentive to affected agents, aching bodies and wounded subjectivities, she relocates documentary's ethical activism in a space that is neither performative nor representational, an in-between that allows private, intimate pains to be understood as the shared affects of a neoliberal social ontology. The productive dissonance she produces between image and sound, voices and bodies, recalls the affective release that films such as *Reprise du travail aux usines Wonder* (1968) and *Le sang des autres* (Bruno Muel, 1973) sought, while giving them new meaning. Jocelyne's exclamation that she will not return to a workplace where they are elbow-deep in nasty grease all day ('on a de la merde jusque là!) echoes with present complaints that new productivity standards force employees to deliver shameful results ('Ils nous font faire de la merde!').

These films cast light on what Danièle Linhart calls 'subjective precarity', which does not always coincide with economic and social precarity, both tied to an 'objective' form of precarity (fixed-term contracts, low-wage employment, seasonal work or gig jobs).[91] Subjective precarity consists in undermining individuals' professional knowledge, *savoir-faire* and self-esteem, invalidating their experience. In *Mon diplôme, c'est mon corps*, Madame Khol's body refracts a multiplicity of sufferings and 'social positionings of insecurity'.[92] As such, it connects Bruneau's sustained aesthetic project to materialise 'affective connections of bodies' and 'mutual affections' with ethics of care. Madame Khol embodies a different, 'minority subject' that has traditionally been invisible and whose voices, values and experiences were not considered valuable.[93] In this film, not only is she given attention, she commands attention to the difference of her suffering, only to be considered as a part of this diffuse precarious affectivity.

# Chapter 5
# Portraits of life in France's folds

Pourquoi filmer, pourquoi regarder un film si ce n'est pour se sentir déplacé dans son rapport au monde, aux autres?

— Denis Gheerbrant.[1]

When it comes to documentaries [...] there are some incredible, real people, but I made them so strong they are like fictional characters.

— Agnès Varda.[2]

Nous aimons le plaisir de la rencontre devant la caméra, avec des gens.

— Claudine Nougaret.[3]

In this final chapter, I follow Denis Gheerbrant, Raymond Depardon (accompanied by Claudine Nougaret) and Agnès Varda (in a rare partnership with JR) in their peregrinations around France. From the 'proletarian Marseille' threatened by gentrification to the farmers of the Massif Central, from the *France des villes moyennes* to small villages dotting the country's heterogeneous landscapes, they uncover distinct *petits mondes* of different scales.[4] These geographies, which invoke familiar tropes, clichés even, of sociality and communality, simultaneously ground us in a distinct social reality and appear to us reimagined and revitalised. Depardon and Nougaret's immersion in France's rurality in their farm trilogy

(*Profils paysans: L'approche*, *Le quotidien* (2001, 2006) and *La vie moderne/Modern Life* (2009)) recalls snapshots from France's past. Mostly, it celebrates the precarious resilience of these farmers who have decided to spend their lives in remote valleys. In *Les habitants* (2016), Depardon crosses the country in a caravan. On every stopover, he invites strangers to step inside, sit at the kitchen table and continue their conversations in front of the camera. *Visages villages/Faces Places* (2017) follows Agnès Varda and JR's road trip through equally picturesque and bucolic scenery, where they orchestrate, in cooperation with locals, beautiful displays of social vitality. Finally, Gheerbrant's *La République Marseille* (2009) examines what it means to live in the Mediterranean city's northern *quartiers* or *cités* for ageing, lifelong residents and more recently arrived immigrants.[5]

Agnès Varda, Raymond Depardon and Denis Gheerbrant use cinema to question their position in the (social) world, as artists and human beings.[6] The following analyses address a central tension in their films in that regard. Whereas their settings convey a certain *empaysement* (rooting), the film-makers' *errance* (wandering) mobilises 'nostalgic pathways of affect and desire' that 'provide [reactivate] what the present lacks': communality, friendship and hospitality.[7] I contend that they reimagine the documentary encounter as a praxis intended to '(re)connect [unnoticed, abandoned, ordinary] people to the rest of humankind', forging with these subjects a 'minimal community' that the presence of the camera and the spectator instantly opens to more connections and, therefore, institutes as the primordial form of restored sociality.[8]

### *Errance*(s) and silence: Raymond Depardon's human topographies

Since the late 1990s, Depardon's documentary and photographic work has deepened this ethical (dis)position while narrowing the geographical reach of his travels. What started as a twofold desire to reconnect with his rural roots and to drive around France, photographing the country's diverse landscapes and human faces, resulted in a series of interrelated photographic and cinematic projects: the farm trilogy (*L'approche*, 2001, *Le quotidien*, 2006, *La vie moderne*, 2009), *Journal de France* (2014) and *Les habitants* (2016); several books and exhibitions including 'La France' (BnF, 2010–11) and 'La Terre des Paysans'. *Les habitants*, for instance, directly echoes with, and complements, the documentary film *Journal de France* (2012) and the collection of photographs *La France* (2010), though each adopts a different perspective. *Journal de France* focuses on Depardon himself, his career and his lasting relationship to photography and France's landscapes. *La France* aims at producing a well-documented portrait of '*la France du milieu*': 'the France that is only mentioned "when something happens, an incident that makes the news or a natural disaster" [...] a France "without any picturesque quality", "not too joyful" but " not depressed" either'.[9] During the second half of the 2000s, Depardon crisscrossed the country alone in his converted van, taking thousands of photographs that show us France 'at eye level' or 'on a human scale' ('à hauteur d'homme').[10] These images are, for the most part, empty of any human presence.[11] Hence the idea for *Les habitants* – translated in English as *France*, an unfortunate choice that shifts attention back to geography, away from the people who inhabit it.

Depardon went back on the road for this last film with Claudine Nougaret and a wild casting director during the summer of 2015. Together, they logged in hundreds of miles, stopping in fifteen different towns, 'from Charleville-Maizière to Nice, from Sète to Cherbourg'.[12] The final product is an enlivened 'study of its inhabitants' speech' – an oral, as much as an aural, embodiment of the *France du milieu*:

> We invited them to take a seat inside the trailer, but it was important not to ask them any questions. Not to cut their intentions. We did not expect anything in particular. There was a screen that separated them from us, the shooting crew, on the other side. We wanted them to feel as alone as possible. At first, people would say something very banal. Our premise was to keep the microphones on. Some people have a strong presence when they speak, or speak with the right person, maybe. Sometimes, we see a more egalitarian relationship

between the two people sitting face to face; other times, one person dominates. When it works well, it is as much thanks to the person who speaks as it is to the person who listens.[13]

This premise echoes with Luce Irigaray's statement that 'our capacity for remaining silent' should be 'the first word that has to be said to each other by way of welcome', challenging common assumptions about greetings and silence.

In *Les habitants*, this willingness to 'leave the circle of [their] own discourse – or usual house of language – to listen to what the other wants to say, wants to address to him or her, from a horizon of language that is unknown to them' finds in the caravan a place that is outside everyone's world.[14] A cultural cliché, the caravan can evoke different things. A popular symbol of a freedom accessible to all, it can also denote marginality, either deliberate or forced. In the film, Depardon's caravan is both an inconspicuous element in the landscape and a slightly odd presence, especially when parked by a town square or on the side of the street. For all these reasons, the caravan functions as a space that is unattached to a specific place, yet contiguous to both the world of the people invited to step inside it and that of the film-makers who use it to wander through France.

Creating a hospitable space for their subjects' speech has always been a core principle of Raymond Depardon and Claudine Nougaret's collaborative partnership as film-makers. Starting a film with silence is, as Nougaret explains, crucial for the viewers; it provides them time and space to 'empty their minds' and make themselves available for the subjects they are about to encounter.[15] 'Silence is the speaking of the threshold', Luce Irigaray remarks.[16] 'If this silence does not remain present and active, the whole discourse loses its most important function: communicating and not merely transmitting information. Then dialogue becomes impossible.'[17] For this reason, 'silence is', in Judith Still's words, 'the temporalization of the threshold, a gap that cannot easily be stepped over, but not a chasm – for there can be an encounter.'[18] On this note, Nougaret mentions that, in their films, silence is often maintained up to a point when it becomes almost unbearable for the viewer. In some instances, the subjects themselves endorse such 'temporalization of the threshold', forcing Depardon to exist as an interviewer, against his will. No films better encapsulate this dynamism of silence than *Profils paysans* and *La vie moderne*.

For Alain Bergala, the work that Depardon has produced alone and in collaboration with Claudine Nougaret since the 1970s constitutes the only large-scale portrait of France done to this day – a portrait that presents French life through 'language, gestures and bodies'.[19] At times, this attention to the texture and physicality of speech can be revealed as very economical, as is the case in the farming trilogy, reflecting the subjects' economy of language; other times, as in *Les habitants*, words continuously flow, filling in the tight space of the caravan-studio. Because of their commitment to '*dégager l'écoute*' (to clear out space and time for the speech of the subjects filmed to emerge, flow and be heard), their films have captured the attention of sociolinguists, eager to mine a body of work that constitutes a rich repository of France's linguistic diversity and fabric, from everyday language to the more codified and contextual speech heard in courts, hospitals or police stations.[20]

The place given to silence, speech and the possibility for dialogue in their films opens up Depardon's camera work to Claudine Nougaret's skilful sound recording, making her work neither marginal nor supplemental but integral to the documentary encounter. While typically considered the *auteur* of his films, Depardon himself often refers to his lasting partnership with Nougaret, using the pronouns *nous* (we) to describe their creative process. While their collaboration conforms to a division of labour that has traditionally placed males behind the camera and women behind microphones, it does not subordinate sound to the image. Undoing the 'gender hierarchies' does not occur through a simple inversion of roles but by shifts that promote different modalities of being and knowing the world that appeal to senses other than vision.[21] Later in this chapter, we will see that the enactment of an ethic of mutual hospitality between masculine and feminine hierarchies is also at work in Agnès Varda and JR's *Visages villages*, albeit through different strategies.

In the films discussed in this chapter, Depardon fully embraces his status as an outsider, though to different end goals. His embodied ambulation, his *errance*, is central to their commitment to a more hospitable future. If *Les habitants* relies on the spontaneity and unpredictability of circumstantial/fortuitous encounters, *Profils paysans* and *La vie moderne* needed a much longer mutual commitment from both the film-makers and the farmers. Whereas *Les habitants* offers a series of snapshots with nameless participants, the farm trilogy mixes documentation – of the extraordinary resilience of these farmers surviving, on their own, for the most part – and introspection. Both projects could not be more different. Nevertheless, they are moved by a similar desire to crack open vague territorial concepts/constructs, such as '*La France du milieu, des villes moyennes*' and '*la France rurale*', by seeking out people who inhabit these abstract geographies. In Jean-Michel Frodon's words, Depardon's approach leaves us with 'impressionist cartographie[s]'; more importantly, we are left 'waiting' for a clear position on the film-makers' part. In *Les habitants*, it fails to materialise, and by the end of *La vie moderne*, we are led to ponder our position in the world.[22]

In the large-format photo-text *Errance*, published in 2000, Depardon wrote at length about his 'ethics in relation to the (visual) world', positing '*errance*' (wanderings) as a vital force in his work.[23]

> Most importantly, wandering is not about taking something from someone. It does not mean appropriating a place [...] It neither reflects a dominant gaze or observing or participant gaze; it is about adopting another gaze entirely [...] The wanderer is someone who shares, who comes from elsewhere and who does not stay long [...] It is someone for whom sharing is essential, even if they have their own opinion and are on a quest of their own.[24]

In *Profils paysans* and *La vie moderne*, wandering implies coming back, even briefly, to show that one cares and does not forget each other. 'We often return to visit but not without reason. We are delighted to see each other again [...] We make sure not to bother them. It's important not to bother them; yet it's essential to come back.'[25] In her review of *La vie moderne*, Catherine Soulard underscores the film-makers' willingness to 'take their time, visit and come back time and again for twenty years [...] to make the trip for a smile, to provide some support, to leave without a single image, no audio recordings, putting it off to a later time', in other words, their commitment to 'give time and human beings pre-eminence again'.[26]

If the shooting of *Profils Paysans* and *La vie moderne* officially started in 1998, the genesis of this long-term project can be traced back to the late 1980s–early 1990s. Born on a farm near Lyon, Depardon left relatively young for Paris to become a photographer. While he never photographed or filmed his parents, he documented the political activism of farmers in the south of France in the 1970s. He also collaborated with the DATAR Photographic Mission in the 1980s, contributing to their efforts to redefine landscape photography. In 1987, the French magazine *Le Pélerin* commissioned him to produce a series entitled 'Voyage au bout de la France'. His book, *Images politiques* (2004), ends with the first photograph he ever took of Jean Maneval, one of the farmers featured in the trilogy, in 1990 in the confines of Haute-Loire. In the caption, Depardon explains:

> [This photo was] taken the first time I stepped into the Manevals' home – I have been back regularly since that day. I met Jean while working on a reportage about Lignon's farmers for *Libération*. This trip made me realise how much I needed to return to rurality, the world of my parents, of my childhood. I wanted to show this agriculture that still takes places in the mountains at medium altitude [...] I knew there were still farms up there [...] like when I was a child. I found them, checking with an altimeter, at an altitude between 2,000 and 2,600 feet. It's a hilly landscape, which makes it impossible for agriculture to be mechanised. It's not high enough to hold a second job in the ski industry. They indeed are in the middle of nowhere, especially in the Massif Central, in the High Vivarais, in Haute-Loire, and Lozère ... Nobody wants to do this job, nobody wants to buy their farms, so people keep on working until the very end, until they die.[27]

This first encounter took place almost ten years before he returned with his camera to film *L'approche*.[28] The Manevals are recurring characters in the farm trilogy.

Stretching the temporality of these films across three chapters affirms the film-makers' commitment to meet the farmers on their terms, respectfully of their defiance of strangers and their cameras. For ten years, Raymond Depardon made repeated trips to the Massif Central, a vast upland region in south-central France, meeting, getting to know and filming a few enduring farmers, whose stubborn determination to remain, or to start a life, put them at odds with our so-called 'modern life'. In Depardon's words, the trilogy dresses the 'portrait of a craggy culture and a disappearing profession'.[29] *L'approche* introduces the viewers to a few key characters, Paul Argaud, Marcel and Raymond Privat, Alain Rouvière and the Jeanroy family. In *Le quotidien*, the film-maker returns to the farmlands of central and southern France: some old acquaintances have passed away, like Louis Brès, while others are getting ready to sell their farms to younger families, introducing us to two new couples, Nathalie Deleuze and Jean-François Patel and Amandine and Michel Valla. Depardon's presence is more audible in the second part, whereas he stayed at a distance in the first film; this progression mimics Depardon's evolving relationship with these individuals and families and his gradual reacquaintance with the milieu in which he grew up. The third and last episode, *La vie moderne*, is the most carefully constructed, its narrative progression following the cyclical rhythm of the seasons, starting in late summer and ending in the following autumn. René Prédal notes that, in this final opus, 'Depardon fait entrer de l'air, décloisonne et fait sortir les gens' ('Depardon lets the air in, he knocks down walls and takes his subjects outside').[30] Long and slow forward-moving tracking shots, digging into the horizon recur and punctuate the film, highlighting the seasonal transitions and showcasing the landscapes, warm, yet hostile at times.

Depardon's reliance on cinemascope enhances the luminous beauty and texture of these mountains and fields. It is also a format that better honours the land, the ecological territory he immerses himself (and us) in, and the people who live in its folds. The horizontal frame accentuates the road. Tracing the deepening relationships between the film-maker and the farmers, it reconnects the film-maker's present journeys with his past – the son of small farmers near Lyon. Writing on territoriality, temporality and spatiality in *La vie moderne*, Philippe Ragel explains that Depardon '*s'installe-en-circulant*' (settles-in-while-ambulating) in the topography as well as in the cinematic frame. 'In this modus operandi, the trilogy draws its force from life itineraries. It is less concerned with portraits than it is with individual journeys. Its rhythm and central structure, mirroring the lives that it presents, originate in the comings and goings.'[31] Wandering serves as a life force that prevents the landscapes we continuously see unfold before our eyes from turning into fixed panoramic vistas or distant, dominating bird's-eye views. Instead, we experience embedded mobility that simultaneously instils a sense of temporality in spatial movements.

The slow unfolding of the road combines with Raymond Depardon's meditation on the social and cultural oblivion 'too often' suffered by the people he places at the centre of his frame. Could we dare argue, then, that Depardon's process of *empaysement* across this trilogy echoes with Deleuze's topographic conception of time, memory and cinema? May his ambulation within the landscape activate an ecological inscription – in the broadest sense of the word – of our being in the world? In his second book on cinema, *L'image-temps* (1985), Gilles Deleuze invests depth of field with a temporal quality. The primordial functions of this technique, in his view, consist 'of remembering, of temporalization: not exactly a recollection but "an invitation to recollect ..."'.[32] This being said, memory is not individual[ised] for Deleuze; instead, it connects us to the world. 'Memory is not in us', Deleuze states, 'it is we who move in a Being-memory, a world-memory.'[33] Depardon's pursuit of rural territoriality's depth of field 'creates a certain type of direct time-image that can be defined by memory, virtual regions of the past, the aspects of each region'.[34] His cinematic practice traces a sort of topological stratification within the image, using depth of field as a mode of orientation that takes us through different regions and layers of rural sedimentation.

As Raymond Depardon films it, the rural space acquires, in René Prédal's view, a transcending dimension that is all and at once metaphysical and cosmological: '[Depardon's cinema] foregrounds morality and aesthetics, but the ever-present agrarian cartography endows its portraits with metaphysical – time – and cosmological

– space – dimensions.'[35] This dual expansion of France's rurality, as both a world in itself and a memory of our being-in-the-world, comes from Depardon's commitment to recording the resilience of the men and women who still live in this world and uphold its values.

While the topographical 'creases' and 'folds' of the land are endowed with temporality, the people he meets and films, many of old age, embody a relationship to time different from our own. They are not remnants of a bygone era; instead, they exist in the present, fully aware of their precarious conditions as farmers and human beings. *La vie moderne* is not, in Depardon's mind, about the nostalgia he may feel for his childhood farm. The series of living snapshots that concludes the film must not be understood either as a means to freeze these farmers, still alive, into timeless figures. Instead, with these final portraits, they salute us on their own terms. In 1965, Pierre Bourdieu wrote about farmers' relationship with portrait photography:

> The attitude and posture that farmers choose to adopt in front of a camera embody their social values, most significantly a system that structures social relations within farming communities. Individuals often present themselves standing in the middle of the frame, facing the lens, at a respectful distance.[36]

'If it's the memory of the farm in Garet that gave me the energy to make it', he says, these farmers and their farms, lost in the folds of mountains and valleys, are 'not a "disappearing world", or a "separate world", [they are] a world that is not unlike our own.' Most significantly, these men and women 'don't expect anything from anyone anymore. They know they can only count on themselves. Like us.'[37]

The long lapse of time between *L'approche* (released in 2001) and the third chapter, *La vie moderne* (2009), conveys the (extra)ordinary resilience of these people. To do so, Vincent Amiel states, Depardon puts 'the spectators back in their place', refusing them the possibility to believe they are elsewhere and that they can live an/other person's reality for the duration of the film.[38] The goal here is not to merge the spectators with the subjects on the screen. Rather, it aims to bring the spectator to relate to them despite differences in lifestyles and values. Can we relate to them? How does this cinematic relationship affect us and cause us to reflect upon ourselves, our position in the world and our disposition towards other people?

The mutual care and commitment Soulard sees driving the farming trilogy to completion echoes with Derrida's definition of friendship:

> We must give up trying to know those to whom we are linked by something essential; by this, I mean, we must greet them in the relation with the unknown in which they greet us, as well, in our distance. Friendship, this relation without dependence, without episode yet into which all of the simplicity of life enters [...] passes by way of the recognition of the common strangeness that does not allow us to speak of our friends, but only to speak to them, not to make of them a topic of conversations [...] but the movement of understanding in which, speaking to us, they reserve, even on the most familiar terms, an infinite distance, the fundamental separation on the basis of which what separates becomes relation. Here discretion is not the simple refusal to put forward confidences [...] but it is the interval, the pure interval that, from me to this other who is a friend, measures all that is between us, the interruption of being that never authorizes me to use him, or my knowledge of him (were it to praise him) and which, far from preventing all communication, relates us to one another, in the difference and sometimes the silence of speech.[39]

The image of the farmer subtly greeting Depardon and Nougaret in the distance, either to welcome them back or to wish them goodbye, recurs on several occasions in *La vie moderne*, the last opus of the trilogy. After all, the film starts with these words, initiating Depardon's sparse voice-over narration: 'It starts with these roads. At the end of these roads, the farms. I return to these farms, happy to see these men again because, with time, I have gained their trust'

(2"17–2"46).[40] It also ends with a long tracking shot, one of many, with the difference that the camera, filming from the back of the van, slowly moves backwards instead of digging forward into the frame. After a while, Depardon's familiar voice-over narration resumes, one last time (1'16"03–1'18"27).

> Tonight, it is the golden hour. The most beautiful season. It is 6 pm, and it is Fall. Soon, you will glimpse Raymond, standing at the top of the pass, who is always eager to do better. He knows that I will return to Le Villaret. He knows that I am no longer scared to admit my affection for these farmlands. At peace, I will also return to the cold high plateaux and the deep valleys of the Massif. Tonight, I film this light like no other, and I won't forget it soon.[41]

Indeed, suddenly, Raymond appears on the right-hand side, stopping to watch Raymond Depardon (his friend) drive away – for now. This long tracking shot, which gradually pulls us away from Raymond, to the point that his silhouette altogether disappears behind the horizon line, perfectly illustrates the ungraspable nature of friendship that Derrida describes – this essential link, 'this relation with the unknown […] in the distance'.[42] Raymond Depardon's films affirm these farmers, otherwise neglected, as actual contemporary figures of our shared precariousness.

The deep personal ethical bond he maintains with these farmers and these mountains take on a broader existential dimension for the spectators. Neither are we led to identifying with the farmers (the subjects of the films) or with Depardon's guiding subjectivity. The spectator's experience is different; we are invited to contemplate all and at once our ethical engagement with the world and everyone else in it as an experience that evades distinctions between the past, the present and the future. At that moment, we are not only implicated in 'the subjective dynamics' of our 'social engagement […] with a representation of the historical world', but we are also confronted with an unrealised and perhaps unreachable vision of a more hospitable world for the future.[43] Thus, the film operates an inversion. Whereas we expect to be presented with an archaic way of life, we are instead called out on 'our relation with and infinite responsibility to [these] landscapes and other inhabitants, without which we would not be who or where we are today'.[44]

## Spectres of community life in Marseille's *cités populaires*

Wandering also anchors Denis Gheerbrant's cinematic practice, allowing him to immerse himself more deeply within the geography and the social topography of a place, independently of its scale: a country, a region, a city. If Raymond Depardon sinks into '*la France profonde*', Gheerbrant's *La République Marseille* performs a '*cinépratique*' (cinepraxis) of Marseille's marginal territoriality, to excavate fading social values and solidarities in 'a world already almost forgotten'.[45] His most ambitious project to date, this seven-part film portrait marks his return to the south of France, several years after making *Le voyage à la mer* (2001), shot in several camping grounds along the coast between Catalonia, in Spain, and the Camargue, the swampy nature reserve, west of Marseille. Originally from Paris, Gheerbrant first came to the city in the 1980s, when he worked as a cinematographer for film-maker René Allio. From this experience, he preserved the image of 'a largely working-class city that had created a singular sociality, deeply rooted in the uniqueness of each of the localities' incorporated into the larger metro area.[46] Marseille is, first and foremost, an 'imagined country, a world peopled with stories, where speech flows openly', an idea and an ideal.[47] Fully assuming his position as an outsider, Gheerbrant embarks us in this journey.

The screen still black, 'La totalité du monde' starts with the sound of a car driving on the road. The first shot confirms this initial aural experience, revealing a view of the highway that brings us into Marseille. Next, we are looking through the windscreen, signalled by the mirror glimpsed in the top-left corner. The asphalt ribbon goes by in front of us; to the right, we discover the Mediterranean expanse, and to the left, the urban landscape stretches out. Gradually, the sound of a doleful musical score, mixed with intermittent metallic thuds, adds tension to our travelling gaze, guided towards the relief of public housing estates in the background to old industrial façades and manufacturing sites in the foreground. As we slowly dive into the social maze of these neighbourhoods, the sounds of a few distant, unidentified, disembodied voices speaking French and Arabic remind us of the multi-generational and multi-lingual nature of this social fabric. Finally, a brief look up towards the sky, following a bird gliding away, lands us in a café, face to face with a man. The camera positions us very close to him as if we were sitting right across from him, with Denis Gheerbrant, curious to hear his story of how, against his will, he first took a job as a boilermaker in a local factory when he was barely sixteen, before becoming a docker. Similarly, 'Marseille dans ses replis', the sixth chapter, embarks the viewers on a forty-five-minute-long drift through the 15th and 16th arrondissements, once homes to several local industries, all the way to the Plage des Corbières, on the seashore, passing through La Cabucelle, Saint-Louis, Les Aygalades and La Viste. Along the way, the film-maker meets and speaks with residents from different generations and ethnicities, catches up with them at work, at home, in the street or at the beach.

Asked how he envisaged the city's social geography, Gheerbrant explains he truly worked on 'getting his bearings' (*repérer*) for several months first before writing or filming anything. To do so, he looked for people (still) actively involved in preserving the cohesion of neighbourhood life: from the docks to Les Rosiers, once a prized garden city, now a decrepit housing estate riddled with poverty, crime and drugs; from l'Estaque, the village-like port, home to many industries now shut down, to the old working-class estate of Saint-Louis, up for sale. But being an outsider, identifying and locating places and people involved in various forms of community-based social activism left him 'lost' and 'disoriented':

After a few months, I found myself completely lost and disoriented: I had met over two hundred people! I could not figure out how to build solid relationships with individuals and groups. Too often, interlocutors with whom I had nevertheless established a relationship would simply disappear into the blue. So, each time, I had to start again and find new ones! Regardless, I had already successfully found promising leads and, looking back, as soon as I started sorting out all these contacts, connecting them and organising them, the film's structure began to take shape.[48]

*La République Marseille* (2009) prolongs Gheerbrant's ongoing exploration of social vacuity and blighted hopes. Writing about two of his previous films, *Et la vie* (1991) and *Le voyage à la mer* (2001), *Les Inrocks* critic Vincent Ostria explains that 'wandering and digression [are] key [recurring] principles' in his approach that, in the end, bring coherence to his cinema:

> Gheerbrant goes out and meets French people. Some are experiencing the sudden vacuity of their life (unemployment, retirement, disenchantment); others are simply on vacation. The value of his conversations with people of modest origins stems from the unforeseen, impromptu and informal quality of these encounters. These people provide the film-maker with an inexhaustible source of stories, phrases and accents, making fiction heroes look incredibly insipid in comparison.[49]

Stitching together different faces and facets of Marseille's northern neighbourhoods, the film-maker directs his attention to city officials' and private interests' concerted efforts to gut out Marseille of its 'proletarian' history and transform it into (a) global capital for leisure and tourism.[50] Just a few decades ago, these *villages* and *cités* were vibrant centres of Marseille's working-class culture, solidarity and social identity. Now, residents struggle to preserve their relevance and affirm their contributions to local history. They are left to live in the shadows of new constructions and a landscape redesigned for tourists and wealthier newcomers.

As a form of symbolic resistance to this process, *La République Marseille* reveals people who, though 'told they do not exist anymore', get to exist, momentarily, on the screen.[51] In 'The Last Working-Class City in France', Nathalie Rachlin contends that the film's force lies in its ability to make visible, audible and accessible these new 'proletarian' Marseillais who, in a sense, are 'a pure product of the cinema'. She adds that, with this film, Gheerbrant is more interested in filming how people '"recognize" each other, invent new social bonds and a new *ré-publique*'.[52] The *cité phocéenne* has become a case study of the matter in France, compelling film-makers to document protests and grassroots responses condemning and resisting this vast reinvention of Marseille from a working-class city into a world-class cultural capital. Nicolas Burlaud's *La fête est finie* (2014), for instance, picks up where 'La République', the last chapter of Gheerbrant's *La République Marseille*, ends.[53] As an activist-member of Primitivi, a '*téloche de rue*' (a community TV channel), Burlaud focuses on the conflicts that opposed local authorities, real estate interests and international investors to residents and activists about the future of the Rue de la République, a busy artery downtown, in the months that followed Marseille's nomination as the European Capital of Culture in 2013.[54] For Burlaud, culture and artists' contributions to the vitality and renewal of urban sociality were used as a pretext to push lower-income residents further away and out of the new Marseille.[55]

If *La République Marseille* strives to encapsulate 'La totalité [de ce] monde' *marseillais*, the juxtaposition of 'Les Femmes de la Cité Saint-Louis' (part 4) and 'Le Centre des Rosiers' (part 5) draws attention to a gaping hole at the core of this proletarian identity, its shared, yet differentiated, precariousness. These films present us with two incarnations of the *cité populaire* (the housing estate) – the older working-class women of the Cité Saint-Louis and the stranded youths of the Cité des Rosiers. Gheerbrant's cinematic intrusion in their everyday life thus becomes 'the chance to say "we, now"' on terms that reflect the distinct nature of the 'nonpresence of [their] present'.[56]

'Les Femmes de la Cité Saint-Louis' offers a rare feminine view of a working-class world most commonly embodied by male stories and experiences.[57] Most importantly, Denis (Gheerbrant) follows Jeanne, aka Jeannette, around the working-class estate where she has lived since the 1940s when she moved in with her parents and her four sisters. One of them, Joséphine, aka Fifi, is another recurring figure in the film. Starting in 1926, more than two hundred units – many single-family town-homes with adjacent courtyards or gardens – were built for families who needed to be relocated away from derelict downtown neighbourhoods facing demolition. Eighty years later, when Denis Gheerbrant arrives with his camera, the *cité* is changing. As older tenants pass away, their houses are sold to new residents, turning one of the first public social estates into private properties. For Jeanne and her friends, mainly women in their sixties and seventies, the decision is heart-breaking. For them, and for their friend Gracieuse, who until she recently died presided over the local tenants' association, the estate was their whole life, a place of lasting kinship, solidarity and friendship. With 'Les Femmes de la Cité Saint-Louis', Gheerbrant gifts Jeannette and her friends with the opportunity to symbolically reclaim the ownership over their *cité*, while revealing its communal life as already spectral. Throughout the film, the film-maker falls into step behind Jeannette in a '*marche fantastique*' ('fantastic walk') through the streets and alleys of her *cité*, punctuated by conversations with friends and neighbours.

In contrast, 'Le Centre des Rosiers' reveals a public estate that has become utterly inhospitable, riddled with crime, drug trafficking and extreme poverty. Notwithstanding this reality, Gheerbrant searches for signs of sociality, precarious as it may be. Led into the *cité* by a smiling mailman, we are immediately introduced to a small convenience store centrally located. Following the mailman on his daily rounds, we stop by Maria's apartment. Born in Spain, she came as a refugee after Franco came to power and moved into the Rosiers in the 1940s. She never left. Finally, we arrive at the Centre des Rosiers, a community centre that tries to provide local youth with alternatives to drug trafficking and crime. In a neighbourhood where 70 per cent of children have parents who are unemployed or live in extreme precarity, the Centre's primary mission is to foster an environment where residents can enjoy more peaceful and positive interactions. Instead of focusing on their difficulties, the Centre promotes activities and resources that emphasise people's '*savoir-faire*', '*savoir-être*' and 'competences', its director explains to Gheerbrant.[58]

For the rest of the film, so does Gheerbrant's camera. It shows us children practising karate and meditation, mothers taking literacy classes, a group of teenagers having fun at the beach, under the supervision of a social worker and others working on their *résumés*. The film culminates in the community's loud, joyful and proud display of its youth's talents when everyone congregates in the middle of the estate for a summer festival. Nevertheless, though relegated off-frame, the crime and social stigmas that weigh on Gheerbrant's subjects' lives can hardly be forgotten. In the most poignant scene, the film-maker interviews the father of a teenager, who was recently stabbed to death in broad daylight in front of witnesses. Speaking in his apartment, with the curtains drawn, he solemnly tells Gheerbrant: 'What hurts me the most is to know that my son's last words were "Am I going to die, doctor?"' When he asked for help, as he was lying down on the ground, no one helped, he adds. He walked alone to the doctor's office, his hand pressing on his bleeding heart. In the next scene, Gheerbrant comes across a woman, originally from the Comoros. She starts singing in her native language. When Gheerbrant asks what the lyrics mean, she replies that it is a sad lullaby. The mother in the song begs her baby to stop crying because she does not want to be angry with him. Each line adds new information, gradually revealing that she is a single mother, abandoned by the child's father. She does not want her child to go astray, like all the children raised on the street. She then abruptly stops and states, 'We are headed for ruin here, it's sure and certain', alluding to the situation on the estate where, in her view, too many children grow up with no clear frame of reference.

For Gheerbrant, cinema is a shared process that brings the viewer directly into the documentary encounter: 'I use the viewfinder when I film. Bodies therefore coalesce, and the third body is the camera.'[59] An appendage of Gheerbrant's body, the camera does not promote complete identification between the viewers and the film-maker. Instead, the camera body stands in contiguity with his body and point of view. As such, the ethical relationality of Gheerbrant's cinema can adapt to the specific needs and political stakes of the situation filmed.

In the two films considered here, Gheerbrant's position is visibly different. In 'Les Femmes de la Cité', his presence is rapidly, and naturally, embraced by Jeannette and her friends, making the camera essentially inconspicuous. We partake in the documentary encounter, primarily as witnesses to the praxis of hospitality and friendship it enacts between Gheerbrant and his subjects. In contrast, his position and identity as a film-maker are much more apparent in 'Le Centre des Rosiers', but not because it is intrusive. The young residents of the Cité des Rosiers make us aware of the cinematic *dispositif*. As he arrives at the community centre, children playing outside assail Gheerbrant. One boy runs up to him, sticking his face close to the camera as he exclaims: 'On est les plus forts!' ('We are the strongest!'). In response, Gheerbrant asks all of them to introduce themselves. Ensues a cacophony of voices as they start speaking over one another, shout and clown around. The same is true for older ones, teenagers and young adults, whom he films later in the film. In 'Le Centre des Rosiers', the camera is used in a more performative manner. In this second film, we are repeatedly summoned more directly into the encounter.

In each film, the ethical modulation, whether it implies the viewer or not, falls under the subjects' control, enabling them to 'enunciate their "we", their community' in such a way that their participation in the documentary encounter 'is a decision about politics, about if and how [they] allow [their] otherness to exist, to inscribe itself as community and history' – understood as 'the announcement of a "we"', to use Jean-Luc Nancy's words.[60]

In 'Les Femmes de la Cité Saint-Louis', Denis Gheerbrant's gift to these women is reciprocated, not as returned favour but as a co-constitutive disposition to redirect the documentary encounter towards genuine friendship and hospitality. Halfway through the film, a shift occurs in Denis Gheerbrant's and Jeannette's relationship. Whereas she addressed him with the formal pronoun '*vous*' during the first half of the film, she now uses '*tu*', a more familiar form. By that point, the roles have already been redefined: Gheerbrant may be carrying a camera and filming them, but he is first and foremost Denis, and his presence with the group has become completely natural, as the following dialogue illustrates perfectly.

> Jeannette: Fifi, y'a Denis, tu descends. Prends ta chaise. (Fifi, Denis is here, come out. Take a chair with you).
> Fifi: Qu'est-ce qu'il fait Denis? (What's Denis doing?)
> Denis: Il filme Jeannette. (He's filming Jeannette.)
> Jeannette: Il me filme. Alors, filme un peu Nine. (He's filming me. You should film Nine.)

Denis: Elle se cache. (She's hiding.)
Nine: Il m'a déjà filmée. (He's already filmed me.)
Denis: Oui, c'est vrai, mais je ne m'en lasse pas. (True, but I never tire of it!)

It is worth noting that this is the only instance when the camera is explicitly alluded to, and, at that moment, its mention affirms Gheerbrant's adoption by the women of the Cité Saint-Louis. He is joining them for an evening ritual they have been doing every day at sunset for as long as they can remember: they all come together, with their chairs, and sit down on the side of a quiet street, '*à la fraîche*' (after the sun has set and the air has cooled off), for a while, chatting. On that night, Jeannette recounts when she and her family first arrived, after taking refuge for a couple of years during the war in another region, prompting her daughter – who has joined them – to say: 'You are a sort of local historian, aren't you?' Jeannette replies, 'No, I just tell my story.' Then, shortly before it becomes too dark to film, Gheerbrant steps further back to get a shot of all of them, side by side, as if to immortalise this precious moment.

The film alternates between different spaces: the locale where they meet as members of the tenants' association (mainly during the first half of the film), various local sites of memory (the factory where they all worked, the back alley where the '*frottadoux*' would have clandestine rendezvous, a small square where women washed and line dried clothes communally, places where the community would gather for street parties) and private homes. In Jeannette's own words, the *cité* was a self-sufficient world; it contained everything they needed personally and socially – jobs, love, families, community. Today, much of this world has vanished, starting with many of their husbands and friends. This sociality can only be experienced residually from Jeannette's and her friends' friendships, recollections and old photographs. Jeannette's last confession to Denis, the type one voices to a friend, validates the whole documentary encounter we have been witnesses to as these women's enunciation of their community, their world. She has just talked about her husband and the emptiness she feels now that he has gone:

> Jeannette: Let me tell you something. See, I am 73 years old. I wouldn't mind living a little bit longer. Still, sometimes, I think I don't really want to see more. You see (*she smiles at Denis Gheerbrant, sitting behind the camera*).
> Denis Gheerbrant: Yes.
> Jeannette: Considering the circumstance and everything I hear and see … of course, not everything is true. But I am not sure I'm interested in seeing what's to come. It may sound stupid (*she turns towards the camera*). What do you think, Denis? (*she smiles*).

A cut brings us outside the house. We never hear Denis Gheerbrant's answer. Instead, she walks him out, back to his car, and says goodbye.

> Jeannette: Where is your car?
> Denis Gheerbrant (off-screen): Over there, you know, on that little square down there.

Looking in that direction, hands on her hips, she adds, 'Ok, well, I'm going to leave you here, then', letting out one last small smile before seeing *her friend* off. Jeannette's spontaneous decision to follow in Gheerbrant's steps as he walks away that day stems from more than mere politeness. It renders manifest the friendship that the film-maker and his hosts, his local guides, have developed. However, their last exchange before parting ways echoes back to Nancy's description of the community as a form of claiming togetherness in a world that breaches open as 'we' enunciate it: 'A world is neither space nor time; it is the way we exist together. It is our world, the world of us, not as a belonging, but as the appropriation of existence insofar as it is finite.'[61] While Jeannette does not directly address us, the viewers, in this final one-on-one conversation, our contiguity with Denis Gheerbrant's camera-body confers on her words a political dimension. At that moment, the 'minimal community' that Denis Gheerbrant and Jeannette form becomes a pure act of communication and community between two beings contemplating their finitude. It also opens the documentary encounter outward onto the world beyond, when Gheerbrant leaves Jeannette's question in suspension.

In 'Le Centre des Rosiers', in contrast, Denis Gheerbrant maintains his position as an outsider observing a social microcosm in a dire state, bearing witness to France's failures to extend genuine hospitality to immigrants. The previously discussed film mainly left the viewer outside the 'minimal community' formed by Gheerbrant and the women of the Cité Saint-Louis. Here, we are repeatedly summoned into 'partak[ing]' in the scenes. Our participation is constitutive of the political exposition of this community, especially in scenes involving the youths. There, our presence in the contiguous space carved out by Gheerbrant's three-body approach is actualised. Addressing the camera directly, they interpellate us, holding us to account for their systemic exclusion from the national community. Shortly after visiting the community centre and speaking with its director, who explains that the phrase '*les habitants des Rosiers*' (the Rosiers' inhabitants/ residents) is often used to stigmatise residents, Denis Gheerbrant meets a young man, sitting on a bench nearby. He has just finished his first year as a law student at a local university. After receiving his high school diploma with a distinction ('*Assez Bien*') last year, he was hoping to pursue an Associate Degree in Accounting, but he was not accepted. As he talks about his studies and career prospects, his eyes move between Gheerbrant, who films, and the camera, as if he were hoping to speak through it to viewers. These brief, repeated eye contacts hold us to account for the discriminations that preclude a young man like him from making good on his promise to come to France to get an education, even if this means leaving a life, friends and familiar social structures.

'Les Femmes de la Cité Saint-Louis' offers the women the opportunity to reveal their world as it is coming to an end; this second film presents us with a community-to-come, struggling to find ways to exist, together, 'in common', amid violence. Here, Gheerbrant's camera supports this process by bearing witness to, and making visible, various moments when the residents 'allow [their] otherness to exist, to inscribe itself as community and history'.[62] 'Otherness' is a common thread that not only ties the different sequences and interviews that compose the film, but it is also what connects the people we encounter together: from Maria, who came to France as a political refugee from Franco's regime in the early 1940s to African-born women learning how to read French; from the director of the Centre des Rosiers, one of the few white men in the *cité*, to the teenager, born in La Réunion, who grew up speaking Creole and not French.

To a large extent, this film performs the sociality it seeks to imprint on the documentary image, namely: 'To partake of community is to partake of existence, which is not to share any common substance, but to be exposed together to ourselves as to heterogeneity, to the happening of ourselves.'[63] The film propels us forward in that direction, culminating with the final community talent show. On this occasion, the law student we met earlier has become a master of ceremonies, inviting Gheerbrant to join in this celebratory moment: 'Young ones will dance, older ones will sing, and I will be there to represent my neighbourhood, for sure!' He later calls on their parents to go out and vote the next day, to reclaim what being *Les habitants des Rosiers* means from those who see it as a fixed social position, maintained apart from the *cité*, in the Greek sense, meaning a political community of citizens. Instead of ending on what could be seen as a relatively consensual promotion of voting as an act of political enunciation, Gheerbrant ends with a less determining view of *les habitants des Rosiers*, here assembled, in an instance of joyful communion in the middle of the *cité*. The camera starts panning slowly, around the crowd of children watching the show, in a circular motion. As we look at these attentive faces, the call to vote lingers, invoking both the immediate tomorrow and the slightly more distant future. When these children are, in turn, old enough to vote, will their community have 'happened' yet? In the last minutes of 'Le Centre des Rosiers', two visions of democracy come to us, one that is premised on the participation in the political system, by voting, and another that consists in claiming and embodying the right to choose to exist and live together, as a community, against all (deferred) expectations. The film does not create a choice. It simply opens up the field while, as Patrick Leboutte rightly points out, offering itself as a site where this community of otherness can take place.[64]

### The 'village' ethos: hospitality, collaboration and vulnerability

Of the film-makers featured in *Precarious Sociality*, Varda is undoubtedly the most widely known and internationally recognised. In 2017, she was the first woman to receive an honorary Oscar. A few weeks later, *Visages villages*, her collaboration with JR, was added to the list of the 2018 nominees for Best Documentary. Scholarly attention to her work in the Anglophone world picked up in the 1990s, most notably with Sarah Flitterman-Lewis's study of *Sans toit ni loi/Vagabond* and Alison Smith's monograph, *Agnès Varda*.[65] Since then, more books and a plethora of articles, reflecting a wide range of perspectives about her contribution to French and international film-making, have been published in the United Kingdom and the United States.[66]

If Agnès Varda's work epitomises French film auteurism, her unique style foregrounds a singular ethical disposition towards the world and towards humanity. She has authored a cinematic vision anchored in curiosity, kindness and hospitality. Her cinema puts everyone to the contribution, from the people who inhabit it to the viewers who witness it come to life. We can see all these principles at work in *Visages villages*, which follows the cross-generational duo journeying across France in JR's iconic mobile photo booth. Along the way, they stop in different 'villages' where they encounter people from different walks of life. A few of these stop-offs reflect the picturesque postcard image we have when imagining a small French village, bathing in the sound effects of cicadas in the summer. Other instances, however, are more surprising choices: a chemical factory, a row of empty old miners' cottages, the port of Le Havre and the graffiti-covered ruins of 'a ghost town, half-built and abandoned'.[67]

'We hope to inhabit, re-inhabit, bring some life to [a] place where life has vanished', JR explains to a group of people gathered in Pirou-plage for one of the sequences, 'using faces and a bit of energy, even if only for a day' (38"55–39"07).[68] Indeed, life and death are inextricably linked throughout the film, from Varda's repeated references to her mortality to various homages to friends and personalities, dead for a while (Henri Cartier-Bresson, Nathalie

Sarraute, Guy Bourdin) and the loss imprinted on some of the places featured (the miners' village, the D-Day beach in Saint-Aubin-sur-Mer, the ruins of Pirou-plage). While Varda's style is decisively more colourful and playful than Gheerbrant's or Depardon's more sober approaches, her films attest to the same commitment to reactivating the residual vitality of a place, especially when it appears to be encumbered by economic and political forces. In that enterprise, JR is a perfect acolyte, partner, accomplice and heir. The large-scale portraits that JR and his team paste on all sorts of walls bring people together, on- and off-screen, generating some spontaneous community life and honouring lives that have ended.[69] As *Visages villages* revolves around creating these images, Marion Froger's remarks about the (documentary) image's power to produce sociality doubly find resonance in Agnès Varda and JR's artistic adventures. 'Sociality (*le lien à l'autre*)', Froger writes, 'may well be the principal stake of an image offered, created and perceived outside instituted social relations that presuppose the commodification of images.'[70] In that regard, Varda and JR's presumably 'Instagram-ready act' forestalls the very economic logic that it seems to feed on or replicate by continually rerouting our attention towards the creative, collaborative and social processes of production of these images, even if they inevitably end up on social media.

Several scholars have commented on Agnès Varda's ethics of subjective relationality in her artistic practice across her work in photography, cinema and art installations. Writing about *Les glaneurs et la glaneuse*, Claude Murcia describes her documentary practice as eminently generous, hospitable and egalitarian.[71] In his brief review of *Visages villages*, Richard Brons states that what distinguished Varda from 'other famous directors of her "grand" generation' was her 'attentiveness' to 'possible connections between people starting from, but not sticking to, their mutual alienation'.[72] Delphine Bénezet considers the relevance of the term '*cinéaste passeur*' – coined by Dominique Baqué to describe, in particular, Raymond Depardon's work – to account for Varda's 'determin[ation] to capture images of those whom cinema often rejects'.[73] Of specific relevance to *Visages villages*, she adds that, for Varda, the image functions as the trace of her encounters with the people she films, capturing 'the fleeting nature of this "being together"'.[74] Aligned with these readings, my analysis posits that Varda's collaboration with JR is more than anecdotal. It continues and deepens an ethical project that underpins her artistic and cinematic practice and delivers a radically different politics of *auteurism*.

For Varda, politics was never just, nor primarily, about representation and figuration. It was always implicitly alive in the way she addressed (in person or through the camera's body) her subjects and in how she consciously and affectively implicated her spectators in the narratives she crafted. While most critics lauded the film in France and abroad, a few frowned on its lack of social criticism, its 'deeply nostalgic image of [a "blindingly white"] rural working class' and the 'transgenerational duo's Instagram-ready act'.[75] Even Varda's long-time friend and assistant, Bernard Bastide, describes *Visages villages* as her 'Canada Dry': 'it tastes like Varda's cinema, but it is not Varda's cinema.'[76]

Varda's films rarely present themselves as strong indictments of a given social and political reality, but they gently stir the viewer in directions with political implications. In *The Gleaners and I*, for instance, Nathalie Rachlin saw Varda not so much denounce the resurgence of gleaning in cities as a means of survival as compensate for it. By turning her *cinécriture* into acts of love and radical tenderness for her films' vulnerable subjects, Varda moves past social didacticism and turns cinema into social interventions.[77] In *Visages villages*, she and JR choose to embrace positivity as a gift to the people they encounter and film. As she explained, it gives them a chance to see themselves and their environment more favourably, an image that is radical in the current media landscape:

> Throughout, many of the places we filmed are under quite bad social conditions: unemployment for the workers, the bankruptcy of a company, the demolition of a village, and even a strike of the dockworkers. But I kept telling myself, and JR agreed, that we are neither journalists nor sociologists – the former needs news, and the latter needs sociological samples. Although we observed these kinds of social relations and class divisions very clearly, I believe that an artist needs to sense and capture the relationships between the people, give a new angle on them, and then share this perspective.[78]

For Kelley Conway, *Visages villages* 'asserts the necessity of community, friendship, and art in the face of personal loss, isolation, and the fraying of France's social fabric', with Varda and JR 'serv[ing] as guides to navigating the world with one's curiosity, empathy and humour intact'.[79]

Luce Irigaray defines hospitality as 'car[ing] about welcoming the other with respect for the difference or differences between us'. Such position 'requires that we [...] transform ourselves into works of art, through which we unify all that we are – body, sensibility and sensory perceptions, feelings and thoughts, and so forth – and express them to the other with restraint, a welcoming capable of both proximity and distance, with a meeting and a cultural fecundity between us in mind'.[80] The portraits that end up dotting the landscape materialise this transformation. In *Visages Villages*, this meeting of creative and sentient minds concerns as much the artistic friendship and symbiosis between Varda and JR that the film documents and performs as the trusting relationships they forge with the people they meet and 'transform [...] into works of art'. Therefore, JR's large-scale portraits are the products, and the ephemeral trace, of sociality that is, here, conceived and presented as a ludic, fun and convivial work in progress.

The coupling of genders, elements and even narratives is a constant in Agnès Varda's cinematography.[81] The shift from romantic love, present in many of her films starting with *La pointe courte* (1954), to a cross-generational friendship with JR invokes Luce Irigaray's ethic of gender difference as a primordial condition for mutual hospitality. In this instance, gender and age differentiation is visibly posited as a point of origin for creative collaboration:

> Without turning back to a merely natural order, we have to reopen the differentiated places prepared by nature itself in order to resume a cultivation of our natural belonging that takes into account the difference(s) between us at the vertical level of genealogy and, above all, at the horizontal level of difference between the genders.[82]

The film playfully stages these 'difference(s)' between Varda and JR without situating them as either complementary or compensatory qualities. Instead, they reflect mutually supportive positions and worldviews. Vertical and horizontal differentiation animates the film as a whole, typically by bifurcating segments into masculine and feminine elements and/or fostering cross-generational dialogue. Varda's editing intimately connects these narratives while allowing them and the subjects they feature to stay autonomous. Examples of this pattern are found in the sequences filmed at the two goat ranchers, previously mentioned, as well as the decommissioned row of miners' cottages and the port of Le Havre.

In the north of France, a region well known for its coal mines, Varda and JR meet Jeannine, the daughter of a miner who refuses to leave her family house. She is the last resident left on a row of empty cottages. JR's installation consists, therefore, of two parts: a large portrait of Jeannine's face, covering the façade of her house, and a line of full-length portraits of miners, modelled after old postcards found in Varda's archives. Once pasted on the soon-to-be-demolished row of houses, these black and white figures conjure up the spirits and memory of those who once lived on this street. They join the last woman standing in memory of this rich and painful heritage. While JR and his team work, gradually revealing these 'larger than life' figures, brought back from the past, Varda speaks with passers-by who have gathered in awe. Several are retired miners. Seeing these images, they reminisce about what it was like for them, physically, in front of the camera or in voice-over commentaries layered over shots of the old postcards, serving as illustrations. Personal memories anchor the scenes fixed in time on sepia-coloured postcard photographs, while the latter help spectators, unfamiliar with the everyday life of miners, to visualise the situations recollected. At the end of the sequence, a group of local teenagers joins in, taking selfies with JR. Past and present intermesh, told, seen and reimagined from different perspectives. Recounted with present-day art forms, the story of France's northern miners gets a chance to endure, a little bit longer, as generations cross paths. Furthermore, Jeannine, through her resistance, becomes the primary bearer of the local miners' legacy. Varda's insistence that women be recognised on an equal footing with men is clear throughout the film. For JR, the port of Le Havre is a familiar place, having done several projects there already, in collaboration with the dockers.[83] With Agnès Varda in charge, the spotlight turns to the dockers' wives, whom she simultaneously elevates into majestic 'totems' in a men's world and imagines as women-birds (*femmes-oiseaux*). Here, Varda reimagines a historical symbol of male solidarity and militancy, the docks, as a space of female empowerment and recognition.

As mentioned in the main introduction, Varda made precarity and precariousness central questions of her documentary *Les glaneurs et la glaneuse* subtly interlocking the social, economic and ecological dimensions in her multifaceted portrayal of gleaning. In *The Gleaners and I*, Varda crafted an ethic of relationality to others and the 'unknown', as Sarah Cooper points out, by inserting herself in the narrative as another (kind of) gleaner:

> Ageing and change are brought out in relation to the people she films [...] and herself. But as with her potatoes, the focus on Varda leads less to a self-centred portrait than to one in which the self is decentred through its concern for others, being rendered unknown and unknowable in the process.[84]

For Claude Murcia, *The Gleaners and I* carefully stages the awareness of 'shared otherness' as an experience bound to corporeality:

> Far from extruding the body in favour of a purely intellectual consciousness of I ('*le Moi*'), *Les Glaneurs et la glaneuse* resembles an attempt to domesticate the Self ('*le Soi*'), one's own body and anguish about the sense of finitude it produces. A process that implies accepting this alterity constitutive to the Self and the Other.[85]

This conscious embodiedness, which characterised *Les glaneurs et la glaneuse*, became constitutive of her cinematic practice from that time onwards, in films like *Quelques veuves de Noirmoutier*, *Les plages d'Agnès / The Beaches of Agnes* and *Visages villages*. However, a much earlier film, *L'opéra-mouffe* (1958), had already laid down the premises of such later developments. It is important to note that, in all these films, Varda grapples with her body's alteration, either as the result of pregnancy in *L'opéra-mouffe* or ageing in more recent films.

In *Visages villages*, Agnès Varda and JR welcome each other in their art practices and support each other's vision – figuratively and literally. By that time, Varda suffered from an eye disease that had started to impair her vision. Early on in the film, after she shares concerns about her gradually failing body, JR tells Agnès that he plans to help her record as many images as possible before 'everything falls apart!' (13"43).[86] Co-architects of the film, they also become subjects of each other's art. On several occasions, the film documents JR's team-based process, from selecting the photograph to building scaffolding, glueing and putting together the large-scale image to its gradual wear and tear. Similarly, Agnès Varda's toes and eyes end up on a freight train that disappears into the horizon as JR's voice-over explains: 'Your feet and your eyes tell a story; this train will go to other places where you will never go.' After a brief musical pause, Varda's voice-over thanks JR for 'this beautiful trip' as we look forward, in a point-of- view shot that places us on the front of a locomotive (1'20"00–1'21"59).

Despite its playful lightness, *Visages villages* promotes a subtle reflection on 'the fragility of living beings and ecosystems' ('*la fragilité du vivant*').[87] While *Les glaneurs et la glaneuse* made Varda's responsibility to her subjects a central stake of that documentary's ethics, *Visages villages* introduces another dimension, namely, her need to rely on another (artist)'s energy. At close to 90 years old, Varda's body is gradually failing her; her eyesight is impaired – we see her undergoing surgery – and she is often shown sitting, needing to rest. Of course, the famous scene where JR pushes her, as she sits in a wheelchair while running through the Louvre, a direct reference to Jean-Luc Godard's *Band of Outsiders* (1964), encapsulates the distribution of energy in their artistic partnership. JR's presence moves the film along, while Varda generates sideways, asides and pauses.

For Corine Pelluchon, facing the 'alterability' of one's body predisposes us to this ethical responsibility to others and the ecosystems that surround us: 'The alterability of my body and the incompleteness of my psyche underscore the passive nature of living things and our need for others. They are the conditions of this internal experience of alterity that opens me to the other.'[88] Additionally, it encourages us to recognise that our need for others

Figure 24. JR and Agnès Varda walking towards the ocean in Saint-Aubin-sur-mer, *Visages villages/Faces Places* (2017) © 2017 ciné-tamaris – jrsa.

is not a sign of weakness but compels us to consider others and engage ourselves in the ushering of an alternative, more just political, social and ecological ethos.[89] 'This triple experience of alterity', Pelluchon asserts, 'refers [us] back to [...] the public sphere', which is 'the place where I discover myself and the values I hold dear that my political community either reflects or disrespects'.[90] In this context, I thus propose that we see the village, in *Visages villages*, as a social, political and ecological fiction. The expression of an ethos that entwines the experiences of otherness, our responsibility to others and our need for others, the film exceeds the nostalgic trope its title connotes.

Notably, the 'village' ethos brings us to consider hospitality as another necessary condition for the renewal of sociality. Jacques Derrida reminds us that 'the problem of hospitality [is] coextensive with the ethical problem': 'it is always about answering for a dwelling place, for one's identity, one's space, one's limits, for the *ethos* as an abode, habitation, house, hearth, family, home.'[91] The 'minimal community', born of friendship and hospitality, is first and foremost the one that Agnès Varda and JR form and perform through this artistic collaboration (see Fig. 24). This coupling of an

ageing film auteur and a young street artist reimagines auteurism
as a site of hospitality, in contrast to historical conceptions that have
stressed the auteur as an expression of individuality. Varda
henceforth reframes auteurism as an ethic that manifests her
situatedness in the world and her responsibility to, and need for,
others. This hospitable collaboration actuates a process of
differential inheritance and legacy between Varda's and JR's artistic
practices. The success of their project, as a film and as a praxis of
sociality, is premised on the hospitality of the people they involve
in the film. No sequence better encapsulates this reciprocity than
our encounter with Pony, a seventy-five-year-old artist, who is
homeless – or is he? – and, in his own words, never worked.

Halfway through the film, Varda and JR are in the south of
France, where JR is busy creating portraits as part of his Inside Out
project.[92] Pony agrees to have his portrait done and added to the
open-air gallery in progress. Then, he invites the film-makers to
follow him back home, in 'his domain', perched in the hills nearby.
Derrida asks: 'to offer hospitality, is it necessary to start from the
certain existence of a dwelling, or is it rather only starting from the
dislocation of the shelter-less, the homeless, that the authenticity of
hospitality can open up?'[93] Pony indeed is the only one welcoming
them in his actual home. Throughout the film, filmed encounters
tend to occur on the street, at the front door, on the village square
or in open fields. Pony's makeshift home reflects his artistic
existence. It is built from a wide range of materials collected over
the years, assembled in colourful patterns, making it look like a little
dreamlike palace, where all senses can be awakened – colours for
the eyes, wind chimes for the ears, and an open structure that lets
the wind caress the face.

After taking his place in his nest, he exclaims: 'Aren't we good
here?' The camera positions us directly across from Pony as if he
were addressing us as his guests. He goes on, 'We are at peace, on
Planet earth.' After a few shots that reveal some of his art, made from
salvaged materials, we sit again as Pony shares his life philosophy.
'You know, I was born under a lucky star. My mother, the moon,
gave me her freshness. My father, the sun, his heat. And the universe
to live inside of it. Do you realise how blessed I am in life?' (*He
laughs and looks away, wistfully*). Pony embodies this ethos of

consideration that Pelluchon sees enmeshed with the ethics of vulnerability: 'The ethic of vulnerability [...] which is premised on taking into consideration the fragility of life, invites us to rethink our relationship to other species, to sensible animals, as well as to plants, ecosystems and the biosphere.'[94] Interestingly, the film follows this encounter with Pony, which brings us to ponder our place in the natural world with two visits to two different goat farms, opening the village, a human ethos of the habitat, to the ecological question of humans' relationships with animals. It is well known that cats occupy a special place in Varda's cinematography. So without a surprise, we see plenty of cats in *Visages villages*. This film, however, turns the spotlight on another animal, goats, returning us to the question of bodily alterations.

The scene places side by side two farms, two conceptions of agriculture and two ecological visions. First, we meet a farmer, a man, who owns 240 goats and can produce up to 800 cheeses a day. To prevent his goats from injuring each other, he burns their horns shortly after they are born, leaving the goats hornless – a practice that the second farmer, a woman, sees as a complete aberration:

> Varda: You have one of the only herds where the goats have horns.
> The Farmer: To my mind, if a goat has horns, she keeps them. I'm not going to remove them. That just seems ...
> I can find no logical explanation unless you see them as a product required to attain a specific rate of return, so you eliminate any factors that might make them less profitable and cut off their horns. You burn them off. But if you want to do this in a way that respects the animals, you have to leave them intact. If they have horns, they keep them. Sure, they fight. Human beings fight too. (49"24–50"18)

The comparison is drawn between both farms and methods, one resorting to technologies and machinery to enhance productivity, the other putting the animal's well-being first. It thus raises the question of how non-human living beings are valued. In the end, Agnès Varda and JR value the goats with horns, making this

Figure 25. A goat with horns, *Visages villages/Faces Places* (JR and
Agnès Varda, 2017) © 2017 ciné-tamaris – jrsa.

statement clear with a gigantic portrait of the animal on a local
farming depot. Anecdotally, JR's (production) company goes by
the name 'Social Animals'.

Jean-Luc Nancy, writing about painting, states that 'a *visage* was
a portrait before being a face'.[95] I would like to offer a variation
and propose that, in *Visages villages*, a visage is a face that deserves
the gift of a portrait. The portraits the film's subjects and viewers
discover throughout the film take on different functions, according
to the locations and contexts in which they are made and presented.
In Pirou-plage, the ghost village, they manifest 'the presence of what
is absent, a presence in absentia [...] charged [...] with presenting
presence insofar as it is absent: with evoking it (invoking it, even)'.[96]
In other instances, with Pony, Jeannine, the farmer and the waitress,
they confer public recognition to individuals who would otherwise
remain anonymous. At the factory, the twin portraits, joining the
morning and afternoon shifts, materialise an invisible community
that can never be grasped as such because of the dispersion of the
workplace across different times, spaces and professional identities.
As for the goat (see Fig. 25), this portrait, with horns, asserts this

animal's wholeness and subjects us to 'bottomless gaze […] called animal', that for Derrida, unlike Levinas, 'offers to my sight the abyssal limit of the human: the inhuman or the ahuman, the ends of man'.[97]

Meanwhile, this portrait of a goat with horns that JR pasted on an agricultural warehouse by the side of the road confronts us with 'an animal that reciprocates our gaze', maintaining the 'intrinsic value' of its identity and natural integrity.[98] This moment in the film stretches the documentary encounter to account for another difference and another vulnerable body: the animal. In the equality posited between the other human portraits and this animal portrait, what is at stake is not an attempt to anthropomorphise the goat. On the contrary, this portrait reaffirms the documentary's interest in a transforming ethical intervention. Instead of directly denouncing the exploitative nature of modern-day agriculture, Varda and JR leave us, and whoever will come across the large-scale image, face to face with this goat, proudly horned.

Ending this study of early twenty-first-century French social documentary cinema with Agnès Varda institutes the filiation I see between her conception of (*auteur*) cinema and the commitment of French social documentary film-making to a praxis of differential affiliations, sociality and care. While loss and disappearance are an important subtext in *Visages villages*, the film moves away from the social and economic precarity addressed in *Les glaneurs et la glaneuse* to reflect on the ethical force of our shared existential precariousness and vulnerability. This film continues, nonetheless, Varda's pursuit of an ethic that values life. In this regard, the village is not to be dismissed as Varda and JR's nostalgia for homogeneous, bucolic communities, detached from the world. Instead, they embrace it as an ethos, more than an actual geographic space, that mobilises responsibility, fragility and hospitality to regenerate sociality.

## Conclusion

If Agnès Varda's and Raymond Depardon's cinematic practices have been examined side by side, few connections have been made between their work and Denis Gheerbrant's documentary approach.

For a film-maker whose career spans more than four decades, Gheerbrant has received relatively little scholarly attention to date, especially in the Anglophone world. However, in the late 2000s, Editions Montparnasse released a couple of box sets featuring his work, indicating that he had reached the status of a recognised documentary *auteur*, at least in France.[99] In closing *Precarious Sociality* with these film-makers, my main goal has been to reveal contiguity between *auteur* documentary cinema, better known to Anglophone documentary scholars, and the much wider-ranging production of creative social documentaries that have not enjoyed the same attention. This last chapter has stressed, in particular, how *Profils paysans*, *La vie moderne* and *Les habitants*, *La République Marseille* and *Visages villages* use social and geographical fictions that evoke ambiguous socialities – rurality, proletarian *quartiers* and villages. The films represent these *lieux communs* as fertile terrains for envisioning a social ethos that values precariousness, vulnerability and heterogeneity as vital and connective energies. Christophe Guilluy admits that, while cultural representations such as neighbourhoods, villages, regions and homeland are often mythologised, answering to processes of deculturation, they are nonetheless foundational to a grassroots reinvention of sociality.[100]

If they can be criticised for occasionally leaning into utopian ideals and leaving raw social, racial and political fractures unresolved in the background or off-frame, these film-makers have relentlessly probed the ethical force of documentary cinema. Sometimes, cinema's most radical intervention is its capacity to draw us into engagement with the most mundane and ordinary forms of sociality, conviviality and communality. Most importantly, they know when to trust their subjects and the relationships they establish with them, allowing us, the viewers, to trust them into the unknown of their practice and the world they introduce us to. In that regard, these films' genuine ethics of encounters with others bring us to see difference, ambiguity and life as fundamentally precarious gifts.

# Concluding remarks

In 2000, Jean-Louis Comolli described the impossible challenge of filming workers' bodies (*les corps ouvriers*) brought to the point of exhaustion, while simultaneously casting 'this crisis of presence, speech, listening' as a new political project for the future to come.[1] 'Documentary cinema', he stated, is uniquely equipped to 'register the gap [difference/interval] between a cinematic project and a political project (or rather "non-project") as a fundamental lack, pain, malaise.'[2] How film-makers have explored and occupied that gap in the past two decades has been the main focus of this study. The evanescence of working-class bodies and the political solidarities they embodied has been shown to be a new starting point rather than the end of documentary cinema's political projects.

Across this book, I have argued that, in the early decades of this century, French documentary film-makers have re-engaged the political from the standpoint of an ethical inquiry. The connections between the chapters and the socio-political context of precarity have occasionally been tangential. Yet, I argue that, by returning to solidarity, sociality and community as processes to be engaged with through scalable and careful social, political, aesthetic and ethical experiments, they have engaged the double crisis induced by precarity and precarisation: the 'crisis of the collective' and the existential crisis of the social subject.[3] '"Precarious" is as much a description of patterns of worktime as it is the description, experience, hopes and fears of a faltering movement', Angela Mitropoulos writes; therefore, 'a different future, by definition, can only be constructed precariously, without firm grounds for doing so, without the measure of a general rule, and with questions that should, often, shake us, particularly what "us" might mean.'[4] Across the chapters, identities have been shown to come undone, filiations reimagined and minimal communities of all sorts provisionally assembled. At times, they have troubled the film archive to retrieve unrealised filiations; at other times, they have directly confounded the viewer.

From 'a mutual bond *within* a given social group or community' (such as class-based solidarity), the films of the corpus advance 'a democratic notion of solidarity', one that, to use Olivier Marchart's words, 'registers an ethical demand for self-alienation – for de-grounding one's own identity – and translates it into the language of political demand'.[5] The films that I have examined untangle the political demands of democracy, justice and community (in Jean-Luc Nancy's sense of 'being-in-common') from the class-based politics that dominated twentieth-century political film-making practices, by relocating their engagement with social, economic and subjective precarity in the vulnerable ethics of documentary cinema.[6]

This work and mine, as a result, focus on the specific demands that each voice extends, allowing the different *scenes* (labour struggles, work dreams, rural life, post-industrial valleys, housing estates) included in the corpus and in each chapter to be both distinct and resonant with one another. The precarious subjectivities encountered are not presumed to be equal; precarity is understood to involve different social positionings, each subject to individual and collective inflexions. There is no 'precariat' figured in this book, neither is it assumed as the goal of French documentary's political project.[7] Instead, the films invite us to 'attend to voices other than [our] own and to include in [our] judgement other points of view', to see this 'sensitivity to the needs of others' as a moral and political 'responsibility', echoing Carol Gilligan.[8] French documentary cinema invites us to be with others (the subjects in the film, the film-maker) as it decelerates time, removing us from the alienating urgency of our times to allow the corporeality of other voices (and silences) to materialise and confound us.[9]

# Endnotes

## Introduction

[1] Guillaume Le Blanc, *Vies ordinaires, vies précaires* (Paris: Editions Seuil, 2007), p. 13, 'This book was inspired by the oppressive, suffocating nature of our present times and the anger that boils up as we helplessly witness the precarisation of ordinary lives, summoned to justify precarity with new ideologies'.

[2] In July 1998, a Law against Social Exclusion (*Loi d'orientation de lutte contre les exclusions*) was approved by the French government, recognising access to housing, employment, healthcare, justice, education and culture as basic human rights, *https://www.legifrance.gouv.fr/jorf/id/JORFTEXT00000020 6894* (last accessed 15 July 2021): 'La lutte contre les exclusions est un impératif national fondé sur le respect de l'égale dignité de tous les êtres humains et une priorité de l'ensemble des politiques publiques de la nation. La présente loi tend à garantir sur l'ensemble du territoire l'accès effectif de tous aux droits fondamentaux dans les domaines de l'emploi, du logement, de la protection de la santé, de la justice, de l'éducation, de la formation et de la culture, de la protection de la famille et de l'enfance.' For further details, see Sophie Dion-Loye, 'La loi d'orientation relative à la lutte contre les exclusions du 29 juillet 1998', *Le Genre Humain*, 2/38–9 (2002), 113–30.

[3] The emergence of new forms of social movements in France has been the subject of numerous publications, including Sarah Waters, *Social Movements in France: Towards a New Citizenship* (London: Palgrave Macmillan, 2003); Jeremy F. Lane, *Bourdieu's Politics: Problems and Possibilities* (London: Routledge, 2007); Graeme Hayes and Martin O'Shaughnessy, *Cinéma et engagement* (Paris: L'Harmattan, 2005).

[4] 'Interview avec Christophe Otzenberger', *Objectif Cinema*, *http://www.objectif-cinema.com/interviews/014a.php* (last accessed 16 July 2021).

[5] Jean-François Chauvin, 'Fragments sur la misère de Christophe Otzenberger', *Objectif Cinema*, *https://www.objectif-cinema.com/spip.php? article3050&artsuite=2*, 'Il y a effectivement quelque chose d'irrespectueux à déranger les gens dans leur "moderne solitude", ce sentiment où le bien-être ouaté se mêle à une irrépressible envie de pleurer. Otzenberger dérange […] Dérangeant, en effet, car subitement,

les passants ne sont plus ces petites particules d'anonymat fichues d'un flou de cinéma ou de stries vidéo, non, ils s'incarnent au contact du cinéaste qui, volontairement, les choque et réclame d'eux qu'ils fournissent un avis, du discours […] A contrario, les sans-logis, les galériens du quotidien, les noyés en sursis bénéficieraient d'un régime d'écoute a priori favorable: je pose la caméra, prends ton temps, je t'écoute' (link no longer available 2 July 2021).

6   Bill Nichols, *Representing Reality: Issues and Concepts in Documentary* (Bloomington: Indiana University Press, 1992), p. 178.

7   Judith Butler, *Precarious Life: The Powers of Mourning and Violence* (London and New York: Verso, 2004), p. 49, 'I cannot muster the "we" except by finding the way in which I am tied to "you", by trying to translate but finding that my own language must break up and yield if I am to know you. You are what I gain through this disorientation and loss. This is how the human comes into being, again and again, as that which we have yet to know.'

8   Lisa Downing and Libby Saxton, *Film and Ethics: Foreclosed Encounters* (London: Routledge, 2009), p. 93.

9   Pierre Bourdieu, 'Job Insecurity is Now Everywhere', *Acts of Resistance: Against the Tyranny of the Market* (New York: The New Press, 1998), pp. 81–7, p. 85.

10  Bourdieu, 'Job Insecurity is Now Everywhere', pp. 83–4. In 2015, Isabell Lorey expanded Bourdieu's critique of this emerging political regime, 'precarisation', connecting the sociologist's framework with Michel Foucault's examination of biogovernmentality in her book *State of Insecurity: Government of the Precarious*, trans. Aileen Derieg (London and New York: Verso, 2015), prefaced by Judith Butler. In France, unemployment rates have averaged 10 per cent in the 1980s and the late 2010s, and rarely reached below 7.5 per cent of the general population, *https://www.insee.fr/fr/statistiques/3676628?sommaire= 3696937* (last accessed 2 July 2021).

11  Lorey, *State of Insecurity*, p. 12.

12  Lorey, *State of Insecurity*, pp. 13–15.

13  Lorey, *State of Insecurity*, pp. 12–13.

14  Christophe Dejours, 'Alienation and the Psychodynamics of Work', trans. Cadenza Academic Translations, *Actuel Marx*, 39/1 (2006), XVI–XVII, *https://www.cairn-int.info/article-E_AMX_039_0123—alienation-and-the-psychodynamics-of-wor.htm* (last accessed 2 July 2021).

15  Christophe Dejours, 'Alienation and the Psychodynamics of Work', XVI.

16  Danièle Linhart, 'Modernisation et précarisation de la vie au travail',

*Papeles del CIEC*, 43/1 (2009), *https://identidadcolectiva.es/pdf/43.pdf,* 'Que faut-il entendre par «précarité subjective»? C'est le sentiment de n'être pas chez soi dans son travail, de ne pas pouvoir se fier à ses routines professionnelles, à ses réseaux, aux savoirs et savoir faire accumulés grâce à l'expérience ou transmis par les plus anciens; c'est le sentiment de ne pas maîtriser son travail, et de devoir sans cesse développer des efforts pour s'adapter, pour remplir les objectifs fixés, pour ne pas se mettre en danger ni physiquement, ni moralement. C'est le sentiment de ne pas avoir recours en cas de problèmes graves de travail, ni du côté de la hiérarchie (de plus en plus rare et de moins en moins disponibles), ni du côté des collectifs de travail qui se sont effilochés avec l'individualisation systématique de la gestion des salariés et leur mise en concurrence. C'est ainsi le sentiment d'isolement et d'abandon. C'est aussi la perte de l'estime de soi, qui est en lien avec le sentiment de mal maîtriser son travail, avec le sentiment de ne pas être à la hauteur de son travail, de faire du mauvais travail, de ne pas être sûr d'assumer son poste. Et cela parce que le management moderne impose, au nom de l'autonomie et de la responsabilisation, à tous les salariés de gérer les multiples dysfonctions d'organisations du travail défaillantes, (c'est-à-dire qui ne leur donne pas les ressources nécessaires pour affronter les exigences de leur travail) toute en intensifiant de façon spectaculaire les rythmes de travail' (last accessed 30 June 2021).

[17] Jasbir Puar (ed.), 'Precarity Talk: A Virtual Roundtable with Lauren Berlant, Judith Butler, Bojana Cvejic, Isabell Lorey, Jasbir Puar, and Ana Vujanovic', *TDR: The Drama Review*, 56/4 (Winter 2012), 163–77, 172.

[18] 'Precarity Talk: A Virtual Roundtable with Lauren Berlant, Judith Butler, Bojana Cvejic, Isabell Lorey, Jasbir Puar, and Ana Vujanovic', 172–3.

[19] '17 novembre: 282 000 «gilets jaunes» mobilisés, un mort et plusieurs blessés aux abords des barrages', *Le Monde, live feed* (17 novembre 2018), *https://www.lemonde.fr/societe/live/2018/11/17/suivez-en-direct-la-mobilisation-des-gilets-jaunes-a-travers-la-france_5384807_3224.html* (last accessed 30 June 2021).

[20] Dominique Mèda, Pascal Lokiec and Eric Heyer, 'Cette colère des gilets jaunes est le résultat de vingt ans de politiques néolibérales', *Libération* (3 décembre 2018), *https://www.liberation.fr/debats/2018/12/03/cette-colere-des-gilets-jaunes-est-le-resultat-de-vingt-ans-de-politiques-neoliberales_1695787* (last accessed 17 May 2021). They also co-authored *Une autre voie est possible: Le modèle social n'est pas mort!* (Paris:

Editions Flammarion, 2018), a cross-disciplinary manifesto offering
alternative solutions to France's chronic crisis.

[21]  Ludivine Bantigny, 'Un événement', in Joseph Confavreux (ed.), *Le
fond de l'air est jaune: Comprendre une révolte inédite* (Paris: Editions du
Seuil, 2019), pp. 35–44, p. 42, 'Ce soulèvement est une résistance.
Résister? peut-être d'abord aux évidences supposées. Parmi elles, les
préceptes selon lesquels il faudrait s'adapter au monde tel qu'il est, être
plus flexible, plus précaire, corvéable et finalement jetable. Des experts
et des médias parlent du travail d'après son «coût», assimilent la
protection sociale à des «charges», font passer des régressions pour des
«réformes», opposent qui a un travail et qui n'en a pas, qui est né ici et
qui ne l'est pas. Résister à ces grands mots qui cachent mal leur
violence sociale sous le cache-sexe de leur «sagesse», c'est rappeler sans
cesse que tout cela ne va pas de soi. C'est assumer d'évoquer des classes
sociales, qu'on a prétendu disparues. C'est exposer d'autres formes de
violences que celles des vitrines brisées: la violence du mépris social
et des abîmes qui séparent des possédants; la violence du chantage à
l'emploi qui conduit à tout accepter, fait voler en éclats les solidarités
et jusqu'à la dignité parfois; la violence de la souffrance, au travail, au
chômage, la mise en concurrence et le management par l'obéissance.
La révolte révèle. Elle rend visible les invisibles, qu'on n'entend pas
dans les médias. Cette fois, il s'agit de les écouter.'

[22]  Jeremy F. Lane, *Republican Citizens, Precarious Subjects: Representations of
Work in Post-Fordist France* (Liverpool: Liverpool University Press,
2020), p. 245.

[23]  Joseph Confavreux (ed.), *Le fond de l'air est jaune: comprendre une révolte
inédite* (Paris: Éditions Seuil, 2019), p. 8, 'Car si les gilets jaunes ont
*percuté* toute une société, ils ont fait trembler les cadres d'analyse des
chercheurs et des penseurs.'

[24]  Serge Paugam, 'Face au mépris social, la revanche des invisibles', in
Coll. «Gilets jaunes»: *Hypothèse sur un mouvement* (Paris: La Découverte,
2019), pp. 37–42, p. 37, 'Un mouvement social comme celui des «gilets
jaunes» est à bien des égards difficiles à saisir tant il fait remonter à la
surface des formes multiples de ressentiment et de frustration qui se
sont accumulées au fil du temps dans des couches sociales diverses dont
on peine à trouver immédiatement ce qu'elles ont en commun […]
Pourtant, si rien ne pouvait le prédire avec exactitude, il serait faux de
dire qu'aucun signe de ce malaise ne ressortait de nombreuses enquêtes
sociologiques menées au cours des dernières décennies. Un ouvrage
me semble avoir été tout particulièrement annonciateur de ce malaise
social, mais il date de 25 ans! Il s'agit de *La Misère du monde* publié par

Pierre Bourdieu et son équipe (Editions du Seuil, 1993). Diverses formes de souffrances sociales y sont analysées à partir d'entretiens approfondis collectés auprès d'individus appartenant à différentes couches sociales, mais ayant pris pour point commun de faire quotidiennement l'expérience de l'infériorité de leur statut, ce que les auteurs qualifieront de misère de position en opposition à la misère de condition. Il s'agit d'une infériorité à l'origine de différentes formes de détresse psychologique, notamment la perte de confiance en soi et le sentiment d'inutilité. Ce qui frappe à la relecture de cet ouvrage, c'est qu'on y trouve tous les ingrédients du ressentiment qu'éprouvent aujourd'hui les «gilets jaunes».'

25  Christophe Guilluy, *La France périphérique: comment on a sacrifié les classes populaires* (Paris: Editions Flammarion, 2014), pp. 175–6, 'Depuis le début des années 2000, l'édifice est fragilisé, non pas par les "banlieues" mais par les catégories populaires que l'on croyait définitivement sorties de l'Histoire. Depuis les territoires de la France périphérique, c'est le modèle d'une oligarchie triomphante qui est contesté, par le bas. Cauchemar des classes dirigeantes, cette France périphérique fait voler en éclats toutes les croyances dans un modèle unique. Ce qui se joue désormais n'est pas une controverse entre la "gauche" et la "droite", entre "progressistes" et "populistes", entre le "camp du bien" et le "camp du mal", mais un affrontement pour l'émergence d'une contre-société qui puisse assurer la réintégration économique, politique et culturelle des couches populaires. Ce conflit idéologique majeur entre les gagnants et les perdants de la mondialisation, entre les tenants du "village" et celui d'un monde "hors-sol" n'est pas spécifique à la France et explique la recomposition politique à l'œuvre partout en Europe.'

26  *Il suffira d'un gilet* (Aurélien Blondeau, 2019), 'On vit dans des conditions dégueulasses. On mange des trucs dégueulasses. On termine dans un EHPAD pourri à crever d'une maladie du capitalisme.'

27  *Il suffira d'un gilet* (Aurélien Blondeau, 2019), 'La vraie démocratie nous la pratiquons dans nos assemblées sur nos ronds-points. Elle n'est ni sur les plateaux-télé ni sur les pseudo-tables rondes organisées par Macron. Après nous avoir insultés et traités de moins que rien, voilà maintenant qu'il nous présente comme une foule haineuse, fasciste et xénophobe. Mais nous, nous sommes tout le contraire, ni racistes, ni sexistes, ni homophobes. Nous sommes fiers d'être ensemble avec nos différences pour construire une société solidaire.'

28  Sandra Laugier and Albert Ogien, 'Samedi, j'ai insurrection: neuf leçons à tirer d'un mouvement intermittent', in Coll. «Gilets jaunes»: *Hypothèse sur un mouvement* (Paris: La Découverte, 2019), pp. 59–67,

'Chacun ou presque en a fait l'expérience amusante ces dernières semaines: on voit un gilet jaune dans la rue ou le bus en semaine … sur quelqu'un qui fait juste son boulot (aider les enfants à traverser, s'occuper des ordures, travailler sur un chantier). Tout d'un coup, on s'aperçoit de l'existence et de l'importance de ce travail, de toute cette armée qui permet notre vie quotidienne, et reste invisible. La mobilisation nous a appris à la voir. Il n'est pas un hasard que, même si ceux qui «montent» à Paris sont surtout des hommes, les «gilets jaunes» soient très souvent des femmes, qui s'engagent en politique pour la première fois – et des femmes des professions de care (infirmières et aide-soignantes, travailleuses sociales, aides ménagères, employés à temps partiel(s), retraitées …), premières victimes des «réformes» … Le *care*, le souci des autres, c'est la protection des faibles avant les forts; la reconnaissance de la valeur et la contribution de toutes et tous, «gagnants» ou losers. Ce contre quoi on se révolte, c'est une politique de la *carelessness*, ou d'un *care* monstrueusement inversé où l'on demande en fait aux pauvres de prendre soin des plus favorisés. C'est aussi de l'*attention* (un autre mot pour le *care*) qu'ont obtenue les «gilets» en l'endossant: «On a besoin de ce gilet jaune pour exister face à un monsieur qui croit que le peuple est invisible. Vous vous rendez compte? On est obligés de s'habiller en fluo pour qu'on nous voit?»' (*Libération*, 7 décembre).'

[29]   'Precarity Talk: A Virtual Roundtable with Lauren Berlant, Judith Butler, Bojana Cvejic, Isabell Lorey, Jasbir Puar and Ana Vujanovic', 170.

[30]   'Precarity Talk: A Virtual Roundtable with Lauren Berlant, Judith Butler, Bojana Cvejic, Isabell Lorey, Jasbir Puar and Ana Vujanovic', 171.

[31]   Gérard Leblanc, 'Militantisme et esthétique', *CinémAction*, 110, special issue : 'Le Cinéma militant reprend le travail' (2004), 30–4, 30.

[32]   Paul Douglas Grant, *Cinéma Militant: Political Filmmaking and May 1968* (New York: Columbia University Press, 2018), p. 10.

[33]   *CinémAction*, 110 (2004), special issue 'Le Cinéma militant reprend le travail'; Martin O'Shaughnessy, *The New Face of Political Cinema: Commitment in French Film since 1995* (Oxford: Berghahn Books, 2007); Florian Grandena, *Showing the World to the World: Political Fictions in French Cinema of the 1990s and early 2000s* (Cambridge: Cambridge Scholars Publisher, 2008); Martin O'Shaughnessy, *Laurent Cantet* (Manchester: Manchester University Press, 2015); Joseph Mai, *Robert Guédiguian* (Manchester: Manchester University Press, 2017); Alison J. Murray Levine, 'Documentary Film: A French Renaissance, 1990–

2012', in Hilary Radner, Raphaelle Moine and Alistair Fox (eds), *Companion to French Cinema* (London: Blackwell, 2015), pp. 356–75; Alison J. Murray Levine, *Vivre Ici: Space, Place, and Experience in Contemporary French Documentary* (Liverpool: Liverpool University Press, 2018); Derek Schilling, 'Disuse and Affect: Post-Industrial Landscapes of France's Labour Lost', in Ari J. Blatt and Edward Welch (eds), *France in Flux: Space, Territory and Contemporary Culture* (Liverpool: Liverpool University Press, 2019), pp. 35–62; Anna-Louise Milne, 'Sylvain George's Minor Mode, or Cinema at the Margins of its Fragile Community', in Ari J. Blatt and Edward Welch (eds), *France in Flux: Space, Territory and Contemporary Culture* (Liverpool: Liverpool University Press, 2019), pp. 92–113; Sarah Waters, 'Disappearing Bodies: The Workplace and Documentary Film in an Era of Pure Money', *French Cultural Studies*, 26/3 (2015), 289–301.

[34] Van Kelly, 'Cinéma Engagé: Activist Filmmaking in French and Francophone Contexts', *South Central Review*, 17/3 (Autumn 2000), special issue: 'Cinéma Engagé: Activist Filmmaking in French and Francophone Contexts', 1–6, 5.

[35] O'Shaughnessy, *The New Face of Political Cinema*, p. 179.

[36] Jacques Rancière, *The Intervals of Cinema*, trans. Jonathan Howe (London: Verso, 2014), p. 104.

[37] Jacques Rancière, *The Emancipated Spectator*, trans. Gregory Elliott (New York: Verso, 2008), p. 72.

[38] Jane M. Gaines, 'Documentary radicality', *Revue Canadienne d'Etudes Cinématographiques/Canadian Journal of Film Studies*, 16/1 (2007), 5–24, 6.

[39] Gaines, 'Documentary radicality', 6.

[40] Patrick Cingolani, *Révolutions précaires: Essai sur l'avenir de l'émancipation* (Paris: Editions La Découverte, 2014), pp. 51–5, 'L'histoire ouvrière garde la trace de cette tension constitutive de l'expérience précaire, même si elle a été largement effacée par le grand discours stratégique de la révolution prolétarienne […] La fiction de ce dispositif permet d'anticiper une autre existence au sein même des rapports de domination […] c'est sur la disparition de l'ouvrier comme ouvrier que, au même titre que le dispositif plébéien, ouvre l'utopie. L'un comme l'autre amorcent un mouvement de changement, cette négation de soi que l'ouvrier doit produire pour, selon Marx, se muer en acteur de la révolution.'

[41] Gaines, 'Documentary radicality', 12; Jane M. Gaines, 'Political Mimesis', in Jane M. Gaines and Michael Renov (eds), *Collecting Visible Evidence* (Minneapolis: University of Minnesota Press, 1999), pp. 84–102.

42 Jacques Derrida, *Specters of Marx*, trans. Peggy Kamuf (London: Routledge, 1994), pp. 54–5.
43 Butler, *Precarious Life*, p. 22.
44 Thomas Elsässer, *European Cinema and Continental Philosophy: Film as Thought Experiment* (Edinburgh: Edinburgh University Press, 2014), p. 29.
45 Le Blanc, *Vies précaires*, p. 110, 'Les luttes pour la reconnaissance ne s'insèrent donc pas seulement dans les interstices d'une forme sociale nécrosée ; elles font revivre de vieilles histoires, des paroles anciennes qui restent accrochés à un espace particulier. De ces histoires et de ces paroles, qui sont comme l'humus des précaires, émerge une temporalité qui excède le présent spatialisé d'un lieu […] et en laquelle peuvent se nicher les timbres rajeunis des voix des précaires, raccordant un passé souvent ennobli, fait de luttes et de victoires silencieuses, à un avenir, certes incertain, mais désormais ouvert à un futur de la parole et de la contestation.'
46 Stella Gaon, 'Communities in Question: Sociality and Solidarity in Nancy and Blanchot', *Journal for Cultural Research*, 9/4 (October 2005), 387–403, 397.
47 Olivier Marchart, 'Democracy and Minimal Politics: The Political Difference and its Consequences', *The South Atlantic Quarterly*, 110/4 (Fall 2011), 965–73, 966.
48 A detailed overview of the French documentary so-called 'renaissance' in the last two decades, applicable to the corpus of this book, can be found in Alison J. Murray Levine's recent book, *Vivre Ici*, pp. 21–37.

## Chapter 1: The vanishing factory

1 Tangui Perron, 'Les origines du cinéma militant (ou le cinéma militant et la mort)' (2004), *http://www.peripherie.asso.fr/mouvement-ouvrier-et-cinema/le-cinema-militant*.
2 Luc Decaster, quoted in Audrey Mariette, '"Silence, on ferme!" Regard documentaire sur des fermetures d'usine', *Ethnologie Française*, 35/4 (2005), 653–66, 654.
3 Pierre Nora, 'Between Memory and History: Les Lieux de Mémoire', *Representations*, 26 (Spring 1989), Special Issue: 'Memory and Counter-Memory', 7–24, 12.
4 Nora, 'Between Memory and History', 9.
5 Svetlana Boym, *The Future of Nostalgia* (New York: Basic Books, 2001), p. 29.

6   Boym, *The Future of Nostalgia*, p. 50.
7   Boym, *The Future of Nostalgia*, p. 50.
8   Boym, *The Future of Nostalgia*, p. 50.
9   Derrida, *Specters of Marx*, p. 221.
10  Derrida, *Specters of Marx*, p. 10.
11  Boym, *The Future of Nostalgia*, p. 50.
12  Boym, *The Future of Nostalgia*, pp. 53–5.
13  'Les fermetures d'usines en France, de 2009 à 2012, et autres données', *http://www.trendeo.net/les-fermetures-dusines-en-france-de-2009-a-2012/* (last accessed 17 May 2021).
14  Victoria Masson, 'En France, les fermetures d'usines se réduisent mais le chômage ne baisse pas', *Le Figaro* (18 février 2015), *http://www.lefigaro.fr/emploi/2015/02/18/09005-20150218ARTFIG 00225-en-france-les-fermetures-d-usines-se-reduisent-mais-l-emploi-ne-decolle-pas.php* (last accessed 17 May 2021).
15  *http://www.reuters.com/article/france-election-steel-idUSL5E8DK5O X20120220* (last accessed 17 May 2021).
16  See among other references 'How Macron calmed Whirpool workers whipped up by Le Pen', *The Guardian* (27 April 2017), *https://www.the guardian.com/world/2017/apr/27/how-macron-calmed-whirpool-workers-whipped-up-by-le-pen* (last accessed 28 May 2021); 'Amiens: Le Pen upstages Macron at Whirlpool Factory', *Al Jazeera* (26 April 2017), *http://www.alja zeera.com/news/2017/04/amiens-le-pen-upstages-macron-whirlpool-factory-170426161935345.html* (last accessed 28 May 2021); 'Macron ambushed by Le Pen on French presidential campaign trail', *Financial Times* (26 April 2017), *https://www.ft.com/content/6e7d30d8-2a7f-11e7-9ec8-168383da 43b7* (last accessed 28 May 2021).
17  This is a rough estimate of titles catalogued in the database compiled by the association Ardèche Images and La Maison du Documentaire: *http://www.lussasdoc.org/presentation_de_la_base_de_donnees,194.html* (last accessed 17 May 2021). Maintained for over twenty years, this online database provides, according to Ardèche Images, a list of documentary films produced in Francophone Europe that is as exhaustive as possible. A total of over 38,000 titles has so far been added to the database since La Maison du Doc was created in 1994.
18  They come in a wide range of formats – some respect the fitting 52-minute length for television broadcast, others reach the average theatrical feature length of 80 minutes. Whereas many received funding from public television, others, like *Les Conti, gonflés à bloc*, were crowdfunded by the former employees of Continental-Clairevoix themselves.

19  Belen Vidal, *Heritage Film: Nation, Genre, and Representation* (New York: Columbia University Press, 2012), pp. 58–9.

20  See more on this subject in Emmanuel Barrot, *Camera Politica: dialectique du réalisme dans le cinéma politique et militant (Groupes Medvekine, Francesco Rosi, Peter Watkins)* (Paris: Vrin, 2009), p. 49.

21  The term 'spectralisation' is used here in reference to Jacques Derrida's *Specters of Marx*, pp. 30–1.

22  Further details concerning the film and links to reviews published upon its release can be found on the website *www.allociné.fr* (last accessed 17 May 2021).

23  This short film is available, as a bonus feature, on the DVD of *Rêve d'usine* (DVD Zone 2: Edition Cinémalta, 2008).

24  Mariette, '"Silence, on ferme!"', 653–66.

25  Jackie Clarke, 'Closing Moulinex: Thoughts on the Visibility and Invisibility of Industrial Labour in Contemporary France', *Modern and Contemporary France,* 19/4 (2011), 443–58.

26  Clarke, 'Closing Moulinex', 447.

27  Italics in the quotes from the film reflect emphases I make to highlight the intonation of these workers when describing what the factory means to them.

28  Derrida, *Specters of Marx*, p. 30.

29  Derrida, *Specters of Marx*, p. 5.

30  Derrida, *Specters of Marx*, p. 6.

31  Within a few weeks, in September 1999, Michelin announced a 20 per cent increase in the company's annual profits and 7,500 layoffs among its European workforce. Laurence Lasselle and Serge Svizzero, 'Licencier en période de bénéfices, Michelin l'a fait: Mondialisation, fonds de pension américains obligent. Pas si sûr. Michelin, symptôme français', *Libération* (18 septembre 1999), *https://www.liberation.fr/ tribune/1999/09/ 18/licencier-en-periode-de-benefices-michelin-l-a-fait-mondialisation-fonds-de-pension-americains-oblig_284009* (last accessed 28 May 2021); Christian Dufour, 'Michelin announces profits and redundancies', *Eurofound* (27 October 1999), *https://www.eurofound. europa.eu/sr/publications/article/ 1999/mich elin-announces-profits-and-redundancies* (last accessed 17 May 2021).

32  *http://www.senat.fr/seances/s200010/s20001012/sc20001012018.html* (last accessed 28 May 2021).

33  'Travail. *Rêve d'usine*, de Luc Decaster, revient sur six mois de lutte des ouvriers d'Epéda à Mer en l'an 2000', *L'Humanité* (5 March 5 2003), *http://www.humanite.fr/node/280892* (last accessed 28 May 2021); Gunther Capelle-Blancard and Nicolas Couderc, 'Licenciements

boursiers chez Michelin et Danone: beaucoup de bruit pour rien?',
*Revue Française d'Economie*, XXI/2 (2006), 55–73.

34 Derrida, *Specters of Marx*, p. 6.

35 Derrida, *Specters of Marx*, p. 27.

36 Tom Lewis, 'The Politics of "Hauntology" in Derrida's *Specters of Marx*', in Michael Sprinker (ed.), *Ghostly Demarcations: A Symposium on Jacques Derrida's Spectres of Marxism* (New York: Verso, 1999), pp. 134–67, p. 140.

37 Mariette, '"Silence, on ferme!"', 661, 'The closure-event presents cinematographic stakes since it provides the opportunity to create "portraits" of men and women who are facing an uncertain professional and personal future, and who, as a result, become film "characters".'

38 Derrida, *Specters of Marx*, p. 6.

39 *http://www.cci.sfia.fr/L-industrie-Ardennaise* (last accessed 17 May 2021).

40 Simon Edelblutte, *Paysages et territoires de l'industrie en Europe: héritages et renouveaux* (Paris: Ellipses, 2010), p. 75.

41 Simon Edelblutte, 'Que reste-t-il du textile vosgien?' *L'information géographique*, 72 (2008), 66–88, 84–5.

42 This still seemed to be the case in 2013 (*http://www.lunion.fr/region/usine-cherche-repreneur-pour-perenniser-50-emplois-ia3b25n46015* (last accessed 28 May 2021), when two of the leading partners, including the director interviewed in the film, struggled to find buyers for their shares. In 2016, the company was successfully taken over by a French industrialist who manages the factory with one of three previous shareholders.

43 A detailed overview of Marcel Trillat's personal life and film career can be found in Tangui Perron, 'Portrait de Marcel Trillat', *Histoire d'un film, mémoire d'une lutte*, Etranges étrangers, Editions Scope-Périphérie (2009), available online, *http://www.peripherie.asso.fr/patrimoine-marcel-trillat/portrait-de-marcel-trillat* (last accessed 28 May 2021).

44 *Silence dans la vallée* (dir. Marcel Trillat, 2007, VLR Productions)

45 For further details on Ciné-Liberté and these films, see Guy Gauthier, *Un siècle de documentaires français: des tourneurs de manivelle aux voltigeurs du multimédia* (Paris: Editions Armand Colin, 2004).

46 Margaret C. Flinn, *The Social Architecture of French Cinema, 1929–1939* (Liverpool: Liverpool University Press, 2014).

47 Flinn, *The Social Architecture of French Cinema*, p. 39.

48 Two films come to mind more specifically: *Ma mondialisation* (Gilles Perret, 2006)/the Arves valley in the Alps, and *Sur les cendres du vieux*

*monde* (Laurent Hasse, 2001)/the Fensch valley in Lorraine. A more detailed analysis of *Sur les cendres du vieux monde* can be found in chapter 3, 'Precarious filiations'.

49 Simon Edelblutte, 'Le paysage est-il un lieu de mémoire', *France Culture*, 'Planète Terre' (17 octobre 2012), *http://www.franceculture.fr/emissions/planete-terre/le-paysage-est-il-un-lieu-de-memoire* (last accessed 12 July 2021).

50 *Silence dans la vallée* (4"46–5"02).

51 *Ex-Moulinex, Mon travail c'est capital* is an ISKRA/LaSept ARTE production, *Plan social: et après* was produced with the support of Les Films du Grain de Sable, a company founded by Jean-Michel Carré, Serge Poljinski and Yann Le Masson in 1974. Abandoned and in ruins in *Ex-Moulinex*, the factory is hardly recognisable in the second film. Eighteen years after it closed down in 1992, the Bull factory of *Plan social: et après* is converted into mixed-use office spaces.

52 See for instance *300 jours de colère* (Marcel Trillat, 2000), *Un monde moderne* (Sabrina Malek and Arnaud Soulier, 2005), *Calor, une usine en perspective* (Martine Arnaud-Goddet, 2007), *Des temps incertains* (Jean-François Moris, 2007).

53 Pierre Nora, 'From *Lieux de mémoire* to *Realms of Memory*: Preface to the English Language edition', xv–xxiv.

54 Michael Rothberg, 'Between Memory and Memory: From *Lieux de mémoire* to *Nœuds de mémoire*', *Yale French Studies, Nœuds de mémoire: Multidirectional Memory in Postwar French and Francophone Culture*, 118–19 (2010), 3–12, 4.

55 Rothberg, 'Between Memory and Memory', 4.

56 Nora, 'Les lieux de mémoire', 19.

57 Jani Scandura, *Down in the Dumps* (Durham, NC: Duke University Press, 1997), p. 11.

58 Scandura, *Down in the Dumps*, p. 134.

59 Boym, *The Future of Nostalgia*, pp. 351, 55.

60 Boym, *The Future of Nostalgia*, p. 50.

61 Derrida, *Specters of Marx*, pp. 48–9.

62 *http://www.inattendus.com/catalogue/residence-cinematographique/* (last accessed 17 May 2021). I am including here for reference an extended version of this quote in French.

'L'ancien quartier ouvrier de Lyon, Gerland […] était jusqu'en 1990 quasi exclusivement constitué d'usines, d'ateliers, et de logements HLM, et peuplé par les différentes vagues de travailleurs immigrés depuis le début du siècle. La ville de Lyon, depuis dix ans, a lancé un grand plan d'urbanisme, afin de transformer intégralement ce quartier en un nouveau pôle de Recherche et d'Étude, et en un secteur de logement pour les classes moyennes ou aisées. Lentement, les traces du passé ouvrier du quartier disparaissent. J'ai donc décidé de travailler sur un terrain, au sens propre, sur lequel une usine serait encore présente, mais inactive, et de suivre la mutation de ce terrain, lors de la destruction de l'usine, puis la construction de nouveaux logements. Mais également d'étudier les différents types de personnes y ayant vécu ou travaillé.'

63 Doreen Massey, *For Space* (London: Sage, 2005), p. 39.

64 Massey, *For Space*, p. 55. Here, I echo Doreen Massey's plea for a reconceptualisation of space outside the structuralist emphasis upon closure, stasis, and structure.

65 I refer to the English translation, *https://foucault.info/documents/heterotopia/foucault.heteroTopia.en/* (last accessed 12 July 2021).

66 *https://foucault.info/documents/heterotopia/foucault.heteroTopia.en/*.

67 Lyon-based rapper, singer and composer Hassan Guaid plays this part.

68 Boym, *The Future of Nostalgia*, p. 50. This 'home' manifests itself in the chants Amor co-wrote in 1972; two can be heard in the film: one during the archival footage sequence (27"48–29") and one in the sequence with his son (53"41–55"37).

69 Boym, *The Future of Nostalgia*, p. 53.

70 See on this subject Michael Rothberg, Debarati Sanyal and Max Silverman (eds), special issue of *Yale French Studies*, 'Noeuds de mémoire: Multidirectional Memory in Postwar French and Francophone Culture', 118–19 (2010).

71 See Daniel A. Gordon, *Immigrants and Intellectuals: May '68 and the Rise of Anti-racism in France* (London: Merlin Press, 2012), p. 7.

72 Laure Pitti, 'Peñarroya 1971–1979: "Notre santé n'est pas à vendre!"', *Plein Droit*, 83 (2009), *http://www.gisti.org/spip.php?article4461* (last accessed 12 July 2021).

73 In *May 68 and its Afterlives* (Chicago: University of Chicago Press, 2002), Kristin Ross stresses the central role that this methodology played in collective modes of organisation among workers, and explains that several film collectives experimented with filmic applications of the *enquête* in the early nineteen-seventies: 'The *enquête* […] places the project under the direction and control of workers, who discuss and elaborate an initial text sentence by sentence. The *enquête* thus serves the political role of *regrouping* workers around a project, the production of a text acting as a unifying force that initiates or sustains the process of self-formation of the group, reinforcing the group's consciousness of its own existence as a group', pp. 111–13.

74  Ross, *May 68 and its Afterlives*, p. 113.

75  Jérémy Gravayat, *http://www.l-abominable.org/?p=838* (last accessed 17 May 2021). I include here for reference an extended version of this quote in French : 'Depuis une quinzaine d'années, j'alterne la réalisation de films personnels documentant des territoires étrangement habités (lieux de vie et passages de sans-papiers ou de migrants, quartiers en restructuration urbaine) avec des formes de pratiques cinématographiques d'ateliers […] Depuis deux ans, je suis accueilli par L'Abominable, laboratoire cinématographique partagé, installé à La Courneuve en Seine-Saint-Denis, dans une portion vouée à la démolition de la Cité des 4000. J'y travaille à la réalisation d'un film sur le devenir habitant, qui en partant de la collecte de récits oraux, cherche à retisser ce qui cohabite et fait cité dans le recoupement d'expériences passées et présentes du logement en banlieue. Ces récits forment une histoire intime tout autant que collective, celle de la vie des Grands Ensemble, mais aussi de leurs entours, parcours d'habitants des bidonvilles d'hier et d'aujourd'hui, des cités de transit ou des foyers. En prenant le temps de faire de nombreuses rencontres, sans caméra, de me plonger dans des fonds d'archives, d'écrire un film à partir des mots des uns et des autres, d'organiser des débats publics, ou de réaliser et distribuer un journal rendant compte de ces recherches, je souhaite déplacer un peu conjointement la production du cinéma, l'apparition de la parole et certaines formes de représentations ou de participations attendues.'

76  A copy of the film can be streamed online at *https://vimeo.com/69250356* (last accessed 17 May 2021).

77  This information is only revealed in the end credits, so at this point of the film, it remains an unidentified voice that might as well belong to the film-maker himself. What is obvious is that this narration has been post-synchronously added onto the archival footage.

78  Dominique Dubosc on 'les films insérés', *http://www.dominiquedubosc. com/ TEXTES/GREVE/greve01.pdf?-session=natio:42D08B54331C 363E938 D40BDB4317A41* (website no longer active 12 July 2021).

79  Massey, *For Space*, p. 55.

80  Paolo Magagnoli, *Documents of Utopia: The Politics of Experimental Documentary* (New York: Columbia University Press, 2015), p. 44.

81  Magagnoli, *Documents of Utopia*, p. 44.

82  Boym, *The Future of Nostalgia*, p. 50.

83  Ross, *May 68 and its Afterlives*, p. 3.

84  Ross, *May 68 and its Afterlives*, pp. 2–3.

85  Jean-Pierre Rehm, art critic and artistic director of the FID,

International Documentary Festival of Marseille, *https://fidmarseille.org/film/2010-ami-entends-tu-95896/* (last accessed 17 May 2021).

86  Nico Baumbach, 'Impure cinema: political pedagogies in film and theory' (dissertation, Duke University, 2009), p. 224.

87  Rancière, *The Intervals of Cinema*, p. 122.

88  Dominique Belkis and Michel Peroni, 'La mémoire désidentifiante' (6 juin 2015), *EspacesTemps.Net*, *http://www.espacestemps.net/en/articles/la-memoire-desidentifiante/* (last accessed 12 July 2021).

89  Belkis and Peroni, 'La mémoire désidentifiante'.

90  Belkis and Peroni, 'La mémoire désidentifiante'.

91  Rancière, *The Intervals of Cinema*, p. 22.

92  Boym, *The Future of Nostalgia*, p. 342.

93  Belkis and Peroni, 'La mémoire désidentifiante'.

94  Ross, *May '68 and its Afterlives*, p. 14.

95  Bill Marshall, 'Rancière and Deleuze: Entanglements in Film Theory', in Oliver Davis (ed.), *Rancière Now* (London: Polity, 2013), pp. 169–86, p. 184.

96  Baumbach, 'Impure cinema', p. 203, p. 209.

97  Rachlin, 'The Last Working-Class City in France: Gheerbrant's *La République Marseille* and Post-Global Cinema', *Substance*, 43/1 (2014), 44–62, 45.

98  Rachlin, 'The Last Working-Class City in France', 59–60.

99  Interview with Jérémy Gravayat, *https://vimeo.com/10204536* (last accessed 17 May 2021).

100  Jacques Rancière, 'Jacques Rancière and Interdisciplinarity', trans. Gregory Elliott, *Art & Research*, 2/1 (2008), 1–10, 10.

101  Mariette, '"Silence, on ferme!"', 661.

102  Rancière, *The Emancipated Spectator*, p. 72.

## Chapter 2: Global precarity, local struggles

1  François Bégaudeau shared this observation in 2005 during an interview with Christophe Postic, artistic director of the Etats généraux du film documentaire, on the occasion of the DVD release of *Un Monde moderne* (dir. Sabrina Malek and Arnaud Soulier, 2005, Les Films de Mars). François Bégaudeau has been a long-time critic with the *Cahiers du Cinéma*, and Christophe Postic has served as artistic director of the Etats généraux du film documentaire that take place annually in Lussas. This interview is included in the extra features in the DVD.

2   Sophie Béroud and Philippe Bouffartigue (eds), *Quand le travail se précarise, quelles résistances collectives?* (Paris: La Dispute, 2009), p. 154. Looking closely into the use of subcontracting at three large industrial sites – a petrochemical plant, the shipyards in Saint-Nazaire and a manufacturer of parts of Renault-Trucks – the authors found that, across the three sites, more than 20 per cent of the workforce in 2002–3 had been recruited abroad.

3   Béroud and Bouffartigue (eds), *Quand le travail se précarise*, p. 16, 'Le consentement pratique du travailleur sans papiers ou du jeune équipier de McDonald's à sa situation n'est pas adhésion: il peut se rompre dès lors qu'aux côtés de la délégitimation de l'employeur et/ou de la légitimation de la cause, l'espoir d'une amélioration par l'action collective se lève.'

4   For a complete list of the activities and archives of the organisation, see the website *filmerletravail.org*, *https://filmerletravail.org/a-propos-2/* (last accessed 17 May 2021), 'Filmer le travail vise à articuler trois grands objectifs: (1) cinématographique. Faire connaître à un public plus large la production cinématographique sur le thème du travail à un moment où l'on assiste à un retour du travail dans le cinéma, une multiplication des images et à une redéfinition des frontières entre réel et fiction; (2) Scientifique. Analyser et dynamiser l'usage de l'image (fixe ou animée) en Sciences Sociales; (3) Citoyen. Ouvrir un espace de réflexion et de débats sur l'évolution et l'avenir du travail.'

5   *Citroën-Nanterre* (ARC, Guy Devart and Edouard Hayem, 1968) and *Nantes-Sud Aviation* (Michel Andrieu and Pierre-William Glenn, 1968) are good instances of this silent presence in the striking workers' collectives at the factories filmed in 1967–8.

6   Olivier Barlet, 'La figure de l'immigré en 1968, si distante, si actuelle', *Africultures: les mondes en relation* (14 mai 2008), *http://www.africultures. com/php/index.php?nav=article&no=7613* (last accessed 12 July 2021), 'Transplanté personnage le temps d'un film, l'immigré sert une cause avant de regagner l'anonymat de sa condition. L'image ne le saisit que dans ce rôle: parole cadrée dans un corps codé. Ce que l'on retient de son témoignage est l'objet de la lutte, non ce que dirait son "Je" intime. Il n'est là que pour signifier un slogan: "Travailleurs français et immigrés, tous unis", répété sur les affiches et les graffitis, repris en chœur dans les manifestations.'

7   Perron (ed.), *Histoire d'un film, mémoires d'une lutte*, p. 114, 'Les immigrés sont d'abord perçus comme des victimes (des conditions de logement et du racisme), puis des travailleurs (particulièrement exploités) et enfin des combattants en devenir.'

8   Some of these films include *Citroën-Nanterre* (ARC, 1968), *Les trois-quarts de la vie* (Groupe Medvekine-Sochaux, 1971), *Oser lutter, oser vaincre* (Jean-Pierre Thorn, 1968), *Cléon* (Alain Laguardia, 1968), *Flins 68–69* (CRP/Jean-Pierre Olivier de Sardan, 1969), *On vous parle de Flins* (Guy Devart, 1970), *Avec le sang des autres* (Bruno Muel, 1970), *Humain, trop humain* (Louis Malle, 1974), *Lorraine cœur d'acier* (Jean Serres, 1980), *Pour mémoire, la forge* (Jean-Daniel Pollet, 1980), *Voyage au pays de la Peuge, La lutte des ouvriers de Peugeot* (Collectif, Samir Abdallah and Raffaele Ventura, 1991), *L'Usine* (Eric Pittard, 1998), *Sur les cendres du vieux monde* (Laurent Hasse, 2002), *Metaleurop: Germinal 3* (Jean-Michel Vennemani, 2003).

9   See the official website of *The Forgotten Space*, and Noël Burch and Allan Sekula, 'Notes for a Film,' *http://www.theforgottenspace.net/static/notes.html* (last accessed 12 July 2021).

10  Noël Burch and Allan Sekula, 'Notes for a Film' (July 2010), *https://www.theforgottenspace.net/static/notes.html*.

11  In 2005, *Violence des échanges en milieu tempéré/Work Hard, Play Hard* was nominated for a César for the Best First Film. A few years later, in 2011, *De bon matin/Early One Morning* directly addressed a concerning wave of suicides in the workplace that had made headlines a few years earlier. Psychologists connected this unprecedented phenomenon with demanding management methods and the unrealistic criteria used to evaluate employees.

12  It has now been released on DVD, as part of *Le Cinéma de Mai 68, volume 1* (Editions Montparnasse, 2008), and can be viewed on demand on *Cinémutins, https://www.cinemutins.com/le-1er-mai-a-saint-nazaire* (last accessed 10 June 2021).

13  Before directing *Un monde moderne*, Sabrina Malek and Arnaud Soulier had already released two well-received documentaries together: *Chemins de traverse* (1996), which followed railway workers' occupation of the Gare d'Austerlitz in Paris during the 1995 strikes, and *René Vautier, cinéaste franc-tireur* (2002), a homage to the militant film-maker, author of many films about colonialism, the Algerian war, Apartheid, the women's liberation movement and workers' rights, many censored.

14  See in particular Martin O'Shaughnessy, 'Filming Work and the Work of Film', *L'Esprit créateur*, 51/3 (2011), 59–73, and François Bégaudeau, 'La lutte perd sa langue', *Les Cahiers du cinéma*, 605 (2005), 29–30.

15  Judith Holgate, 'Temporary Migrant Workers and Labor Organization', *Working USA: The Journal of Labor and Society*, 14/2 (2011), 191–9, 193.

16  Arnaud Soulier is a sound engineer by training.

17   Marcel Trillat's voice-over describes the general labour organisation on the site in the first few minutes of the sequence.

18   Cingolani, *Révolutions précaires*, p. 78.

19   Cingolani, *Révolutions précaires*, p. 79, 'Imaginer une politique du précariat revient donc à mesurer cette pluralité de conditions et à chercher les moyens culturels et intellectuels favorisant les convergences et les solidarités.'

20   Jean-Michel Denis (ed.), *Le conflit en grève?* (Paris: La Dispute, 2005), p. 37.

21   Michel de Certeau, *The Practice of Everyday Life* (Berkeley: University of California Press, 1984).

22   Certeau, *The Practice of Everyday Life*, pp. 35–7.

23   Certeau, *The Practice of Everyday Life*, pp. 35–7.

24   Denis (ed.), *Le conflit en grève?*, p. 37, 'Il a pour fondation le tout collectif sur le mode théâtral, avec unité de temps (la sirène sonnant le début et la fin de la journée de travail), unité de lieu (l'usine, la mine) et unité d'action (la chaîne). Ce triptyque était tout à fait conforme aux intérêts des trois acteurs de l'époque. Les syndicats désiraient du collectif, sans lequel il ne peut y avoir de syndicat. L'employeur voulait de la discipline. L'État y trouvait aussi son compte car il était facile de contrôler rapidement cette main d'œuvre rassemblée.'

25   Béroud and Bouffartigue (eds), *Quand le travail se précarise*, p. 63, 'En France […] la question du travail précaire relève moins d'une multiplicité de formes d'emploi atypiques poreuses entre elles et allant jusqu'à la clandestinité, voire jusqu'à l'économie criminelle, que d'un mouvement lent et singulier d'émergence de formes d'emploi nouvelles, et l'on peut dire qu'économistes, sociologues et juristes épinglent celles-ci au gré de leur apparition sur le marché de l'emploi.'

26   Sophe Béroud, Bertrand Fribourg, Jean-Robert Pendariès and Jean-Michel Pernot, 'Précarité sous-traitée et innovations syndicales: trois sites industriels, trois expériences significatives', in Béroud and Bouffartigue (eds), *Quand le travail se précarise*, p. 152, 'Le fait d'orienter l'action syndicale vers les salariés précaires relève ainsi non pas d'une nécessité profondément partagée, mais d'un travail militant mené le plus souvent par quelques individus en marge du fonctionnement régulier des organisations.'

27   Guy Standing most famously identifies the precariat as 'a *class-in-the-making*, if not yet a *class-for-itself*, in the Marxian sense of that term' in his book *The Precariat: The New Dangerous Class* (London: Bloomsbury, 2011), p. 11.

28   Certeau, *The Practice of Everyday Life*, pp. 35–7.

29  Certeau, *The Practice of Everyday Life*, pp. 38–9.
30  Official subtitles in *Un monde moderne* (dir. Sabrina Malek, Arnaud Soulier, France, 2005,VLR Productions).
31  Perron (ed.), *Histoire d'un film, mémoires d'une lutte*, p. 112,'En bas de la société, au niveau des bidonvilles, des taudis et des caves survit un peuple de l'ombre, les immigrés aux conditions de vie iniques; au sommet, pécore un patron adroit et cynique, situé dans un bureau confortable, et dont Marcel Trillat essaie de déstabiliser l'assurance par l'impertinence de ses questions et la nonchalance de son attitude. Entre ces deux mondes que tout oppose évoluent, selon une certaine hiérarchie, la population française, un édile politique, maire PCF d'un territoire emblématique, et des militants essentiellement syndicaux (dont certains concluent le film).'
32  *https://www.cnrtl.fr/etymologie/économie//1* (last accessed 17 May 2021).
33  In the years 1997 to 2007, Zalea TV operated as a free, independent TV channel, producing programmes aiming at giving greater visibility to all the persons absent from mainstream media: 'youths, poor, disenfranchised, foreigners, unorthodox thinkers, cultural minorities, communities and marginalized content creators', *https://www.acrimed. org/Zalea-TV-television-associative* (last accessed 17 May 2021). Similarly, Les Mutins de Pangée, which acts as a modest, but invaluable, repository of independent political, libertarian, anarchist and leftist cinema, was founded in 2005 as an 'audiovisual cooperative of production and theatrical and home video distribution', *https://www.lesmutins.org/english* (last accessed 17 May 2021). They have partly produced several films by Pierre Carles and François Ruffin's *Merci Patron!*, among others.
34  'Collectif 360° et plus', *Femmes Plurielles*, 47 (septembre 2014), 6–7, 'Notre cinéma est engagé au cœur du monde dans lequel il émerge et le processus de réalisation est aussi important que le film lui-même. On travaille principalement avec les invisibléEs et les inaudibiliséEs dans un monde où le visible et audible est le plus souvent humain mâle cisgenre blanc hétéro riche valide adulte. Ça donne un point de vue féministe mais pas forcément annoncé comme tel.'
35  *Remue-ménage dans la sous-traitance* (dir. Ivora Cusack, 2011), 'Quatre chambres par heure, une cadence infernale sauf pour la direction de l'entreprise Arcade qui ne voit qu'un problème d'entraînement [...] Ces femmes maliennes, longtemps dociles et malléables, sont devenues grévistes' (France 3, 19–20 archival footage).
36  Olivier Barlet, '*On a grévé!* de Denis Gheerbrant: faire corps!', *Africultures* (4 septembre 2014), *http://africultures.com/on-a-greve-de-denis-*

*gheerbrant-12411/* (last accessed 12 July 2021).

37  Ivora Cusack, 'Dossier de presse *Remue-ménage dans la sous-traitance*', 'Je tente au mieux de trouver une position juste avec ma caméra au sein de l'action militante. Le rôle de témoin que joue la caméra appuie l'action', *http://remue-menage.360etmemeplus.org/wp-content/uploads/ 2010/12/ docpress_rm_fr.pdf* (last accessed 17 May 2021).

38  Jean-Michel Denis, 'Dans le nettoyage, c'est le chantier qui part en grève!' in Béroud and Bouffartigue (eds), *Quand le travail se précarise*, p. 116.

39  The acronym CERFA is used for all official forms used for various administrative procedures in France. In the context of the strikes led by undocumented interim workers between 2008 and 2010 in France, the term was used specifically to refer to the document required for the legalisation of work permits. Interim workers who are undocumented find themselves in a double bind since they hold no right to occupy their workplace – having no lasting connection to a workplace and to an employer. Temping agencies are technically not their employers, but they manage their employment assignments. However, as Pierre Barron, Anne Bory, Sébastien Chauvin, Nicolas Jounin and Lucie Tourette explain, for temping agencies to sign this form goes against their very 'nature' since their *raison d'être* is to provide workers for short-term projects, not to be contractually bound to employing people for a minimum of twelve months out of eighteen, 'L'intérim en grève: la mobilisation des travailleurs sans papiers intérimaires', *Savoir/Agir*, 2/12 (2012), 19–26, 25.

40  Lucie Tourette, '*Coming for a Visit*: press kit' (prod. Vezfilm, 2009), *http://static1.1.sqspcdn.com/static/f/408586/21168367/135465377709 3/Coming+for+a+visit+-+Press+kit.pdf?token=gQYG%2Bus0Vy% 2BDZ9Hdt8IVWcnmP6U%3D* (last accessed 17 May 2021). A co-production between the research collective and Vezfilm, *On vient pour la visite* has screened at a few international labour film festivals in 2013–14, most notably the 5th Festival International 'Filmer le travail' in Poitiers (France), the Ethnographic Film Festival One with a movie camera in Marburg (Germany), the 5th Canadian Labour International Film Festival and the 7th Terra Di Tutti Festival in Bologna (Italy).

41  For more detailed analyses of the movement, see publications by the collective ASPLAN, that sociologists Pierre Barron, Anne Bory, Sébastien Chauvin, Ndèye Amy Fall, Nicolas Jounin and journalist Lucie Tourette formed in 2008 precisely to study the unprecedented mobilisation of undocumented workers: 'La grève des sans-papiers au miroir de la précarité', *Savoir/Agir*, 2/36 (2016), 59–64 ; 'L'intérim en

grève: la mobilisation des travailleurs sans papiers intérimaires', *Savoir/Agir*, 2/12 (2012), 19–26 ; 'Derrière le sans-papier, le travailleur?', *Genèses*, 94/1 (2014), 114–39; 'State Categories and Labour Protest: Migrant Workers and the Fight for Legal Status in France', *Work, Employment and Society*, 30/4 (2016), 631–48 ; *On bosse ici, on reste ici! La grève inédite des sans-papiers: une aventure inédite* (Paris: Editions La Découverte, 2011).

[42] Sophe Béroud, Bertrand Fribourg, Jean-Robert Pendariès and Jean-Michel Pernot, 'Précarité sous-traitée et innovations syndicales: trois sites industriels, trois expériences significatives', in Béroud and Bouffartigue (eds), *Quand le travail se précarise*, p. 190, 'Les organisations, syndicales ou non, qui soutiennent, accompagnent, voire organisent les précaires, évitent difficilement une relation instrumentale ou clientéliste à leur endroit, qui bride le développement chez ces derniers d'un pouvoir d'agir émancipateur.'

[43] '2009–2011: la grève des travailleuses et travailleurs sans papiers, Du côté des intérimaires', (2011), *https://www.convergencesrevolution naires.org/IMG/pdf/brochure_greve_sans_papiers_2011.pdf* (last accessed 17 May 2021).

[44] Carine Eff, 'Journal d'une femme de chambre (2)', *Vacarme*, 3/24 (2003), 62–4, 'On répugne à citer les organisations syndicales, tant leur rôle s'est avéré ambigu, voire contre-productif. Curieusement, les salariés les plus démunis trouvent rarement l'appui escompté auprès de leurs représentants officiels. Trop souvent, ceux-ci se révèlent inaptes à défendre la précarité, la marginalité, le chômage. Les bords, là où ça s'entrechoque, leur échappent. Les intérimaires de Peugeot, les salariés en contrats express de McDo, les caissières à temps partiel des Intermarché. C'est pourtant là, du côté des formes dites atypiques d'emploi, que le salariat se développe et que les inégalités sont les plus criantes. À quoi bon, semblent dire les syndicats, soutenir des demi-salariés, déjà un peu chômeurs, pas encore intégrés, ballottés d'une entreprise, voire d'un secteur à l'autre? Leur potentiel d'adhésion paraît bien trop limité pour intéresser qui que ce soit.'

[45] Todd May, 'Jacques Rancière and the Ethics of Equality', *SubStance*, 36/2 (2007), 'The Future of Anarchism', 20–36, 31–3.

[46] May, 'Jacques Rancière and the Ethics of Equality', 33.

## Chapter 3: Precarious filiations

[1] Laurent Hasse, 'I remember a moribund region [...]. I remember wanting to leave, to leave early, far and forever...For ever?And yet, in 2000, I came back. I came back because running away always leaves a bitter taste in your mouth, like leaving things unfinished, the haunting sensation that when I left, a piece of myself stayed behind...a piece that I could maybe recover by filming.' *http://voiretagir.org/SUR-LES-CENDRES-DU-VIEUX-MONDE.html* (last accessed 17 May 2021).

[2] Régis Sauder (dir.), *Retour à Forbach/Return to Forbach* (2017), 'I was ashamed of my social background. I wanted to be like the sons of engineers, doctors and pharmacists with whom I went to school uptown. I left Forbach thirty years ago. Forbach never left me. Today, I come back reminiscing about feelings we don't say.'

[3] Thomas Faverjon, *Fils de Lip* (2007), 'Yes, I am the son of Lip [workers/militants], who still believes that it is possible.'

[4] Nicolas Mathieu, *Leurs enfants après eux (The Children Who Came after Them)* (Paris: Actes Sud, 2018) ; Benoît Coquard, *Ceux qui restent: Faire sa vie dans les campagnes en déclin* (Paris: La Découverte, 2019).

[5] Lauren Berlant, *Cruel Optimism* (Durham, NC: Duke University Press), p. 10.

[6] Le Blanc, *Vies précaires*, p. 110, 'Les luttes pour la reconnaissance sont des luttes pour le retour de voix inaudibles. La reconnaissance porte les voix méprisées dans tous les interstices de la vie sociale. Elle reconstruit un moule narratif dans lequel le méprisé peut à nouveau se loger, redécouvrant, comme une condition positive cette fois, l'enchevêtrement de la narration de soi et des modes d'adresse auxquels cette narration renvoie.'

[7] Derrida, *Specters of Marx*, p. 67.

[8] Jacques Derrida and Elisabeth Roudinesco, *For what tomorrow ... A Dialogue* (Stanford: Stanford University Press, 2004), p. 3.

[9] Samir Haddad, *Derrida and the Inheritance of Democracy* (Bloomington: Indiana University Press, 2013), p. 46.

[10] Haddad, *Derrida and the Inheritance of Democracy*, p. 117.

[11] Berlant, *Cruel Optimism*, p. 9.

[12] Sociologist Denis Merklen hinted at possibly new solidarities emerging in the *quartiers/banlieues* in the early twenty-first century in his book, *Quartiers populaires, quartiers politiques* (Paris: La Dispute, 2009). Commonly understood as the equivalent of the English word 'neighbourhood', the word *quartiers* in its plural form became synonymous in the 1980s with *les cités* (housing estates), typically

located on French urban centres' outskirts. The semantic shift intimately captures the geographical and demographic stigmas and, according to Merklen, leads to new processes of identification. Whereas professional activity used to structure group solidarity, residential affiliation is playing a stronger role, especially among younger generations – a trend that may promote cohesion, in Merklen's view.

13 Le Blanc, *Vies ordinaires, vies précaires*, p. 73.

14 Froger, *Le cinéma à l'épreuve de la communauté*, p. 11, 'La question de l'énonciation (documentaire) prend acte de l'hétéronomie du geste artistique et tente de relier l'acte créateur non pas à un imaginaire social, mais à un acte d'affirmation de la puissance d'être d'un "nous" à travers un "je", un "nous" qui ne se serait pas laissé dompter et piéger par les rapports de pouvoir et d'assignation de rôles sociaux.'

15 Laurent Chalard, 'Des villes françaises en net déclin démographique: le cas des communes anciennement industrielles', *Population et Avenir*, 3/683 (2007), 15–19, 16; INSEE, *https://www.insee.fr/fr/statistiques/3303389? sommaire=3353488* (last accessed 17 May 2021).

16 Full results, *https://www.lemonde.fr/alsace-champagne-ardenne-lorraine/moselle,57/moyeuvre-grande,57491/elections/presidentielle-2017/* (last accessed 17 May 2021).

17 In a private email exchange, Laurent Hasse informed me that the score for *Sur les cendres du vieux monde* was written by Kat Onoma's lead Rodolphe Burger. Kat Onoma was formed in Alsace, drawing inspiration from Lou Reed and the Velvet Underground. Hasse decided to use their song 'Le déluge', written by another band member, Thomas Lago, for the end credit sequence because he felt the lyrics echoed the state of the Fensch valley as he saw it, 'C'est le déluge d'après moi/Chacun fait son temps/Le bleu seul me grise/rhabillez la nue/Je partirai à l'heure/où blêmit ma compagne/en larmes on s'appelle/pourvu qu'on dessale/à l'eau mon amante tu ondules/tu souris jaune, ma souris blanche/j'ai vu qu'il t'a plu des ions des yeux/voilà que la science dépasse l'affliction/C'est le déluge d'après moi/arrêtez l'acide/tu t'atomises/ma chère âme/à l'eau mon amante [...]/C'est le déluge d'après moi/Chacun fait son temps/le ciel nous lessive/allons voir ailleurs.'

18 Annick Peigne-Giuly, 'Lussas en croisade pour le réel', *Libération* (27 août 2002), *https://next.liberation.fr/culture/2002/08/26/lussas-en-croisade-pour-le-reel_413438* (last accessed 17 May 2021).

19 *Sur les cendres du vieux monde* (dir. Laurent Hasse, 2002), 'Après plus d'une année à revenir en Lorraine, mon voyage s'achève. Derrière moi, l'industrie agonise dans un siècle dévolu à l'argent. Pour les habitants

de la vallée de la Fensch, seul importe le devenir de la région. Mais le prochain chapitre de l'histoire, la maternité ayant elle-aussi fermé, y aura-t-il encore des enfants pour le raconter?'

[20]　*Retour à Forbach/Return to Forbach* (dir. Régis Sauder, 2017), 'J'avais honte de mon milieu. Je voulais ressembler à ceux que j'avais rejoints dans le haut de la ville: les fils d'ingénieurs, de médecins, de pharmaciens avec qui je partageais mon lycée. J'ai quitté Forbach il y a plus de trente ans. Mais Forbach ne m'a jamais quitté. Et je reviens avec le souvenir de ces sentiments qu'on ne dit pas. J'ai en vrac devant moi ce que j'ai longtemps méprisé. Injustement. La mémoire de ma famille, chamboulée. Même les planches scannées du cerveau de mon père ont été sorties de leur étui. Sa maladie, une démence de type Alzheimer, l'empêche aujourd'hui de se souvenir. Cette maladie me semble tellement liée à la région. A Forbach, on ne raconte pas. On laisse la mémoire s'effacer. Tout ce qu'il ne me dit pas aujourd'hui disparaîtra bientôt définitivement. Ne pas chercher à se souvenir. Oublier plutôt que penser. La maladie du siècle. Moi, je filme pour me souvenir. Mais comment montrer l'histoire sans archives, sans récits du passé? Dans l'amnésie collective.'

[21]　Dominique Widemann, 'Régis Sauder: «J'avais rendez-vous avec Forbach», *L'Humanité* (19 avril 2017), *https://www.humanite.fr/regis-sauder-javais-rendez-vous-avec-forbach-634953* (last accessed 2 July 2021).

[22]　Régis Sauder, 'Forbach trahit sa mémoire car nous avons trahi Forbach', *Libération* (24 mars 2014), *https://www.liberation.fr/france/2014/03/24/forbach-trahit-sa-memoire-car-nous-avons-trahi-forbach_989787* (last accessed 2 July 2021).

[23]　Sauder, 'Forbach trahit sa mémoire car nous avons trahi Forbach', 'Si j'ai pu haïr individuellement des gens de là-bas, que je peux mépriser individuellement ceux qui votent FN, pour autant je peux comprendre ce qui les mène collectivement dans cette impasse. Car ils ne sont pas là où je suis, ils vivent parfois sans emploi, sans argent, sans librairie, sans vrai cinéma, souvent sans perspectives, sans tout ce qui permet de construire autre chose que la haine, de tenir debout, sujets pensants et agissants … Oui je comprends ce qui se passe et je sais la lourde responsabilité de ceux qui ont contribué à cette situation. Forbach trahit sa mémoire car nous l'avons trahie, abandonnée … pour nous libérer.'

[24]　Robert Castel, *L'insécurité sociale, qu'est-ce qu'être protégé?* (Paris: Seuil, 2003), p. 29.

[25]　Ariane Chottin-Burger and Stany Grelet, 'Rencontre avec Laurent Hasse', *Vacarme*, 21 (2 octobre 2002), *https://vacarme.org/article*

*1464.html* (last accessed 2 July 2021).

26  Le Blanc, *Vies précaires*, pp. 72–3.

27  *Retour à Forbach*, 'Tu trahis pas ton milieu d'origine, Régis. Regarde ta démarche d'aujourd'hui, tu reviens, tu reviens là, t'a envie d'en parler, t'as envie de dire les choses. Euh, voilà, le Front National qui prend de l'ampleur à Forbach, ça te dérange. Je veux dire, ça t'est même insupportable puisque tu reviens, et t'as envie de faire quelque chose, de dire quelque chose, pour que, qu'on en arrive pas là, tu vois Régis. Donc, t'es pas parti complètement. On est de quelque part Régis. Tu vois, moi, je suis de Forbach, puis une fille du Konelberg. Enfin, j'en suis pas fière, mais ça me paraît pas, ça me paraît plus aussi dur qu'avant. Tu vois, parce que j'me dis que ce qu'je suis aujourd'hui, c'est, fin, je m'suis construite avec ça. Je prends du recul aussi par rapport à tout ça, des gens qui me disaient que je venais manger le pain des Français, hein, c'est ce que je te disais, moi, fille d'immigré italienne, j'ai souffert de ça aussi, mais finalement, ben voilà, je me dis qu'il y a toujours une explication. J'arrive à comprendre [...] sur quelle peur joue le Front National' (31"00).

28  Le Blanc, *Vies précaires*, pp. 73–4.

29  Lorey, *State of Insecurity*, p. 38.

30  Robert Castel, quoted in Lorey, *State of Insecurity*, p. 52.

31  Claudine Offredi, 'La précarité des années 1980 ou un phénomène social en gestation dans la société', *International Review of Community Development/Revue internationale d'action communautaire*, 19 (1988), 21–31.

32  Le Blanc, *Vies précaires*, p. 84.

33  Le Blanc, *Vies précaires*, pp. 119–21, 'la précarité, qui se joue d'abord d'un point de vue subjectif, dans le sentiment de l'inutilité que porte avec lui le précaire [...] Le précaire est toujours en excès par rapport à son inscription dans un site social particulier [...] Ainsi le précaire est-il dans et hors de la cité [...] Le précaire n'est pas l'homme (le sujet) détaché, capable de mobiliser une critique sociale vigoureuse, d'organiser sa rage en contestation [...] Le précaire désire encore s'attacher au jeu disqualifiant des normes sociales par lesquelles il continue d'être ce "quelqu'un" qui n'est pas totalement perdu de vue, qui est maintenu à flot.'

34  Judith Butler, 'Foreword', in Lorey, *State of Insecurity*, p. viii.

35  Donald Reid, *Opening the Gates: The Lip Affair, 1968–1981* (New York: Verso, 2018), p. 377.

36  Reid, *Opening the Gates*, p. 385.

37  Reid, *Opening the Gates*, p. 3.

[38] Reid, *Opening the Gates*, p. 3.

[39] 'Entretien avec Thomas Faverjon', *Images de la Culture/CNC, http://www.voiretagir.org/FILS-DE-LIP.html* (last accessed 22 January 2022).

[40] Reid, *Opening the Gates*, pp. 464–5.

[41] In his portfolio, *http://www.cndp.fr/crdp-lille/PartAGER/IMG/pdf/ Dossier_ CLEA_nume_urique_et_patrimoine_de_Thomas_Faverjon.pdf.*, Thomas Faverjon cites Chris Marker's praising words for *Fils de Lip,* 'Il fallait sans doute le temps passé, une position privilégiée dans l'arbre généalogique de la lutte, et un tempérament exceptionnel de cinéaste, mais le fait est là: voici le film le plus vivant, le plus juste et le plus nécessaire sur la saga des Lip. Et dont les réflexions qu'il va provoquer devraient s'étendre bien au-delà d'une seule histoire et d'une seule époque' (link no longer active when verified 17 May 2021).

[42] *http://www.cndp.fr/crdp-lille/PartAGER/IMG/pdf/Dossier_CLEA_ nume_urique_et_patrimoine_de_Thomas_Faverjon.pdf.*

[43] Jacques Derrida, 'Archive Fever: A Freudian Impression', *Diacritics,* 25/2 (Summer 1995), 9–63, 43.

[44] Derrida, 'Archive Fever', 43.

[45] Reid's *Opening the Gates* (pp. 82, 87) provides some background information about Jacky Burtz and François Laurent, who were young OS workers in the 1970s. We thus learn that it is after being 'challenged' by François Laurent, 'an OS who cleaned the machines with trichloroethylene', that Jean Raguènès started paying attention 'to those marginalized within the union' and decided to create the Action Committee. Like Laurent, Jacky Burtz, who was initially close to CGT-LIP, later joined the Action Committee and CFDT-Lip. Both virulently denounced the decision in 1979 to divide *les Lip* into three lists.

[46] Reid, *Opening the Gates*, pp. 464–5.

[47] Thomas Faverjon, *Fils de Lip* (2007), 'Oui, je suis un fils de Lip qui croit encore que c'est possible.'

[48] Joëlle Beurier, 'La mémoire Lip ou la fin du mythe autogestionnaire?', in Frank Georgi (ed.), *Autogestion, la dernière utopie* (Paris: Publications de la Sorbonne, 2003), pp. 451–66; in *Opening the Gates*, Reid suggests a similar contrast, but from varying interpretations of Lip's slogan, 'It is Possible', that Faverjon also evokes in his final statement. Reid explains thus: 'For supporters of the Lip struggle, the slogan "it is possible", written on a banner hung on the factory, referred to the workers' democratic self-management (*autogestion*), as a prefiguring of socialism. For the skilled workers who initiated the movement, however, "it is possible" referred to a firm with no layoffs, no dismantling and no loss

of benefits, and not initially to a change in the exercise of authority and practices on the shop floor', pp. 9–10.

49 Reid, *Opening the Gates,* p. 453.

50 Beurier, 'La mémoire Lip ou la fin du mythe autogestionnaire?', 455–6.

51 *Puisqu'on vous dit que c'est possible/We maintain It's Possible* (dir. Chris Marker and Roger Louis, 1973), *Lip, le goût du collectif* (dir. Dominique Duboc, 1976), Carole Roussopoulos's six-part video series (1973–6), *A pas lentes* (Cinélutte, 1977), *L'Affaire Lip, 1973–1974* (dir. Dominique Dubosc, 1976), and *La lutte des femmes à Lip et ailleurs* (1975) made by the Women's Group in collaboration with Cahiers de Mai, are some of the best-known militant films and videos. For further information regarding this corpus and its significance in the history of French militant film-making, see for instance the interactive report on 'Expériences vidéo dans les conflits LIP' by the research group 'Vidéo des premiers temps', *https://earlyvideo.hypotheses.org/111* (last accessed 17 May 2021); Hélène Fleckinger (ed.), *Carole Roussopoulos: Caméra militante. Luttes de libération des années 1970* (Geneva: Editions MétisPresses, 2010).

52 I will return to this point later; to put it briefly for now, in 1979, the decision to divide *les Lip* into three groups, A, B and C, with the intention to lay off everyone listed in the C group, came in response to the French government's demands that 108 employees be laid off and that Lip be relocated outside Palente before they could commit to legalising the newly established L.I.P. Industrial Cooperative. For further details on these negotiations, see Reid, *Opening the Gates*, pp. 374–86.

53 Christian Rouaud, 'Que reste-t-il de ces beaux jours ?' (2007), *https://medias.unifrance.org/medias/103/106/27239/presse/les-lip-l-imagination-au-pouvoir-presskit-french.pdf* (last accessed 17 May 2021).

54 Rouaud, 'Que reste-t-il de ces beaux jours?', 'Qui, parmi ceux qui ont vécu cette période, ne porte pas en lui un petit bout de LIP, un lambeau de mémoire en éveil, sa façon à lui d'avoir vécu le conflit? LIP, on y est tous un peu pour quelque chose. Qu'on soit d'ici ou de là, on a fait des grèves de soutien, collé des affiches, diffusé le journal Lip-Unité, participé à des galas, vendu des montres. On est allé à Besançon visiter l'usine, on a fait la manif monstre sous la pluie, tenté de boycotter la banque qui étranglait les Lip. On a diffusé des films, des cassettes, des chansons, fait des meetings, on est allés sur le Larzac, on a encouragé d'autres travailleurs à imiter les Lip [...] Tracer ces portraits, c'est aussi essayer de comprendre ce qui a poussé ces gens

comme vous et moi à se lancer dans une lutte collective radicale, et puis faire résonner les modes de réflexion, d'intervention, d'organisation d'il y a 30 ans aux oreilles d'aujourd'hui, car je suis convaincu que cette histoire, pour de nombreuses raisons, nous parle de nous, ici et maintenant.'

55   The film consists primarily of interviews with Charles Piaget (skilled worker/CFDT-Lip), Fatima Demougeot (OS worker/Action Committee), Jean Raguènès (worker-priest/Action Committee), Raymond Burgy (skilled worker/CFDT-Lip), Jeanine Pierre-Emile (OS worker/CFDT-Lip), Roland Vittot (OS worker/CFDT-Lip), Michel Jeanningros (commercial manager/CFDT-Lip), Noëlle Dartevelle (union delegate, CGT-Lip) and Pierre Neuschwander (CEO, Publicis/Lip President-Director-General, 1974–6), who share their memories, anecdotes and reflections on their individual and collective actions directly with the audience.

56   Tangui Perron, 'Le territoire des images: Pratiques du cinéma et luttes ouvrières', *Le Mouvement Social*, 1/230 (2010), 127–43, 128 n. 5.

57   'Entretien avec Thomas Faverjon', *Images de la Culture/CNC*, 'En 1978, j'avais six ans et ma mère travaillait à Lip. Elle ne m'avait pas expliqué qu'elle était en lutte et que ce n'était pas une usine comme les autres. Je croyais que c'était normal que les ouvriers fassent des tours de garde le dimanche pour garder l'usine. Il y avait une garderie et tout le monde se connaissait' ('In 1978, I was six years old, and my mother was working at Lip. She had never explained to me that she was on strike and that Lip was not a typical factory. At the time, I thought it was normal for the workers to watch guard on Sundays. There was daycare, and everyone knew one another').

58   Reid, *Opening the Gates*, p. 28.

59   Reid, *Opening the Gates*, p. 28.

60   Derrida, 'Archive Fever', 50, 'At once, and at the same time [...] the One forgets to remember itself to itself, it keeps and erases the archive of this injustice that it is. Of this violence that it does. *L'un se fait violence*. The One makes itself violence. It violates and does violence to itself, but it also institutes itself as violence. It becomes what it is, the very violence – that it does to itself. Self-determination as violence.'

61   'Voilà en juin 1980, Je me retrouve à la case départ du Chômageopoly, "Débrouille-toi toute seule!"'

62   Reid, *Opening the Gates*, pp. 376–7.

63   For further information on the subject, see Reid, *Opening the Gates*, pp. 377, 151, 144.

64   Reid, *Opening the Gates*, pp. 12, 468. It is worth noting that, in 1983,

Piaget retired early and 'quit the CFDT over what he saw as the confederation's fatalism with regard to unemployment', 'returning to the origins of his own radicalism'. Ten years later, in 1993, he joined AC! Action contre le chômage, a network of activists fighting against unemployment which has played a key role in drawing public and political attention to the social and economic insecurity of a growing number of French citizens since the 1990s. In 1994, AC! Action contre le chômage sponsored several marches against unemployment across France, helping the unemployed to affirm themselves as political activists and subjects fighting for their social and political recognition. The initiative was repeated on a European level in 1997. AC! Action contre le chômage has since maintained a comprehensive website, providing activists and individuals facing precarious working and living conditions with information, legal resources, and news about ongoing campaigns and upcoming events, here: *http://www.ac-chomage.org* (last accessed 17 May 2021).

65  Reid, *Opening the Gates*, p. 377. Between the beginning and the end of the conflict, the national unemployment rate doubled. Averaging 2.6 per cent before 1973, national unemployment had doubled by 1980, creeping upward of 5 per cent, *https://www.insee.fr/fr/ information/3537088* (link inactive when last verified 17 May 2021). It has hovered between 8 and 10.5 per cent since the mid-1980s.

66  Derrida, 'Archive Fever', 43.

67  The text was recently republished as *C'est possible: Une femme au coeur de la lutte de Lip (1973–1974)* (Paris: L'Echappée, 2015).

68  In 'Archive Fever', Derrida asks, 'Is it possible that the antonym of forgetting is not "remembering" but justice?', 50; Thomas Faverjon has equated the seven-year-long process of making *Fils de Lip* to undergoing a psychoanalysis; see 'Entretien avec Thomas Faverjon', *Images de la Culture/CNC*, 'C'est une longue histoire. Le travail s'est étalé sur sept ans – la durée moyenne d'une psychanalyse!' For Laurent Devanne, another documentary film-maker, the family trauma revealed in the film echoes with those of an entire social class, completely decimated and neglected, *http://www.ville-gardanne.fr/IMG/article_ PDF/article_a12896.pdf* (last accessed 17 May 2021).

69  O'Shaughnessy, *The New Face of Political Cinema*, p. 45. *Reprise* repeatedly uses a short clip from 'Reprise du travail aux usines Wonder' (1968), a ten-minute-long take recorded by two IDHEC students, Pierre Bonneaud and Jacques Willemont, on 10 June 1968, as the workers of the Wonder factory, mainly female OS workers, were resuming work after a strike. Their attention is drawn to a small group

of people gathered around a young woman, screaming that she will not go back in, in the midst of the crowd. She is surrounded with union representatives, local politicians – all male – who try to convince her to accept the decision that was made. A young leftist student comes to her defence. Le Roux explained in interviews that he first encountered this woman when he saw a poster of *Reprise du travail* at the Fémis; he became fascinated with her and decided to search for her.

[70] I am referring here to Xavier Vigna's thesis about the lasting effects of female and immigrant workers' insubordination during 1968, which he developed in *L'insubordination ouvrière dans les années 68. Essai d'histoire politique des usines* (Rennes: Presses Universitaires de Rennes, 2007).

[71] For a critical analysis of *Reprise*'s reassertion of a masculine discourse, see Yvette Delsaut, 'Ephémère 68: A propos de *Reprise*, de Hervé Le Roux', *Actes de la Recherche en Sciences Sociales*, 3/158 (2005), 62–95.

[72] See note 68.

[73] Reid, *Opening the Gates*, p. 12.

[74] Lorey, *State of Insecurity*, p. 12.

[75] Reid, *Opening the Gates*, p. 13.

[76] 'Entretien avec Thomas Faverjon', *Images de la Culture/CNC*, 'La question que continue à me poser Lip, c'est celle de la démocratie. Ça apparaît clairement après le vote du 3 octobre 1979. Jusque-là, les articles dans Lip Unité n'étaient pas signés. À partir de ce moment de rupture, chacun reprend ses positions et les noms apparaissent. Dans les colonnes du journal se développe entre les leaders du mouvement un débat très intéressant sur la démocratie, avec Fatima, Jacky, Charles Piaget. Chacun parle en son nom et ils s'opposent sur la question de la pratique au sein des coopératives. Ces textes sont tellement passionnants que j'ai eu un moment l'envie d'en tirer une pièce. J'aimerais revenir sur la pratique concrète de la démocratie au sein des luttes et dans la société. Comment instaurer un ordre sans en même temps imposer un pouvoir? Voilà ce qui m'intéresse.'

[77] Derrida and Roudinesco, *For What Tomorrow*, p. 3.

## Chapter 4: No pain, no gain: the ordinary brutality of (the) work(place)

1   Philippe Ansellem, 'Sophie Bruneau: "Les rêves permettent de résister"', *La Marseillaise* (10 décembre 2018), *http://www.lamarseillaise. fr/culture/ cinema/73898-s-bruneau-les-reves-permettent-de-resister* (link no longer active 2 July 2021).

2   Pierre Bourdieu, 'L'essence du néolibéralisme', *Le Monde Diplomatique* (mars 1998), 3, *https://www.monde-diplomatique.fr/1998/03/BOUR DIEU/3609* (last accessed 2 July 2021), 'Can we wait until, someday, the extraordinary mass of suffering produced by such a political and economic regime generates a movement capable of stopping us from falling into the abyss? [...] The transition to "liberalism" takes place insensibly, hence imperceptibly, like continents drifting, thus masking its effects, especially those that will be the most horrific in the long term.'

3   Christine Renon's letter is available online, *http://www.cafepedagogique. net/lexpresso/Documents/docsjoints/renon.pdf* (last accessed 17 May 2021).

4   'Christine Renon, directrice d'école épuisée jusqu'au suicide', *Places de la République*, saison 3 (2/12), *Les Pieds sur Terre*, France Culture, *https://www.franceculture.fr/emissions/les-pieds-sur-terre/places-de-la-republique-saison-3-212-christine-renon-directrice-decole-epuisee* (last accessed 17 May 2021).

5   Louise Tourret, 'Le suicide de Christine Renon n'a pas eu l'écho qu'il aurait dû avoir', *Slate.fr* (2 octobre 2019), *http://www.slate.fr/story/ 182301/education-nationale-suicide-lettre-christine-renon-directrice-ecole-souffrance-mal-etre-enseignants* (last accessed 17 May 2021); Marie Pezé, *Ils ne mouraient pas tous mais tous étaient frappés: Journal de la consultation Souffrance et Travail 1997–2008* (Paris: Editions Flammarion, 2010).

6   Tourret, 'Le suicide de Christine Renon', '[Christine Renon] est une personne qui avait à cœur son travail, qui était portée par son sens du devoir, comme beaucoup de fonctionnaires, avec une haute idée du service public [...] Nous avons affaire à un suicide dédicacé, un message qui a une dimension politique, et l'Education nationale doit rendre des comptes.'

7   Sarah Waters, 'Suicide Voices: Testimonies of Trauma in the French Workplace', *Medical Humanities*, 43 (2017), 24–9, 24; Sarah Waters, 'Suicides Voices: Neoliberal Globalisation and Workplace Trauma', *https://gtr.ukri.org/projects?ref=AH/N004299/1* (last accessed 17 May 2021). One outcome of Waters's AHRC-funded research investigation has been the publication of *Suicide Voices: Labour Trauma in France*

(Liverpool: Liverpool University Press, 2020), an interdisciplinary examination of suicide notes and narratives left by more than sixty individuals who decided to kill themselves between 2005 and 2015.

8    Yves Clot, *Le travail à cœur: Pour en finir avec les risques psychosociaux* (Paris: Editions La Découverte, 2010), p. 11.

9    Danièle Linhart and Nelly Mauchamp, *Le travail* (Paris: Le Cavalier Bleu, 2009), p. 11.

10   Clot, *Le travail à cœur*, p. 12.

11   Among her publications, see in particular *Le travail. Une valeur en voie de disparition* (Paris: Editions Flammarion, 1995), *Travail: la révolution nécessaire* (Editions de l'Aube, 2010), and *Einstein avait raison, il faut réduire le temps de travail* (Paris: Les Editions de l'Atelier, 2016), written in collaboration with agronomist and economist Pierre Larrouturou.

12   Yves Clot, *La fonction psychologique du travail* (Paris: Presses Universitaires de France, 2006) ; Dejours, *Souffrance en France. La banalisation de l'injustice sociale* (1998) and *Travail, usure mentale* (Paris: Bayard Editions, 2000).

13   Christophe Dejours, Jean-Philippe Deranty, Emmanuel Renault and Nicholas H. Smith, *The Return of Work in Critical Theory: Self, Society, Politics* (New York: Columbia University Press, 2017), p. 114, 'The idea of the centrality of work has been widely repudiated. A major reason for this has been the popularity of the "end of work" scenario among social theorists, philosophers, and social commentators generally [...] From this point of view, the only possible progressive responses to the malaises around work would then be, on the one hand, to struggle against the centrality of work, in order that people learn to achieve self-realisation outside of work, and, on the other hand, to reduce the quantity of time spent at work, as well as the material dependence on work, in order that people suffer less from the necessary evils of work.'

14   Jean-Philippe Deranty, in Jean-Philippe Deranty, Danielle Petherbridge, J. Rundell and Robert Sinnerbrink (eds), *Recognition, Work, Politics: New Directions in French Critical Theory* (Leiden and Boston: Brill, 2007), p. 15.

15   Sarah Waters, 'Disappearing bodies: The workplace and documentary film in an era of pure money', *French Cultural Studies*, 26/3 (2015), 289–301, 291.

16   Waters, 'Disappearing bodies', 291. During the following decade, a few fiction films picked up on the subject, including *De bon matin* (Jean-Marc Moutout, 2011) and, more recently, *Corporate* (Nicolas Silhol, 2017).

17   This film has already toured the world, screening at numerous

international festivals since 2018, including the Cinéma du Réel 2018 (Paris), the Etats Généraux du Documentaire 2018 (Lussas), the Vancouver International Film Festival, the Festival des Droits de l'Homme (Lugano), Bobines sociales 2019 (Paris), Festival Filmer le travail 2019 (Poitiers), and many more. Along the way, Sophie Bruneau has collected several prizes, including the Award for Best Documentary Film at the MARFICI 2018 Festival in Mar del Plata (Argentina).

[18] Sophie Bruneau, 'A propos de Frederick Wiseman', *Communications*, 71 (2001), 225–33, 226–7.

[19] Kathleen Stewart, *Ordinary Affects* (Durham, NC: Duke University Press, 2007), p. 1.

[20] Stewart, *Ordinary Affects*, p. 1.

[21] Stewart, *Ordinary Affects*, p. 1.

[22] Stewart, *Ordinary Affects*, p. 2.

[23] Chapter IV of the 'LOI n°2002-73 du 17 janvier 2002 de modernisation sociale', passed on 17 January 2002, explicitly stipulated that procedures could be engaged to fight against such practices in the workplace, *https://travail-emploi.gouv.fr/publications/picts/bo/05022002/A0020008. htm* (last accessed 17 May 2021). While Christophe Dejours was instrumental in calling public attention to the question of suffering in the workplace, another psychoanalyst, Marie-France Hirigoyen, first introduced the concept of moral harassment, in *Le Harcèlement moral: La violence perverse du quotidien* (*Stalking the Soul*), also published in 1998. In 2001, in *Malaise dans le travail*, she refined her definition to account more precisely for practices of moral harassment, or workplace bullying, laying the groundwork for what became law in 2002. She has since published another book, *Le harcèlement moral au travail* (Paris: Presses Universitaires de France, 2014).

[24] On 20 December 2019, France Télécom and three of the company's former chief executives were found guilty of promoting an unhealthy work environment, sentenced to spend some months in prison and pay money fines, *https://www.lemonde.fr/societe/article/2019/12/20/le-tribunal-rend-son-jugement-dans-le-proces-inedit-de-france-telecom_6023561_3224.html* (last accessed 17 May 2021); Angelique Chrisafis, 'Former France Télécom bosses given jail terms over workplace bullying', *The Guardian* (20 December 2019), *https://www.theguardian.com/world/2019/dec/20/former-france-telecom-bosses-jailed-over-workplace-bullying* (last accessed 17 May 2021). See also Waters, *Suicide Voices* (2020).

[25] Marie Alderson, 'La psychodynamique du travail: objet, considérations épistémologiques, concepts et prémisses théoriques', *Santé mentale au*

*Québec*, 29/1 (printemps 2004), 243–60, 'The psychodynamic approach to work developed in the 1970s in France by Christophe Dejours [… ] consists of an interdisciplinary approach that views the organisation of work as both a source of pleasure and suffering as well as the origin of defensive strategies of individuals who strive to reconcile the demands of the workplace with personal efforts to protect their health.'

26   Christophe Dejours, 'Subjectivity, Work, and Action', in Jean-Philippe Deranty, Danielle Petherbridge, J. Rundell and Robert Sinnerbrink (eds), *Recognition, Work, Politics* (2007), pp. 71–87, 76.

27   Dejours, 'Subjectivity, Work, and Action', pp. 71, 79.

28   Dejours, 'Alienation and the Psychodynamics of Work', XVII.

29   Dominique Martinez, 'Le travail à cœur: entretien avec Yves Clot', *La Nouvelle Vie Ouvrière* (16 juillet 2010), 44–7, 45, *http://www.snupfen.org/ IMG/pdf/Le_travail_a_coeur-Yves-Clot.pdf* (last accessed 17 May 2021).

30   The first French translation of Carol Gilligan's book was published in 1986.

31   Early publications include Patricia Paperman and Sandra Laugier (eds), *Le souci des autres. Ethique et politique du care* (Paris: Editions de l'Ecole des Hautes Etudes en Sciences Sociale, 2005), Pascale Molinier, Sandra Laugier and Patricia Paperman (eds), *Qu'est-ce que le care? Souci des autres, sensibilité, responsabilité* (Paris: Petite Bibliothèque Payot, 2009). Other contributors include Guillaume Le Blanc, author of *Que faire de notre vulnérabilité?* (Paris: Editions Bayard, 2011), Frédéric Worms, *Le Moment du soin. A quoi tenons-nous?* (Paris: Presses Universitaires Françaises, 2010), as well as Fabienne Brugère, *L'éthique du 'care'* (Paris: Presses Universitaires de France, 2010) and *Care Ethics: The Introduction of Care as Political Category* (Leuven: Peeters, 2019), co-written with Joan C. Tronto. Efforts to conceive of care as a new, radical alternative ethos have been spurring debates and fostering cross-pollinations across a broad matrix, ranging from feminism to disability studies, from class, labour and social injustice to animal and non-human studies, from psychiatry to environmental studies.

32   Patricia Paperman, Caroline Ibos, Aurélie Damamme and Pascale Molinier (eds), *Vers une société du care: une politique de l'attention* (Paris: Editions Le Cavalier Bleu, 2019), pp. 155–6, 'Lucide, le regard du *care* accepte le tragique d'une humanité dont il reconnaît la fragilité ontologique en même temps que l'ingéniosité, sans en dénier le potentiel de méchanceté. Pour autant, il refuse l'adhésion à un modèle indissociablement moral, économique et politique, qui, pour l'intérêt de quelques privilégiés nommant "rationalité" leur défaillance morale, précipite la majeure partie de l'humanité justement dans le tragique.

La voix de cette humanité rejetée dans la pauvreté, la solitude ou la fuite nous manque. L'éthique du *care* engage alors à l'action plus qu'à la plainte.'

33  Sandra Laugier, 'L'éthique du care en trois subversions', *Multitudes*, 3/2 (2010), 112–25, 115–16.

34  Gilligan cited in Laugier, 'L'éthique du care en trois subversions', 122.

35  Pascale Molinier, 'Souffrance, défenses, reconnaissance. Le point de vue du travail', *Nouvelle Revue de Psychosociologie*, 10/2 (2010), 99–110.

36  Scarlett Salman, 'Fortune d'une catégorie: la souffrance au travail chez les médecins du travail', *Varia* 50/1 (janvier–mars 2008), 31-47. Salman notes that, by the late 1990s, occupational medicine had lost its legitimacy. By 2005, approximately 70 per cent of occupational doctors were women working part-time.

37  'Rencontre avec Sophie Bruneau', *Causes Toujours* (16 décembre 2018), *https://www.gsara.be/causestoujours/sophie-bruneau/* (link no longer active 2 July 2021).

38  Jean-Philippe Deranty, 'Work and the Precarization of Existence', *European Journal of Social Theory*, 11/4 (2008), 443–63, 455, 'Work seems to have deeper formative effects on democratic habits than most other forms of social experience, workplaces, we want to argue, are a central learning place of democracy. And this is true not only in the positive, to the extent that work can make democratic habits possible, but also in the negative, insofar as deleterious work can corrode democratic habits and strengthen their corresponding vices: intolerance, voluntary servitude, the acceptance of injustice, and even evil being done to others.'

39  *Ils ne mouraient pas tous mais tous étaient frappés* (dir. Sophie Bruneau and Marc-Antoine Roudil, 2005).

40  Molinier, 'Souffrance, défenses, reconnaissance', 106–7.

41  Molinier, 'Souffrance, défenses, reconnaissance', 106.

42  Molinier, 'Souffrance, défenses, reconnaissance', 107.

43  Philippe Simon, 'Sophie Bruneau et Marc-Antoine Roudil à propos de *Ils ne mouraient pas tous…*', *cinergie.be* (février 2006), *https://www.cinergie.be/actualites/sophie-bruneau-et-marc-antoine-roudil-a-propos-de-ils-ne-mouraient-pas-tous* (last accessed 2 July 2021). The decision to film first encounters between doctors and patients only added complications and uncertainties to the project. They warranted their subjects the rights to rescind their agreements to appear in the film's final cut until the very last minute.

44  Molinier, 'Souffrance, défenses, reconnaissance', 107–8, 'L'analyse de la souffrance dans le travail ne signifie pas, comme certains le

prétendent, devoir nécessairement adopter un point de vue moraliste sur le travail [...] Être attentif à ce que les gens ont à dire, et chercher avec eux les solutions, fussent-elles de compromis, pour que ça aille mieux, seule cette *attention au détail* est susceptible de déplacer les défenses [...] Qu'on parle de risques psychosociaux, de stress, de souffrance, qu'importe, notre vigilance doit porter sur ce que ces mots disent et surtout *ne disent pas*, et sur la façon dont ils sont sans fin reconfigurés au service des défenses.'

45    Pascale Molinier and Anne Flottes (eds), 'Travail et santé mentale: approches cliniques', *Travail et Emploi*, 129 (2012), 51–66, 53, 'La "souffrance" est un concept-clé de la psychodynamique du travail. Or la souffrance n'est pas le *stress* (Molinier 2009): les théories du *stress* établissent en effet des corrélations entre des facteurs organisationnels et des variations biologiques ou comportementales au niveau individuel. La psychodynamique du travail cherche à comprendre *ce que vit* le sujet en relation avec son travail. L'accent est porté sur la capacité à donner un sens à la situation, à se défendre de la souffrance et à conjurer la maladie en mobilisant les ressources individuelles de l'intelligence et de la personnalité, mais aussi celles de la coopération et du collectif. Dans cette perspective, l'être humain est un *être-affecté*, le corps, une corporéité et la souffrance, un affect. La souffrance désigne une dimension intrinsèquement subjective du vécu psychique par différence avec une description neurologique des états mentaux qui, peut-être, leur correspond, mais ne dit rien de ce que nous ressentons et encore moins de ce que nous pensons de ce que nous ressentons.'

46    Molinier, 'Souffrance, défenses, reconnaissance', 107–8, 'En revanche, on ne peut comprendre la souffrance au travail sans s'intéresser aux questions éthiques. Non pas prendre de la hauteur pour développer un point de vue surplombant sur le Bien, le Mal, les bons, les méchants, les victimes, les bourreaux. Mais s'en tenir au socle des évidences, *à ce qui compte pour les gens, à ce qui a de l'importance pour eux*. Et s'en tenir là, de façon insistante. Or maintenir cette insistance est sans doute l'une des tâches les plus ingrates qui soient pour des chercheurs, parce que c'est faire corps avec l'ordinaire, l'anecdote, le détail et renoncer à ce que Wittgenstein appelait "la pulsion de la généralité", ou le désir d'énoncer des règles générales, pour apprendre à voir ce qui est important et non remarqué parce que sous nos yeux (Laugier, 2009).'

47    Carol Gilligan, 'Le care, éthique féminine ou éthique féministe? Entretien', *Multitudes*, 2/37–8 (2009), 76–8, 78, 'Ecouter est un acte politique [...] C'est donc une manifestation de l'éthique du care (faire

attention, répondre) et d'une résistance au cadre patriarcal, qui décide de qui doit être entendu (la voix du père) ou pas.'

48 *Ils ne mouraient pas tous mais tous étaient frappés* (dir. Sophie Bruneau and Marc-Antoine Roudil, 2005).

49 This term underscores the film's multidirectional address, considering its etymology, *https://www.cnrtl.fr/definition/viatique/substantif/0* (last accessed 17 May 2021).

50 Simon, 'Sophie Bruneau et Marc-Antoine Roudil à propos de *Ils ne mouraient pas tous …*'.

51 *https://www.cnrtl.fr/definition/viatique/substantif/0* (last accessed 17 May 2021).

52 Philippe Roger, 'Critique – *Ils ne mouraient pas tous*', *Etudes: Revue de Culture Contemporaine*, 4/404 (2006), 534–5, 535.

53 Marie Pezé, 'Le territoire, pas la carte', *Souffrance et Travail*, (12 février 2016), *https://www.souffrance-et-travail.com/magazine/emploi-chomage/marie-peze-le-territoire-pas-la-carte/* (last accessed 17 May 2021), 'Nous sommes en 2016. Les ¾ du capital des entreprises cotées dans le monde sont devenus la propriété des fonds d'investissements et des fonds de pension. On ne déduit plus les objectifs de dividendes à répartir du travail accompli. On accomplit le travail nécessaire pour atteindre les dividendes décidés au préalable. Il faut donc transformer le travail réel en données comptables, chiffrées. Une nouvelle bureaucratie managériale impose ses outils. Le comptable devient contrôleur de gestion. Et voilà comment le travail humain, avec sa sensorialité, ses muscles, ses efforts cognitifs, son endurance, son honneur, son âme, disparaît au profit d'une grammaire financière: rythme, temps, cadence, flux, tendus si possible, plus de stock, 0 délai, 0 mouvement inutile, 0 surproduction … une entreprise rêvée, virtuelle sans corps.' By 2016, the *Santé et Travail* consultation, which Pezé had opened in Nanterre twenty years earlier, had grown into a vast network of over 120 practices across France and its overseas territories, Anne-Marie Boullet, 'Les consultations souffrance et travail débordées', *Santé & Travail*, 94 (avril 2016), *http://sante-et-travail.net/page.php?controller= article&action =htmlimpression&id_article=75823&id_parution=1434* (link no longer active 2 July 2021).

54 Gérald Hanotiaux, 'Rêver sous le capitalisme', *Ensemble*, 96 (avril 2018), 42–6, *http://www.asbl-csce.be/journal/Ensemble96chomage42* (last accessed 2 July 2021). An English translation of Georges Didi-Huberman's book by Lia Swope Mitchell was published in 2018 by University of Minnesota Press; Charlotte Beradt, *The Third Reich of Dreams* (Wellingborough: The Aquarian Press, 1985).

55  Beradt immigrated to the United States in 1939.
56  Beradt, *The Third Reich of Dreams*, p. 9
57  Beradt, *The Third Reich of Dreams*, pp. 9, 11.
58  Deranty, 'Work and the Precarization of Existence', 456.
59  Deranty, 'Work and the Precarization of Existence', 457.
60  Deranty, 'Work and the Precarization of Existence', 456–7.
61  Ansellem, 'Sophie Bruneau: "Les rêves permettent de résister"'.
62  *Rêver sous le capitalisme / Dreaming under Capitalism* (dir. Sophie Bruneau, 2017, alter ego Films).
63  Georges Didi-Huberman, *Survival of the Fireflies*, trans. Lia Swope Mitchell (Minneapolis: University of Minnesota Press, 2018), p. 62.
64  Didi-Huberman, *Survival of the Fireflies*, p. 61.
65  Didi-Huberman, *Survival of the Fireflies*, p. 72.
66  Didi-Huberman, *Survival of the Fireflies*, p. 20.
67  Two dreams underscore this dynamic more overtly, the first one and another told shortly before the film reaches its conclusion.
    Dream 1 – The large majority of this narrative unfolds over a long, fixed shot of an empty office building, at night. Close attention reveals a cleaner working on a floor in one view, and two employees working late at night, each framed in a small window, isolated. Night was falling. It must have been winter. I noticed that a few colleagues had changed. In my dream, they looked more like zombies than colleagues. They had completely changed and they were slow, which left me a certain freedom. At one point, I said to myself: 'I must do something, get rid of them.' I went to the broom cupboard, where the cleaning ladies keep their tools: hoovers, brooms, dustpans, little carts and stuff. I found a shovel. A metal shovel with a nice wooden handle. I took it. There's no basement in the building, but I realised that I could open the lift and bat the colleagues into it with the shovel, and trap them in there. And just at that moment, I woke up *[laughs]*. I must have got a bit excited batting them into a corner. If I have to link that to the ambience at work, there is a sort of torpor. Sometimes, there are tensions from management, which are totally devoid of interest. Then there's a sort of diffuse ambience of unease. A kind of end-of-era feel. Sometimes we joke amongst ourselves. When saying goodbye we say 'see you tomorrow … perhaps.' Or in the morning, we see each other, and say: 'How many of us are here today?' Because sometimes you go into the offices and there's a sinister atmosphere. Obviously, everyone's busy working in their office and so it feels like Sunday whereas things should be dynamic and alive. Another trivial example is the drink when someone leaves. You sense that after an hour, things wind down,

because they don't see the point of getting together simply because someone's forty-year career is ending. It's a waste of time (2"44–5"39). Dream 2 – Images, unusually shot by day, reveal the inside of a bright office building, with a glass façade and an atrium, which recalls the architecture of the workplace described in this dream. I've been working in an insurance company for twenty-eight years. For the last five years, I've been working in a unit that is part of a call centre, an acceptance unit, which deals with more complicated decisions. I have a lot of dreams these days, because I've been on sick leaves since February. I dreamed I was back at work and couldn't keep up. What was routine for my colleagues was complicated for me and when my colleagues tried to help me, the boss told them it would slow them down. So no one could help me. I'm terrified of restarting work. I'm really panicked […] After that, I dreamed there was a sinister administrator, who told me I had to phone supplies to get him a pair of scissors. It made me angry […] I got angry, told him that he could do it himself, that I wasn't a telephone operator. I shouted so loud that my voice broke and no sound came out. I continued raving at him in silence. In that same dream, there was a guardrail, high up, and a colleague was very sad because her child had died. She climbed up, and I sensed she was about to do something stupid, I took her in my arms and held her close to me, out of danger. In fact, there had been a suicide at work. It was very sinister. There's the building and a terrace, which gives onto the canteen. The person fell to the terrace at lunchtime, in front of the executives having lunch. They saw him hit the ground (48"27–50"44).

[68] Ansellem, 'Entretien avec Sophie Bruneau', 'D'une certaine façon, que ces gens soient en souffrance est plutôt rassurant, s'ils souffrent, c'est qu'ils sont en rejet, qu'ils ont conscience de l'injustice qu'ils vivent.'

[69] Emmanuel Renault, *Souffrances sociales. Philosophie, psychologie et politique* (Paris: La Découverte, 2008), p. 107.

[70] Renault, *Souffrances sociales*, p. 107.

[71] Dejours, Deranty, Renault and Smith, *The Return of Work in Critical Theory*, p. 202, 'When the work collective is undermined, the work experience can no longer be a learning process of courage, and it is likely that it becomes in fact a learning process of voluntary servitude, a voluntary servitude at work that, once again, will have direct and powerful side effects on life outside work. The same argument applies to justice and habituation to injustice.'

[72] Dejours, Deranty, Renault and Smith, *The Return of Work in Critical Theory*, p. 204.

73  Marcel Trillat and Cécile Mabileau co-directed *Rêver le travail* as part
    of the larger 2012 electoral campaign led by Front de Gauche. Created
    in 2008, the Front de Gauche resulted from the alliance of several
    French leftist parties committed to returning the left to strong social
    values and to bringing together trade unions, ecologists, alter-globalists
    and the working classes behind its new anti-liberal agenda. The film-
    makers interviewed various people, asking them to talk about their
    work, why they do it and how it has changed over time. The film ends
    with a few remarks by Yves Clot on reasons that may explain why
    politicans continue to neglect the question of work: 'Quand on voit à
    quel point il est pas simplement présent dans la société mais à quel
    point il agite chacun individuellement, chacun subjectivement, à quel
    point [...] les gens sont traversés par cette question-là, comment ils
    sont taraudés par cette question-là, comment ils sont éveillés aussi par
    cette question-là, comment ils rêvent par cette question-là ... Quand
    on voit à quel point il y a une ressource, une énergie vitale de ce côté-
    là, la question qui se pose c'est comment se fait-il que la politique
    n'aille pas se ressourcer à ce point-là? [...] C'est pas seulement le travail
    qui est absent [...] peut-être c'est la politique tout court. Parce que
    c'est ça la politique, les enjeux civiques qui sont dans tous les gestes
    professionnels [...] c'est la question de la noblesse de l'acte [...] le sens
    même de la vie en société est questionné par ces questions-là. C'est
    donc pour moi le centre de gravité de la politique [...] Cultiver la
    fierté de ce que font les gens, lutter pour que les gens soient fiers de
    ce qu'ils font, c'est le ressort même de la vie politique. Et donc refouler
    cette question du travail dans la politique, de mon point de vue c'est
    refouler la politique elle-même.'

74  Yves Clot, 'Réhabiliter la dispute professionnelle', *Le Journal de l'Ecole
    de Paris du Management* 1/105 (2014), 9–16, 9–10.

75  *Ils ne mouraient pas tous mais tous étaient frappés* (dir. Sophie Bruneau and
    Marc-Antoine Roudil, 2005, Bodega Films), 'Nous avons réalisé ce
    court-métrage pendant le tournage du film *Ils ne mouraient pas tous
    mais tous étaient frappés*. C'est un récit que nous avons pensé de façon
    autonome, à part, car, contrairement aux situations retenues, il ne faisait
    pas directement le lien entre les souffrances individuelles et les
    nouvelles formes d'organisation du travail apparues dans les années 80.
    En ce sens, *Mon diplôme c'est mon corps* n'est pas la prolongation du film
    précédent mais bien une évocation de la souffrance au travail, d'hier
    comme d'aujourd'hui.'

76  Carol Gilligan, *In a Different Voice* (Cambridge, MA: Harvard University
    Press, 1982).

77 Paperman, Ibos, Damamme and Molinier, *Vers une société du care*, p. 12, 'Le regard du *care* […] zoome sur la vie ordinaire et invite à une réflexion éthique sur l'expérience sensible: les gestes et les pratiques de soin, ce qui se joue entre des personnes liées les unes aux autres et qui tiennent à ces liens, les formes de la compassion et de l'attention, les situations de dépendance qui n'excluent ni la fatigue, ni le désespoir, ni la violence. Mais la perspective du *care* dézoome aussi, pour réinscrire ces situations singulières dans une critique globale de la division sociale, sexuelle et raciale des charges générées par le soin d'autrui et la maintenance du monde commun, et pour rendre saillante l'injustice d'une hiérarchisation des besoins qui exprime aussi une hiérarchisation des personnes.'

78 This is what Nicolas Sandret, one of the doctors featured in *Ils ne mouraient pas tous*, explains to a patient who is struggling to accept that her boss downgraded her to get rid of her and push her to leave, not because she was not doing her job well (42"05–58"18).

79 Sandra Laugier, 'L'éthique du care en trois subversions', *Multitudes*, 3/42 (2010), 112–25, 114–15.

80 Corine Pelluchon, *Eléments pour une éthique de la vulnérabilité: Les hommes, les animaux, la nature* (Paris: Les Editions du Cerf, 2011), p. 312.

81 *Mon diplôme, c'est mon corps* (dir. Sophie Bruneau and Marc-Antoine Roudil, 2005, alter ego Films/Bodega Films).

82 Laugier, 'L'éthique du care en trois subversions', 124.

83 Patrick Leboutte, 'Jean-Louis Comolli – Sur la parole filmée d'une femme de ménage. La parole libère', *Des Images (*25 mai 2005), *http://www.desimages.be/spip.php?article137* (last accessed 2 July 2021).

84 Gilligan, *In a Different Voice* (1982). In their more recent book, *Vers une société du care*, Patricia Paperman, Caroline Ibos, Aurélie Damamme and Pascale Molinier reassert the ethic of care's commitment to supporting the voices of all the persons who toil, every day, to maintain our world but rarely receive any recognition for it.

85 Pelluchon, *Eléments pour une éthique de la vulnérabilité*, pp. 285–7.

86 *Mon diplôme, c'est mon corps* (dir. Sophie Bruneau and Marc-Antoine Roudil, 2005, alter ego Films/Bodega Films), 'C'est vrai que je suis rentrée à la France, j'ai besoin de travailler, je vois que mon mariage c'est pas ça. J'ai cherché mes diplômes, qu'est-ce que j'ai? Je sais faire un peu broder, un peu couture, mais ça marche pas. J'ai pas de diplôme de … j'ai trouvé un diplôme c'était mon corps, que je peux bouger, je peux me plier, je peux monter les escaliers. Bon, je vais utiliser ce diplôme pour vivre. Mais, voilà, les diplômes ils se cassent pas, ils se tombent pas malades. Mais mon diplôme à moi, il est cassé, il est pas

bien. Alors, ils m'ont dit, "bon, restez à côté, votre diplôme, il est pas bien, vous avez rien fait" … et voilà.'

87 Fatima Elayoubi published two books, *Prière à la lune* (Paris: Editions Bachari, 2006), which she wrote while working with Marie-Pezé, and *Enfin, je peux marcher seule* (Paris: Editions Bachari, 2011).

88 Stephen Holden, 'In *Fatima*, a Muslim Mother Working in France Hits Her Limit,' *The New York Times* (25 August 2016), *https://www.nytimes.com/2016/08/26/movies/fatima-review.html* (last accessed 28 May 2021).

89 Elayoubi, *Prière à la lune*, pp. 72–4.

90 'Rencontre avec Sophie Bruneau' (16 décembre 2018), *https://www.gsara.be/causestoujours/sophie-bruneau/* (link no longer active 2 July 2021).

91 Danièle Linhart, 'Les formes modernes de l'emprise managériale' (2019), *https://doi.org/10.1590/ES0101-73302019219374* (last accessed 15 July 2021).

92 Lorey, *State of Insecurity*, p. 12.

93 Patricia Paperman and Pascale Molinier, 'L'éthique du *care* comme pensée de l'égalité', *Travail, genre et sociétés*, 26 (novembre 2011), 189–93.

## Chapter 5: Life in France's folds

1 Camille Bui, 'Le corps et la parole: Entretien avec Denis Gheerbrant', *Les Cahiers du Cinéma* (janvier 2019), 43–4, 44, 'What is the point of filming, of watching a film, if not to experience a shift in the way one relates to the world around us, and to others?'

2 T. Jefferson Kline (ed.), *Agnès Varda Interviews* (Jackson: University Press of Mississippi, 2014), p. 181.

3 Alain Bergala, 'Donner la parole: Dialogue avec Raymond Depardon et Claudine Nougaret', *Canal-U* (2013), *https://www.canal-u.tv/video/cinematheque_francaise/donner_la_parole_dialogue_avec_raymond_depardon_et_ claudine_nougaret.13948* (last accessed 2 July 2021), 'Nous aimons le plaisir de la rencontre devant la caméra, avec des gens.'

4 Rachlin, 'The Last Working-Class City', 59.

5 Alèssi Dell'Umbria, 'La vie retrouvée de Marseille', *Le Monde Diplomatique* (mai 2010), *https://www.monde-diplomatique.fr/2010/05/DELL_ UMBRIA/19119* (last accessed 2 July 2021).

6 Sarah Elkaïm and Laurine Estrade, 'Denis Gheerbrant, l'arpenteur', *Critikat* (6 octobre 2009), *https://www.critikat.com/panorama/entretien/denis-gheerbrant/* (last accessed 2 July 2021).

7 'Empaysement' refers to Jean-Christophe Bailly's neologism, which he introduced in *Le dépaysement: Voyages en France* (Paris: Editions Seuil, 2017); Jenny Chamarette, *Phenomenology and the Future of Film* (London: Palgrave Macmillan, 2012), p. 131.

8 Jacques Derrida, 'Politics of Friendship', trans. Gabriel Motzkin and Michael Syrotinski, with Thomas Keenan, *American Imago*, 50/3 (Fall 1993), 353–91, 372; Luce Irigaray, 'Toward a Mutual Hospitality', in T. Claviez (ed.), *The Conditions of Hospitality: Ethics, Politics, and Aesthetics on the Threshold of the Possible* (Bronx: Fordham University Press, 2013), pp. 42–54.

9 'Raymond Depardon présente "sa" France à la Bibliothèque nationale de France' (30 septembre 2010), *https://www.lepoint.fr/culture/raymond-depardon-presente-sa-france-a-la-bibliotheque-nationale-de-france-30-09-2010-1243088_3.php* (last accessed 2 July 2021), 'Restait "la France du milieu", "de l'entre-deux". Celle dont on ne parle "que lorsqu'il y survient un fait divers ou une catastrophe naturelle", souligne Depardon. Une France "sans pittoresque", "pas très gaie" mais "pas déprimée" pour autant, estime le photographe.'

10 *Journal de France* weaves together archival footage from Depardon's lifelong career as a photographer and a film-maker – assembled by Nougaret – and images showing him using his large-format chamber-camera on his tour of France.

11 Pascale Robert-Diard, 'Une certaine France vue par Raymond Depardon', *Le Monde* (13 novembre 2013), *https://www.lemonde.fr/a-la-une/article/2005/06/09/les-bouts-de-france-de-raymond-depardon_660146_3208.html* (last accessed 2 July 2021).

12 *Les habitants* (dir. Raymond Depardon, 2016, Palmeraie et Désert), 'Je pars sur les routes de France, du Nord au Sud, de Charleville-Maizière à Nice, de Sète à Cherbourg. Je vais m'arrêter devant des habitations, des commerces, des places de mairies' (2"57–3"13).

13 Marine Chassagnon, 'Interview. Raymond Depardon nous dévoile les coulisses de son nouveau film Les Habitants', *HuffPost* (5 octobre 2016), *https://www.huffingtonpost.fr/2016/04/27/depardon-les-habitants-film-francais_n_9772006.html* (last accessed 2 July 2021), 'Pas de questions et pas de commentaires. C'est une méthode de cinéma basée sur l'étude de la parole. On les faisait s'installer mais il ne fallait surtout pas leur poser de questions sinon ça casse l'intention. Nous, on a rien voulu. Un paravent était installé entre eux et l'équipe de tournage pour qu'ils se sentent le plus seul possible. Les gens disaient des choses très banales. On est partis de l'idée de laisser les micros ouverts. Il y a des gens qui ont vraiment une puissance quand ils disent quelque chose, ou peut-être quand ils le disent à la personne qu'il faut. On s'aperçoit que le binôme est parfois égalitaire dans l'échange ou parfois qu'un

des deux domine. Quand c'est réussi et fort, c'est aussi bien dû à celui qui écoute qu'à celui qui parle.'

14 Irigaray, 'Toward a Mutual Hospitality', p. 48, p. 46.

15 'Entretien avec Claudine Nougaret', Claudine Nougaret: dégager l'écoute, Le son dans le cinéma de Raymond Depardon, Exposition BnF (janvier–mars 2020), *https://www.bnf.fr/sites/default/files/2020-01/dp_ degager_ecoute.pdf* (last accessed 2 July 2021).

16 Irigaray quoted in Judith Still, '*Sharing the World*: Luce Irigaray and the Hospitality of Difference', *L'Esprit Créateur*, 52/3 (2012), 40–51.

17 Irigaray quoted in Still, '*Sharing the World*', 45.

18 Still, '*Sharing the World*', 46.

19 Alain Bergala, 'Donner la parole: Dialogue avec Raymond Depardon et Claudine Nougaret', 'Objectivement, en France, les films de Raymond et après les films avec toi [Claudine Nougaret], c'est le seul grand portrait de la France sur quarante ans. Et ce portrait, il est précieux […] ça devient un document formidable sur quarante ans de la vie française (le langage, les gestes, les corps).'

20 Early 2020, the Bibliothèque Nationale de France hosted an exhibition dedicated to the role of sound in Raymond Depardon's cinema, focusing on Claudine Nougaret's essential contribution to the aural texture of these films, in collaboration with sociolinguist Gabriel Bergounioux, *https://www.bnf.fr/fr/agenda/claudine-nougaret-degager-lecoute*. For the sociolinguists in the Laboratoire Ligérien de Linguistique at the Universities of Tours and Orléans, *Les Habitants* efficiently records everyday conversations between people who know one another well. The film offers them opportunities to track how social relations are enunciated and conveyed into words.

21 Cooper, *Selfless Cinema?*, p. 27. Cooper refers, in particular, to feminist critiques of the cinematic apparatus who, from the 1970s onwards, have denounced 'the logic of male activity–female passivity' and 'the predominant identification of the camera operator as male' that had defined cinema's ethics from its beginnings.

22 Jean-Michel Frodon, 'Avec Les Habitants de Depardon, la parole est à la "France du centre"', *Slate.fr* (7 novembre 2016), *http://www.slate.fr/story/117205/habitants-depardon-cinema* (last accessed 2 July 2021), 'La diversité des personnes et la multiplicité des sujets [qui ne constituent pas un "échantillon représentatif" de la société française] composent une sorte de cartographie impressionniste […] Depardon construit une "position d'attente", il établit les principes rigoureux d'une disponibilité qui ne fait certes pas disparaître sa subjectivité, mais vise à ne pas l'asservir à une idée préconçue.'

23 Andy Stafford, *Photo-texts: Contemporary French Writing of the Photographic Image* (Liverpool: Liverpool University Press, 2010), pp. 85–6, 104.

24   Raymond Depardon, *Errance* (Paris: Editions Points, 2003), p. 136, 'L'idée forte de l'errance, c'est qu'on ne prend rien à personne. On ne s'accapare pas un lieu […] ce n'est ni un regard dominant, ni un regard observant ou participant; c'est un regard qui est complètement autre […] L'errant est quelqu'un qui partage, qui vient d'ailleurs, qui ne reste pas longtemps […] C'est quelqu'un qui a cette idée de partage, même s'il est dans sa propre pensée, dans sa propre quête.'

25   Raymond Depardon, 'Donner la parole. Dialogue avec Raymond Depardon et Claudine Nougaret, animé par Alain Bergala', *Canal-U* (16 novembre 2013), 'On y retourne beaucoup mais pas pour rien. Avec du plaisir de se revoir […] On les embête pas. Faut pas les embêter et, en même temps, il faut revenir.'

26   Catherine Soullard, 'Visages Paysans: A propos de Raymond Depardon', *Revue des Deux Mondes* (septembre 2008), 147–52, 149, 'On ne fait pas advenir ce qui est à l'œuvre (dans ce film) sans avoir vécu, souffert, donné, sans qu'il y ait eu entre ces paysans sur l'écran et Raymond Depardon qui les filme [et Claudine Nougaret qui les écoute, *my insertion*], avec le temps, bien autre chose qu'une amabilité et une connivence de circonstance. On ne fait pas un film comme La Vie moderne en claquant dans les doigts. Il faut ce qu'on ne sait plus guère faire aujourd'hui, prendre son temps, venir et revenir, approcher, s'approcher et repartir souvent et longtemps bredouille, revenir et revenir sur vingt ans, rendre visite à l'hôpital, faire le voyage pour un sourire, un soutien, repartir sans image, sans son et remettre à plus tard, redonner au temps et aux êtres leur éminence.'

27   Raymond Depardon, *Images politiques* (Paris: Editions La Fabrique, 2004), p. 101, '[Cette photo a été] prise la première fois que je suis entré chez les Maneval – j'y retourne régulièrement depuis. J'avais rencontré Jean pour un reportage sur les paysans du Lignon que nous avons fait pour *Libération*, et ce séjour m'avait fait prendre conscience de la nécessité que j'avais à revenir dans le monde paysan, celui de mes parents, de mon enfance. Je voulais montrer cette agriculture qui reste accrochée en moyenne montagne […] Je savais qu'il y avait encore des fermes […] comme dans mon enfance. Je les ai trouvées à l'altimètre, entre six et huit cents mètres d'altitude. Le terrain est en pente et l'agriculture mécanisée n'est pas possible. Ce n'est pas assez haut pour faire un deuxième métier, comme le tourisme, les sports d'hiver. Ce sont des coins perdus, surtout dans le Massif Central, dans le haut-Vivarais, en Haute-Loire, en Lozère … Personne ne veut faire ce métier, personne ne veut acheter leur ferme, alors les gens continuent à bricoler, jusqu'au bout, jusqu'à la mort.'

28   Depardon, *Images politiques*, pp. 104–5.

29   Robert Daudelin, 'Filmer les paysans', *24 Images*, 143 (septembre 2009), 6–8.

30   René Prédal, 'La mise en scène de La vie moderne (ou le portrait de l'artiste en paysan cévenol)', in Didier Coureau (ed.), *Raymond Depardon: L'immobilité et le mouvement du monde* (Paris: L'Harmattan, 2015), p. 43.

31   Ragel, P., '"Nul, après nous, ne témoignera que nous avons été"', in D. Coureau (ed.), *Raymond Depardon: L'immobilité et le mouvement du monde* (Paris: l'Harmattan, 2015), pp. 53–70, p. 63, 'Dans ce mode opératoire, cette trilogie tire d'ailleurs toute sa force, une trilogie non pas tant de portraits que de parcours, d'itinéraires d'existence où le rythme des allées et venues [...] par un effet de miroirs, fait aussi retour sur elle-même, où le rythme donc de ces allées et venues devient central au regard de la structure générale.'

32   Gilles Deleuze, *Cinema 2: The Time-Image*, trans. Hugh Tomlinson and Robert Galeta (Minnesota: University of Minnesota Press, 1989), p. 109.

33   Deleuze, *Cinema 2*, p. 98.

34   Deleuze, *Cinema 2*, p. 109.

35   Prédal, 'La mise en scène de La vie moderne (ou le portrait de l'artiste en paysan cévenol)', p. 30, 'Esprit du moraliste et souci esthétique sont au premier plan, mais la cartographie agraire, toujours présente, dote les portraits d'une dimension métaphysique – de la durée – et cosmologique – de l'espace.'

36   Pierre and Marie-Claire Bourdieu, 'Le paysan et la photographie', *Revue française de sociologie*, 2/2 (avril–juin 1965), 164–74, 171–2, 'Il n'est pas jusqu'à l'attitude que le paysan adopte devant l'objectif qui ne semble exprimer les valeurs paysannes et plus précisément le système des modèles qui régissent les rapports avec autrui dans la société paysanne. Les personnages se présentent le plus souvent de face, au centre de l'image, debout et en pied, c'est-à-dire à distance respectueuse.'

37   Raymond Depardon, 'Interview with Raymond Depardon and Claudine Nougaret', Press Kit *Modern Life* (2009), *https://medias.unifrance.org/medias/84/144/36948/presse/la-vie-moderne-dossier-de-presse-anglais.pdf* (last accessed 2 July 2021), 5.

38   Vincent Amiel, 'De l'instant à la pose: Le cinéma documentaire de Raymond Depardon', *Esprit,* 355/6 (juin 2009), 47–55, 53, 'Aucun effet d'identification, qui donnerait au spectateur, par le découpage, la proximité, la profondeur de champ, l'impression d'être "au contact" de la réalité filmée. En cela, Profils paysans amendent très nettement le *cinéma direct*: ils restituent au spectateur sa véritable place, sans lui laisser croire qu'il est ailleurs et qu'il peut, le temps d'un film, vivre la réalité d'un autre.'

[39] Derrida, 'Politics of Friendship', 386–7.

[40] *La vie moderne* (dir. Raymond Depardon, 2009, Palmeraie et Désert), 'Au commencement, il y a ces routes. Au bout de ces routes, il y a les fermes. Je reviens dans ces fermes, heureux de revoir ces hommes, car avec le temps, j'ai gagné leur confiance.'

[41] *La vie moderne* (dir. Raymond Depardon, 2009, Palmeraie et Désert), 'Ce soir, c'est la plus belle ore. La plus belle saison. Il est 18h, nous sommes en automne. Vous allez voir Raymond en haut du col qui s'accroche à sa passion de vouloir toujours mieux faire. Il sait que je reviendrai au Villaret. Il sait que je n'ai plus peur de dire mon attachement à la terre des paysans. Apaisé, je retournerai aussi sur les hauts plateaux froids et les vallées profondes du Massif. Ce soir, je filme cette lumière qui n'est pas comme les autres, et je ne suis pas près de l'oublier.'

[42] Derrida, 'Politics of Friendship', 386–7.

[43] Nichols, *Representing Reality*, p. 178.

[44] Sarah Cooper, 'Looking back, looking onwards: selflessness, ethics, and French documentary', *Studies in French Cinema*, 10/1 (2010), 57–68, 67.

[45] I borrow this term from Camille Bui who identifies Denis Gheerbrant as one of these cinepractioners in *Cinépratiques de la ville*, p. 155. At stake in this 'cinépratique' of urban spaces is the 'co-construction' of 'une corporéité nouvelle, à la fois vécue et cinématographique' for both the film-maker and the ordinary people filmed. Dell'Umbria, 'La vie retrouvée de Marseille', 'Gheerbrant a filmé un monde qui est déjà donné pour disparu. Il n'y a plus d'ouvriers, dit-on; l'avenir de Marseille se trouverait dans le tertiaire haut de gamme et le culturel, martèlent depuis quinze ans ceux qui font de cette ville un produit marketing.'

[46] Gheerbrant, '*La République Marseille*: une suite cinématographique par Denis Gheerbrant', 6, 'Marseille […] est une grande ville populaire qui a su s'inventer une socialité propre, profondément ancrée dans chacun de ses territoires particuliers.'

[47] Gheerbrant, '*La République Marseille*: une suite cinématographique par Denis Gheerbrant', 5, 'Marseille travaillait en moi comme un pays imaginaire, un monde peuplé de récits, le lieu d'une parole ouverte, où l'on pouvait avancer l'hypothèse que l'autre soit considéré comme une richesse avant de représenter une menace.'

[48] Gheerbrant, '*La République Marseille*: une suite cinématographique', 7, 'Repérer est bien le mot: j'ai cherché d'abord à me repérer dans cette ville, entre ses quartiers villages et ses réseaux sociaux. Puis j'ai cherché à identifier des endroits où se fabriquait du social: clubs, centres de quartiers, syndicats, mouvements de chômeurs etc. Au bout de

quelques mois, j'étais complétement perdu et désorienté: j'avais rencontré plus de deux cents personnes! J'avais l'impression de ne pas arriver à ancrer assez solidement des relations avec des individus ou des groupes. Trop souvent des interlocuteurs, avec qui pourtant une relation déjà s'était construite, décrochaient brutalement. Alors, chaque fois, je repartais en découvrir de nouveaux! Pourtant j'avais bien ouvert des pistes et, avec du recul, dès que je me suis mis à trier toutes ces rencontres, les raccorder et les organiser, une forme cinématographique a commencé à se dégager.'

49   Vincent Ostria, 'Et la vie/Le voyage à la mer', *Les Inrockuptibles* (1er janvier 2002), *https://www.lesinrocks.com/cinema/films-a-l-affiche/et-la-vie-le-voyage-a-la-mer/* (last accessed 2 July 2021), 'L'errance et le coq-à-l'âne semblent érigés en principe dans ces deux documentaires complémentaires où Gheerbrant rencontre des Français en vacance (chômage, retraite, désillusion) et en vacances. C'est ce côté inopiné, à l'improviste et à la bonne franquette qui fait le prix de ces conversations avec des gens de condition modeste dans l'ensemble, qui se révèlent d'inépuisables réservoirs d'histoires, d'expressions, d'accents, auprès desquels les héros des fictions actuelles semblent d'une insoutenable fadeur.'

50   Rachlin, 'The Last Working-Class City in France', 59.

51   Sylvain Gonzalez, '*La République Marseille* – Denis Gheerbrant', *Grenouille: Radio & Création* (11 juin 2009), *http://www.radio grenouille.com/audio theque/la-republique-marseille-denis-gheerbrant-presente-sa-collection-de-huits-films-documentaires/* (last accessed 2 July 2021).

52   Rachlin, 'The Last Working-Class City in France', 59, 56.

53   Primitivi (*http://www.primitivi.org/-a-propos-*) is a free media channel, a 'téloche de rue' (street TV network), based in Marseille, that was founded in 1998 with the goal, to 'share stories, relay information, and support those who fight to keep Marseille a bubbling, diverse, and untameable city' ('un média local qui raconte, relaie, rassemble, aux côtés de ceux qui se battent pour une Marseille bouillonnante, indomptable et mélangée'). In addition to producing short videos denouncing 'the steam-rolling liberal doxa' ('le rouleau compresseur libéral'), the network produces features, organises screenings and various cultural and community events, and has even set up a 'Guerrilla PhD programme' ('un Doctorat Sauvage') where media and activist practices 'of the people' ('populaires') can be critically examined (last accessed 17 May 2021).

54   *La fête est finie* (dir. Nicolas Burlaud, 2014, Les Mutins de Pangée). More recently, Philippe Pujol, the 2014 Albert Londres Prize recipient for several *reportages* on Marseille's northern neighbourhoods, directed a documentary for ARTE, *Péril sur la ville* (Maximal Productions, 2020).

Pujol filmed in Butte Bellevue, France's most impoverished neighbourhood, during the summer of 2019, as its residents started joining forces against a vast construction project that would most likely result in their displacement. Like Gheerbrant, Pujol's interest lies in the question of how people come together, what ties them to one another, and how they can mobilise this communality to assert themselves politically and claim their collective and individual right to existence in the here and now.

55 Christine Thépenier, 'Entretien avec Nicolas Burlaud', press kit *La Fête est finie*, *http://lafeteestfinie.primitivi.org/wp-content/uploads/2015/09/lfef _doc_press.pdf* (last accessed 2 July 2021), 'J'ai commencé ce film parce que j'éprouvais la sensation de me faire piéger par la "Capitale de la Culture". C'est la grande farce de ce genre de dispositifs qui servent des projets de villes et de société contre lesquels on devrait pouvoir argumenter mais qui, parés de l'aura de la Culture, deviennent inattaquables [...] j'avais vraiment une sensation de simulacre, de piège, quelque chose qui nous endormait par sa beauté.'

56 Jean-Luc Nancy, *The Birth to Presence*, trans. Brian Holmes and others (Stanford: Stanford University Press, 1994), p. 166.

57 'La Totalité du monde', 'Les Quais' and 'L'Harmonie' feature mainly male characters, dockers, union delegates, members of the Communist Party.

58 Denis Gheerbrant, 'Le Centre des Rosiers' (2009).

59 Elkaïm and Estrade, 'Denis Gheerbrant, l'arpenteur', 'Je filme au viseur. Il se constitue donc une rencontre de corps, et le troisième corps, c'est la caméra.'

60 Nancy, *The Birth to Presence*, p. 166, p. 164.

61 Nancy, *The Birth to Presence*, p. 163.

62 Nancy, *The Birth to Presence*, p. 166.

63 Nancy, *The Birth to Presence*, p. 166.

64 Patrick Leboutte, 'Le peuple qui vient', included in the DVD released by Editions Montparnasse (2009), 3, 'D'une exigence éthique depuis longtemps perdue de vue dans les médias, *La République Marseille* [... ] déplac[e] les lignes et [...] rejou[e] sans cesse sur le terrain du cinéma, tout à la fois bien commun et forme donnée à l'existence, façon d'abord d'être là ensemble en dépit des souffrances, de part et d'autre de la caméra, partenaires du même film envisagé comme possible habitat.'

65 Sandy Flitterman-Lewis, *To Desire Differently: Feminism and the French Cinema* (Urbana-Champaign: University of Illinois Press, 1990); Alison Smith, *Agnès Varda* (Manchester: Manchester University Press, 1998).

66 Here are a few books that have been influential in bringing greater and wider recognition of her unique artistic interventions: Geneviève

Sellier, *Masculine Singular: French New Wave* (Durham, NC: Duke University Press, 2008), Rebecca J. DeRoo, *Agnès Varda Between Film, Photography, and Art* (Berkeley: University of California Press, 2017), Kelley Conway, *Agnès Varda* (Urbana-Champaign: University of Illinois Press, 2015), Delphine Bènezet, *The Cinema of Agnès Varda: Resistance and Eclecticism* (New York: Columbia University Press, 2014).

67  At the beginning of the scene, JR's voice-over identifies the new location as 'un village à demi-construit et abandonné, devenu fantôme' (38"30–38"35). It is Pirou-Plage, a holiday village, the construction of which started in the 1990s but was never completed. Demolition of the village started shortly after JR and Agnès Varda came to film the sequence that appears in *Visages villages* during the summer of 2016. For further information, see Solène Lhénoret, 'Le dernier soupir du "village fantôme" de Pirou', *Le Monde* (12 décembre 2016), *https://www.lemonde.fr/francaises-francais/visuel/2016/12/12/le-dernier-soupir-du-village-fantome-de-pirou_5047734_4999913.html* (last accessed 2 July 2021).

68  JR, *Visages Villages* (dir. Agnès Varda and JR, 2017, Ciné-Tamaris), 'Nous, on essaye d'animer, d'habiter, de ré-habiter un endroit où la vie a un peu disparu, avec des visages, avec un peu d'énergie au moins, même si ce n'est que pour une journée.'

69  The large majority of critics praised the playful, moving and tender tone of Varda and JR's collaboration in the film, which grossed close to four million dollars and was an instant success with many audiences abroad. A few voices found the 'feel-good' nature of the film problematic and aggravating. In her review for *Cinemascope*, *https://cinema-scope.com/ currency/visages-villages-agnes-varda-jr-france/* (last accessed 2 July 2021), Erika Balsom deplored the film-makers' avoidance of 'antagonism and unpleasantness', saying: 'the airbrushed image of village life that accumulates across *Visages villages* has something spooky about it. This documentary is a fiction.'

70  Marion Froger, 'Don et image de don: esthétique documentaire et communauté', *Intermédialités: Histoire et théorie des arts, des lettres et des techniques*, 4 (Fall 2004), 115–40, 117, 'Le lien à l'autre serait alors le principal enjeu d'une image offerte, créée et perçue hors des cadres institués des rapports sociaux qu'implique ce commerce de l'image.'

71  Claude Murcia, 'Soi et l'autre (*Les Glaneurs et la glaneuse*)', in Antony Fiant, Roxane Hamery and Eric Thouvenel (eds), *Agnès Varda: le cinéma et au-delà* (Rennes: Presses Universitaires de Rennes, 2009), pp. 43–8.

72  Richard Brons, '"A place gets a face" – Agnes Varda's attentive compassion with the social', *Ethics of Care* (5 June 2018), *https://ethics ofcare.org/place-gets-face-agnes-vardas-attentive-compassion-social/*.

73  Bénezet, *The Cinema of Agnès Varda: Resistance and Eclecticism*, p. 82.

74  Bénezet, *The Cinema of Agnès Varda*, p. 79.

75  Balsom, '*Visages villages* (Agnès Varda & JR, France)'; Didier Péron, 'La tournée des papotes', *Libération* (19 mai 2017), *https://next.liberation.fr/cinema/2017/05/19/la-tournee-des-papotes_1570887* (last accessed 2 July 2021).

76  Stéphane Cerri, 'Agnès Varda, la "liberté de ton, de mouvement, de création"', *L'Ar(t)penteur: Blog d'actualité culturelle* (12 avril 2019), *https://scerri6.wixsite.com/lartpenteur/single-post/2019/04/12/agnès-varda-la-liberté-de-ton-de-mouvement-de-création* (last accessed 2 July 2021), 'Je suis moins "fan" de Visages villages (2016) qui a été surtout monté comme une opération commerciale destinée à ajouter les publics de Varda et ceux du photographe JR. On y retrouve le goût de l'errance et des petites gens chers à Varda mais de façon un peu dévoyée, caricaturale. Pour moi c'est le film "Canada Dry" de l'œuvre de Varda: cela a le goût du cinéma de Varda, mais ce n'en est pas.'

77  Nathalie Rachlin, 'L'Exclusion au cinéma: le cas d'Agnès Varda', *Women in French Studies*, special issue (2006), 88–111, 91–2.

78  Wang Muyan, 'We can be heroes: interview with Agnès Varda', *Film Comment* (September–October 2017), 24–30, 30.

79  Kelley Conway, '*Visages Villages*: documenting creative collaboration', *Studies in French Cinema*, 19/1 (2019), 22–39, 29, 38.

80  Irigaray, 'Toward a Mutual Hospitality', p. 51.

81  Nathalie Mauffrey, 'Un imaginaire collectif au féminin/masculin: *Les Veuves de Noirmoutier* d'Agnès Varda', *Studies in French Cinema*, 19/2 (2019), 135–49, 136, 142, 'Ce qui caractérise le mieux la spécificité du cinéma d'Agnès Varda [est] la manière dont elle a renouvelé l'image à la fois des femmes et des hommes, en mettant au centre de son cinéma le couple dans lequel "l'homme voit lui échapper son rôle [unique] de démiurge" (Prédal 1984, 122) et qui métaphorise son geste de création qu'elle nomme cinécriture […] Le féminisme de Varda repose sur la quête d'une juste mesure entre les hommes et les femmes qui déconstruit la hiérarchie entre les sexes tout en cultivant leur différence réciproque.'

82  Irigaray, 'Toward a Mutual Hospitality', p. 45.

83  Images of his projects are available on his website, *http://www.jr-art.net* (last accessed 17 May 2021).

84  Cooper, *Selfless Cinema?*, p. 87.

85  Murcia, 'Soi et l'autre (*Les Glaneurs et la glaneuse*)', p. 48, 'Loin d'expulser le corps au profit d'une conscience purement intellectuelle du Moi, Les Glaneurs et la glaneuse ressemble à une tentative d'apprivoisement de Soi, de son propre corps et de l'angoisse de la finitude qu'il génère. Démarche qui implique l'acceptation de cette altérité constitutive de Soi et de l'Autre.'

86  JR, *Visages Villages* (dir. Agnès Varda and JR, 2017, Ciné-Tamaris), 'Alors ce que j'te propose c'est que je t'aide à emmagasiner le plus d'images avant que tout foute le camp!'

87  Pelluchon, *Eléments pour une éthique de la vulnérabilité*, p. 40.

88  Pelluchon, *Eléments pour une éthique de la vulnérabilité*, p. 320, 'L'altérabilité de mon corps et l'incomplétude de mon psychisme qui soulignent la passivité du vivant et le besoin d'autrui sont les conditions de l'expérience de l'altérité en moi qui est l'ouverture à l'autre.'

89  Pelluchon, *Eléments pour une éthique de la vulnérabilité*, p. 323, 'La vulnérabilité relie ma dépendance à l'égard des autres hommes et des autres formes de vie ou de la nature *et* l'effort pour organiser leur coexistence.'

90  Pelluchon, *Eléments pour une éthique de la vulnérabilité*, p. 42, 'Nous appelons éthique de la vulnérabilité cette triple expérience de l'altérité qui permet de concevoir le rapport de l'homme à autrui selon deux modalités essentielles de l'ouverture à l'autre: la responsabilité pour l'autre et le besoin de l'autre. Cette altérité en soi ne se borne pas à la rencontre entre moi et l'autre […] mais elle renvoie ultimement à ma non-indifférence aux institutions politiques et au monde public. Celui-ci n'est pas un simple décor ni un carcan dont je doive m'extraire pour atteindre ma vérité, mais il est le lieu de la découverte de moi et des valeurs auxquelles je tiens et que ma communauté politique reflète ou, au contraire, qu'elle ne respecte pas.'

91  Jacques Derrida and Anne Dufourmantelle, *Of Hospitality*, trans. Rachel Bowlby (Stanford: Stanford University Press, 2000), p. 149.

92  JR and Varda stopped by the Lubéron, in the south of France, where they created 273 portraits with local residents to be exhibited outside, in an open-air gallery: *http://www.insideoutproject.net/luberon/fr/portraits/* (last accessed 17 May 2021).

93  Dufourmantelle and Derrida, *Of Hospitality*, p. 56.

94  Pelluchon, *Eléments pour une éthique de la vulnérabilité*, p. 330.

95  Jean-Luc Nancy, *Portrait* (Bronx: Fordham University Press, 2018), p. 57.

96  I channel Jean-Luc Nancy's notion of the portrait here, though he only considers pictural portraiture, whereas JR's portraits originate in photographs, p. 5.

97  Jacques Derrida and David Willis, 'The Animal That Therefore I Am (More to Follow)', *Critical Inquiry*, 28/2 (Winter 2002), 369–418, 381.

98  Holmes Rolston III, 'Value and the Nature of Value', in Robin Attfield and Andrew Belsey (eds), *Philosophy and the Natural Environment* (Cambridge: Cambridge University Press, 1994), pp. 13–30, 16, 'There is somebody there behind the fur or feathers. Our gaze is returned by an animal that itself has a concerned outlook. Here is value right before

our eyes, right behind those eyes. Animals are value-able, able to value things in their world [...] We may not think that animals have the capacity, earlier claimed for humans, of conferring intrinsic value on anything else. Mostly they seek their own basic needs, food and shelter, and care for their young [...] Else, we have an animal world replete with instrumental values and devoid of intrinsic values, everything valuing the resources it needs, nothing valuing itself. That is implausible. Animals maintain a valued self-identity as they cope through the world. Valuing is intrinsic to animal life.'

99  Editions Montparnasse published two boxsets in 2009 and 2010, *Denis Gheerbrant l'arpenteur*, an anthology presenting five films released between 1984 and 2001, and *La République Marseille*.

100 Guilluy, *La France périphérique*, p. 163, 'Si ces représentations culturelles sont le plus souvent mythifiées, apparaissant comme une réponse à la déculturation, elles servent aussi de base à une réinvention par le bas du lien social.'

## Concluding Remarks

1  Jean-Louis Comolli, 'Travail au noir', *Images documentaires*, 37/8, «Parole ouvrière» (2000), 101–20, 118.

2  Comolli, 'Travail au noir', 118, 'Crise de la présence, de la parole, de l'écoute: exactement ce que le cinéma met en jeu, ici exaspéré et déçu [...] La relation documentaire accuse ce décalage entre projet cinématographique et projet (ou plutôt "non projet") politique comme un manque essentiel, une souffrance, un malaise. C'est ce malaise qui est filmé, qui rend ces [...] films si douloureux. Il faut du cinéma pour nous apprendre à quel point la parole ouvrière est devenue, aujourd'hui, inaudible.'

3  Lorey, *State of Insecurity*, p. 5; Le Blanc, *Vies ordinaires, vies précaires*, p. 19, p. 73.

4  Angela Mitropoulos, 'Precari-Us?', *Transversal* (2005), https://transversal. at/transversal/0704/mitropoulos/en (last accessed 15 July 2021).

5  Marchart, 'Democracy and Minimal Politics', 969–70, 'A democratic notion of solidarity runs counter to this idea [for a long-time solidarity referred to a mutual bond *within* a given social group or community]. As a political concept, and it *is* a political concept, solidarity still registers an ethical demand for self-alienation – for degrounding one's own identity – and translates it into the language of political demands.'

6  Jean-Luc Nancy, *La communauté désœuvrée* (Paris: Christian Bourgeois Editeur, 2004), pp. 199–200.

7   In *The Precariat:The New Dangerous Class* (London: Bloomsbury, 2011), p. 10, p. 17, Guy Standing defined the precariat as possibly 'a class-in-the-making, if not yet a class-for-itself, in the Marxian sense of the term', including 'people who lack the seven forms of labour-related security': labour market (adequate wages), employment, job ('ability to retain a niche), work (protection against health and accident hazards), skill reproduction, income (wage stability) and representation.

8   Carol Gilligan, *In a Different Voice: Psychological Theory and Women's Development* (Cambridge, MA: Harvard University Press, 1982), pp. 16–17.

9   Jean-Louis Comolli, 'L'action parlée' (2004), in Comolli, *Corps et cadre*, pp. 110–15, 110–11, 'La parole filmée donne effet de chair au corps filmé qui la porte. Elle le déploie non seulement dans la sphère des sons (le grain de la voix: effet de réalité majeur) mais dans la durée. Derrière la disparition des paroles: celle du temps. Toute parole se donne dans une durée peu compressible, peu manipulable, peu taillable à merci […] Apparemment dociles, les images, elles, semblent se prêter à tous les jeux de montage. Alors que les sons, et les paroles plus encore, résistent aux accélérations, trahissent les coupes et les trafics de formes ou de rythmes […] Désarticulation de toute puissance d'énonciation. Les paroles deviennent obstacles au rythme accéléré des montages. Voilà pourquoi le cinéma documentaire – qui n'est que si peu dans le marché – s'offre le luxe de déplier les formes de la parole, de laisser les corps filmés se prendre dans le filet du langage.'

# Films cited

The information below was collected, as available, from Film-documentaire.fr (*http://www.film-documentaire.fr*), a centralised online database dedicated to documentary film-making. For the few fiction films mentioned, details were found on *imdb.com*.

*1er Mai à Saint-Nazaire (Le)*, Hubert Knapp, Marcel Trillat, France, 1967, 24 minutes

*1336 jours, des hauts, débats, mais debout*, Claude Hirsch, France, 2015, 73 minutes

*28 de Morlaix (Les)*, Kristen Falc'hon, Eric Le Lan, France, 2010, 55 minutes, DV Cam

*300 jours de colère*, Marcel Trillat, France, 2002, 80 minutes, Betacam SP

*A Fabrica de Nada/The Nothing Factory*, Pedro Pinho, Portugal, 2017

*A Lua Platz*, Jérémy Gravayat, France, 2018, 94 minutes, 16 mm & Super 8 mm & HD

*Atlantide, une histoire du communisme (L')*, Maurice Failevic, Marcel Trillat, France, 2010, 180 minutes

*Au Prix du gaz*, Karel Pairemaure, France, 2011, 85 minutes, DV Cam

*Autre jour sur la plage (Un)*, Jérémy Gravayat, France, 2002, 20 minutes, Mini DV

*Avec le sang des autres*, Bruno Muel, France, 1974, 52 minutes, 16 mm

*Bâtisseurs (Les)*, Jean Epstein, France, 1938, 54 minutes, 35 mm

*Brukman, une usine sans patron*, Valéria C. Selinger, France, 2004, 26 minutes, Beta numérique & DV Cam

*Ce vieux rêve qui bouge*, Alain Guiraudie, France, 2001, 51 minutes, 35 mm

*Citroën-Nanterre*, Guy Devart, Edouard Hayem, France, 1968, 63 minutes

*Classe de lutte*, Groupe Medvekine de Besançon/SLON, France, 1969, 38 minutes, 16 mm

*Conflit Metaleurop (Le)*, Stéphane Czubek, Gilles Lallement, France, 2004, 80 minutes, DV Cam

*Conti gonflés à bloc (Les)*, Philippe Clatot, France, 2010, 130 minutes, DV Cam

*Dancer in the Dark*, Lars von Trier, United States, 140 minutes, DV Cam and 35 mm

*Demain / Tomorrow*, Cyril Dion, Mélanie Laurent, France, 2015, 118 minutes

*Dernier continent (Le)*, Vincent Lapize, France, 2015, 77 minutes, HD

*Dernier navire (Le)*, Jean-Marc Moutout, France, 2000, 74 minutes, Betacam SX and DV

*Disparaissez les ouvriers*, Christine Thépenier, Jean-François Priester, France, 2011, 73 minutes, Vidéo

*Dossier Peñarroya: les deux visages du trust*, Dominique Dubosc, France, 1972, 18 minutes, 16 mm

*Et la vie*, Denis Gheerbrant, France, 1991, 90 minutes, 16 mm

*Étrangers dans la ville (Des)*, Marcel Trillat, France, 2014, 70 minutes

*Étranges étrangers*, Marcel Trillat, Frédéric Variot, 1970, 60 minutes, 16 mm

*Être là*, Régis Sauder, France, 2012, 97 minutes, HD

*Europe après la pluie (L')*, Jérémy Gravayat, France, 2006, 50 minutes, DV Cam & Super 8 mm

*Ex-Moulinex: Mon travail, c'est capital*, Marie-Pierre Brêtas, Raphaël Girardot, Laurent Salters,

France, 2000, 88 minutes, Digital video

*Femmes précaires*, Marcel Trillat, France, 2005, 81 minutes, Beta numérique

*Fête est finie (La)*, Nicolas Burlaud, France, 2014, 74 minutes, HDV

*Fils de Lip*, Thomas Faverjon, France, 2007, 50 minutes, Digital Video

*Florange, dernier carré*, Tristan Thil, France, 2012, 61 minutes, HDCam

*Forgotten Space (The)*, Allan Sekula, Noël Burch, The Netherlands, 2012, 113 minutes

*Fragments sur la misère*, Christophe Otzenberger, France, 1998, 85 minutes, Betacam

*Grève des ouvriers de Margoline (La)*, Jean-Pierre Thorn, France, 1974, 40 minutes

*Habitants (Les)*, Raymond Depardon, Claudine Nougaret, France, 2015, 84 minutes, 35 mm

*Hommes debout (Les)*, Jérémy Gravayat, France, 2010, 76 minutes, Super 8 & Mini DV

*Glaneurs et la glaneuse (Les)*, Agnès Varda, France, 2000, 82 minutes, 35 mm

*Il suffira d'un gilet*, Aurélien Blondeau, France, 2019, 73 minutes

*Ils ne mouraient pas tous mais tous étaient frappés*, Sophie Bruneau, Marc-Antoine Roudil, France/Belgium, 2005, 80 minutes, Beta numérique

*J'ai très mal au travail*, Jean-Michel Carré, France, 2006, 82 minutes, HDV

*Journal de France*, Raymond Depardon, Claudine Nougaret, France, 2012, 100 minutes

*Jusqu'au bout*, Collectif Cinélutte, France, 1973, 40 minutes

*J'veux du soleil*, Gilles Perret, François Ruffin, France, 2019, 75 minutes

*Lip I: Monique*, Carole Roussopoulos, France, 1973, Umatic

*Lip V: Christiane et Monique*, Carole Roussopoulos, France, 1976, Umatic

*Lip, L'imagination au pouvoir (Les)*, Christian Rouaud, France, 2007, 118 minutes, DVC Pro

*Lip 1973 ou le goût du collectif*, Dominique Dubosc, France, 1975, 60 minutes, Betacam SP

*Metaleurop: Germinal 2003*, Jean-Michel Vennemani, France, 2003, 85 minutes, DV Cam

*Métallos (Les)*, Jacques Lemare, France, 1938, 38 minutes, 35 mm

*Mise à mort du travail (La)*, Jean-Robert Viallet, France, 2009, HD

*Modern Times*, Charles Chaplin, United States, 87 minutes, 35 mm

*Molex, des gens debout (Les)*, José Alcala, France 2010, 90 minutes, HDCam

*Monde moderne (Un)*, Sabrina Malek, Arnaud Soulier, France, 2004, 84 minutes, DV Cam

*Mon diplôme, c'est mon corps* Sophie Bruneau, Marc-Antoine Roudil, France/Belgium, 2006, 18 minutes, Beta numérique

*Moulinex, la mécanique du pire*, Gilles Balbastre, France, 2003, 52 minutes, Beta digital

*Nous, princesses de Clèves*, Régis Sauder, France, 2010, 69 minutes, DVC Pro

*On a grévé*, Denis Gheerbrant, France, 2013, 70 minutes, HD

*On n'est pas des steaks hachés*, Alima Arouali, Anne Galland, France, 2002, 54 minutes, DV Cam

*Peñarroya: comment se mettre d'accord*, Dominique Dubosc, France, 1973, 54 minutes

*Péril sur la ville*, Philippe Pujol, France, 2019, 57 minutes

*Pieds sur terre (Les)*, Bertrand Hagenmüller and Batiste Combret, France, 2016, 82 minutes, HD

*Planches, Clous, Marteaux*, Jérémy Gravayat, France, 2015, 13 minutes

*Plan social! Et après?*, Laurent Lutaud, France, 2010, 70 minutes, XDCam

*Profils Paysans: L'Approche*, Raymond Depardon, Claudine Nougaret, France, 2001, 90 minutes, Beta Digital

*Profils Paysans: Le Quotidien*, Raymond Depardon, Claudine Nougaret, France, 2005, 81 minutes, 35 mm

*Prolos (Les)*, Marcel Trillat, France, 2002, 91 minutes, Beta numérique

*Puisqu'on vous dit que c'est possible / We Maintain It's Possible*, Chris Marker & collective, France, 1973, 47 minutes, 16 mm

*Remue-ménage dans la sous-traitance*, Ivora Cusack, France, 2008, 69 minutes, Mini DV

*Reprise*, Hervé Le Roux, France, 1997, 190 minutes, 35 mm

*Reprise du travail aux usines Wonder (La)*, Jacques Willemont, France, 1968, 10 minutes, 16 mm

*République Marseille (La)*, Denis Gheerbrant, France, 2009, HDV

*Retour à Forbach*, Régis Sauder, France, 2017, 78 minutes

*Rêve d'usine*, Luc Decaster, France, 2001, 96 minutes, Betacam

*Rêver le travail*, Marcel Trillat, Cécile Mabileau, France, 2012, 26 minutes

*Rêver sous le capitalisme / Dreaming Under Capitalism*, Sophie Bruneau, Belgium, 2017, 63 minutes

*Saga des Conti (La)*, Jérôme Palteau, France, 2011, 97 minutes, DV Cam

*Sans Toit Ni Loi / Vagabond*, Agnès Varda, France, 1985, 105 minutes, 35 mm

*Silence dans la vallée*, Marcel Trillat, France, 2007, 83 minutes, Beta numérique

*Sortie des usines Lumière*, Auguste and Louis Lumière, France, 1895

*Strike*, Sergei Eisenstein, USSR, 1925, 82 minutes, 35 mm

*Sur les cendres du vieux monde*, Laurent Hasse, Belgium/Luxemburg/France, 2001, 73 minutes, Vidéo

*Sur les routes d'acier*, Boris Peskine, France, 1938, 39 minutes, 35 mm

*Varda par Agnès / Varda by Agnès*, Agnès Varda, France, 2019, 115 minutes

*Vie moderne (La)*, Raymond Depardon, Claudine Nougaret, France, 2008, 90 minutes, 35 mm

*Visages villages / Faces Places*, Agnès Varda, JR, France, 2017, 90 minutes

*Vivre ici*, Jérémy Gravayat, France, 2008, 55 minutes, Mini DV

*Voyage à la mer (Le)*, Denis Gheerbrant, France, 2001, 84 minutes, Digital Vidéo

# Bibliography

'Donner la parole. Dialogue avec Raymond Depardon et Claudine Nougaret, animé par Alain Bergala', *Canal-U* (16 novembre 2013), *https://www.canal-u.tv/video/cinematheque_francaise/donner_la_parole_dialogue_avec_raymond_depardon_et_claudine_nougaret.13948* (last accessed 17 May 2021).

'Entretien avec Thomas Faverjon', *Images de la Culture*, 23, CNC (2007), *http://www.voiretagir.org/FILS-DE-LIP.html* (last accessed 17 May 2021).

'Entretien avec Claudine Nougaret', Claudine Nougaret: dégager l'écoute, Le son dans le cinéma de Raymond Depardon, Exposition BnF (janvier–mars 2020), *https://www.bnf.fr/sites/default/files/2020-01/dp_degager_ecoute.pdf* (last accessed 17 May 2021).

'Entretien entre Christine Thépenier et Fabienne Yvert' (2011), *http://www.iskrafilms.com/Disparaissez-les-ouvriers-24* (last accessed 28 May 2021).

'Raymond Depardon présente "sa" France à la Bibliothèque nationale de France', *Le Point* (30 septembre 2010), *https://www.lepoint.fr/culture/ raymond-depardon-presente-sa-france-a-la-bibliotheque-nationale-de-france-30-09-2010-1243088_3.php* (last accessed 17 May 2021).

'Rencontre avec Sophie Bruneau', *Causes Toujours* (16 décembre 2018), *https://www.gsara.be/causestoujours/sophie-bruneau/* (last accessed 17 February 2020, link inactive when last verified 28 May 2021)

Alderson, M., 'La psychodynamique du travail: objet, considérations épistémologiques, concepts et prémisses théoriques', *Santé mentale au Québec*, 29/1 (Printemps 2004), 243–60.

Amiel, V., 'De l'instant à la pose: le cinéma documentaire de Raymond Depardon', *Esprit,* 355/6 (juin 2009), 47–55.

Ansellem, P., 'Sophie Bruneau: "Les rêves permettent de résister"', *La Marseillaise* (10 décembre 2018), *http://www.lamarseillaise.fr/culture/cinema/73898-s-bruneau-les-reves-permettent-de-resister* (link inactive when last verified 17 May 2021)
.
Aroca, M., 'Chap 17: Chronique belge de maux modernes', *Cinéma en Atelier, http://cinemaenatelier.be/timeline-event/chap-17-ils-ne-mourraient-pas-tous-mais-tous-etaient-frappes/* (last accessed 2 July 2021).

Balsom, E., '*Visages villages* (Agnès Varda and JR, France)', *Cinemascope,* 74 (2017), *https://cinema-scope.com/currency/visages-villages-agnes-varda-jr-france* (last accessed 17 May 2021).

Barlet, O., 'La figure de l'immigré en 1968, si distante, si actuelle', *Africultures: les mondes en relation* (14 mai 2008), *http://www.africultures.com/php/index.php?nav=article&no=7613* (last accessed 28 May 2021).

Barlet, O., '*On a grévé!* de Denis Gheerbrant: faire corps!', *Africultures* (4 septembre 2014), *http://africultures.com/on-a-greve-de-denis-gheerbrant-12411/* (last accessed 17 May 2021).

Barrot, E., *Camera Politica: dialectique du réalisme dans le cinéma politique et militant (Groupes Medvekine, Francesco Rosi, Peter Watkins)* (Paris: Vrin, 2009).

Bauer, F., 'Du bruit au discours: la domestication de la voix des précaires', *Vie sociale,* 1/1 (2013), 41–51.

Baumbach, N., 'Impure cinema: political pedagogies in film and theory' (dissertation, Duke University, 2009).

Belkis, D., and Peroni, M., 'La mémoire désidentifiante', *EspacesTemps.Net* (6 juin 2015), *http://www.espacestemps.net/en/articles/la-memoire-desidentifiante* (last accessed 17 May 2021).

Bénezet, D., *The Cinema of Agnès Varda: Resistance and Eclecticism* (London and New York: Wallflower Press, 2014).

Bénezet, D., '"Varda en vadrouille/Agnès on the Road Again", an Extended Review of *Visages Villages* by Agnès Varda & JR', *Contemporary French and Francophone Studies*, 22/4 (2018), 406–17.

Beradt, C., *The Third Reich of Dreams* (Wellingborough: The Aquarian Press, 1985).

Berlant, L., 'Slow Death (Sovereignty, Obesity, Lateral Agency)', *Critical Inquiry*, 33/4 (Summer 2007), 754–80.

Berlant, L., *Cruel Optimism* (Durham, NC: Duke University Press, 2011).

Beurier, J., 'La mémoire Lip ou la fin du mythe autogestionnaire?', in Frank Georgi (ed.), *Autogestion, la dernière utopie* (Paris: Publications de la Sorbonne, 2003), pp. 451–66.

Bonnaves, P., '"Merci Patron !" ou comment François Ruffin réinvente la révolution en faisant des films', *Le Blog Documentaire* (30 novembre 2016), *http://leblogdocumentaire.fr/merci-patron-francois-ruffin-reinvente-revolution-faisant-films/* (last accessed 17 May 2021).

Boullet, A. M., 'Les consultations souffrance et travail débordées', *Santé & Travail*, n°094 (avril 2016), *http://sante-et-travail.net/page.php? controller=article&action=htmlimpression&id_article=75823&id_parution =1434* (link inactive when last verified 17 May 2021).

Bourdieu, P., 'L'essence du néolibéralisme', *Le Monde Diplomatique* (mars 1998), *https://www.monde-diplomatique.fr/1998/03/ BOURDI EU/3609* (last accessed 17 May 2021).

Bourdieu, P. and Bourdieu, M.-C., 'Le paysan et la photographie', *Revue française de sociologie*, 2/2 (avril–juin 1965), 164–74.

Boym, S., *The Future of Nostalgia* (New York: Basic Books, 2001).

Brons, R., '"A place gets a face" – Agnes Varda's attentive compassion with the social', *Ethics of Care* (6 May 2018), *https://ethicsofcare.org/place-gets-face-agnes-vardas-attentive-compassion-social/* (last accessed 17 May 2021).

Brugère, F., *L'éthique du 'care'* (Paris: Presses Universitaires de France, 2010).

Brugère, F., and Tronto, J., *Care Ethics: The Introduction of Care as Political Category* (Leuven: Peeters, 2019).

Bruneau, S., 'A propos de Frederick Wiseman', *Communications*, 71 (2001), 225–33.

Bui, C., *Cinépratiques de la ville: Documentaire et urbanité après Chronique d'un été* (Aix-Marseille: Presses Universitaires de Provence, 2018).

Bui, C., 'Le corps et la parole: Entretien avec Denis Gheerbrant', *Les Cahiers du Cinéma* (janvier 2019), 43–4.

Bürch, N., and Sekula, A., 'Notes for a Film' (July 2010), official website of *The Forgotten Space*, *https://www.theforgottenspace.net/static/notes.html* (last accessed 17 May 2021).

Butler, J., *Precarious Life: The Powers of Mourning and Violence* (New York: Verso, 2004).

Capelle-Blancard, G., and Couderc, N., 'Licenciements boursiers chez Michelin et Danone: beaucoup de bruit pour rien?', *Revue Française d'Economie*, XI/2 (2006), 55–73.

Castel, R., *L'insécurité sociale, qu'est-ce qu'être protégé?* (Paris: Seuil, 2003).

Castel, R., 'La citoyenneté sociale menacée', *Cités*, 35/3 (2008), 133–41.

Cerri, S., 'Agnès Varda, la "liberté de ton, de mouvement, de création"', *L'Ar(t)penteur: Blog d'actualité culturelle* (12 avril 2019), *https://scerri6.wixsite.com/lartpenteur/single-post/2019/04/12/agnès-varda-la-liberté-de-ton-de-mouvement-de-création* (last accessed 17 May 2021).

Chalard, L., 'Des villes françaises en net déclin démographique: le cas des communes anciennement industrielles', *Population et Avenir*, 3/683 (2007), 15–19 (last accessed 17 May 2021).

Chamarette, J., *Phenomenology and the Future of Film* (London: Palgrave Macmillan, 2012).

Chassagnon, M., 'Interview. Raymond Depardon nous dévoile les coulisses de son nouveau film Les Habitants', *HuffPost* (5 octobre 2016), *https://www.huffingtonpost.fr/2016/04/27/depardon-les-habitants-film-francais_n_9772006.html* (last accessed 17 May 2021).

Chauvin, Jean-François, 'Fragments sur la misère de Christophe Otzenberger', *Objectif Cinema* (1999), *https://www.objectif-cinema.com/spip.php?article3050&artsuite=2* (link removed when last verified 28 May 2021).

Chauvin, J. F., 'Entretien avec Christophe Otzenberger', *Objectif Cinéma* (15 janvier 1999), *http://www.objectif-cinema.com/interviews/014.php* (last accessed 28 May 2021).

Chottin-Burger, A. and Grelet, S., 'Rencontre avec Laurent Hasse', *Vacarme*, 21 (2 octobre 2002), *https://vacarme.org/article1464.html* (last accessed 17 May 2021).

Clarke, J., 'Closing Moulinex: Thoughts on the Visibility and Invisibility of Industrial Labour in Contemporary France', *Modern and Contemporary France*, 19/4 (2011), 443–58.

Clot, Y., *La fonction psychologique du travail* (Paris: Presses Universitaires de France, 2006).

Clot, Y., *Le travail à cœur: Pour en finir avec les risques psychosociaux* (Paris: Editions La Découverte, 2010).

Clot, Y., 'Réhabiliter la dispute professionnelle', *Le Journal de l'Ecole de Paris du Management*, 1/105 (2014), 9–16.

Coll. «Gilets jaunes», *Hypothèses sur un mouvement* (Paris: La Découverte, 2019).

Confavreux, J. (ed.), *Le fond de l'air est jaune: Comprendre une révolte inédite* (Paris: Editions du Seuil, 2019).

Conway, K., *Agnès Varda* (Urbana-Champaign: University of Illinois Press, 2015).

Conway, K., '*Visages Villages*: Documenting Creative Collaboration', *Studies in French Cinema*, 19/1 (2019), 22–39.

Cooper, S., *Selfless Cinema? Ethics and French Documentary* (London: Legenda, 2006).

Cooper, S., 'Looking Back, Looking Onwards: Selflessness, Ethics, and French Documentary', *Studies in French Cinema*, 10/1 (2010), 57–68.

Cusack, I., 'Dossier de presse *Remue-ménage dans la sous-traitance*', *http://remue-menage.360etmemeplus.org/wp-content/uploads/2010/12/docpress_rm_fr.pdf* (last accessed 17 May 2021).

Daudelin, R., 'Filmer les paysans', *24 Images*, 143 (septembre 2009), 6–8.

Dejours, C., *Souffrance en France. La banalisation de l'injustice sociale* (Paris: Editions du Seuil, 1998).

Dejours, C., *Travail, usure mentale* (Paris: Bayard Editions, 2000).

Dejours, C., 'Alienation and the Psychodynamics of Work', *Actuel Marx*, 39/1 (2006), 123–44.

Dejours, C., J. P. Deranty, E. Renault and N. H. Smith, *The Return of Work in Critical Theory: Self, Society, Politics* (New York: Columbia University Press, 2017).

Deleuze, G., *Cinema 2: The Time-Image*, trans. Hugh Tomlinson and Robert Galeta (Minneapolis: University of Minnesota Press, 1989).

Dell'Umbria, A., 'La vie retrouvée de Marseille', *Le Monde Diplomatique* (26 mai 2010), *https://www.monde-diplomatique.fr/2010/05/DELL_UMBRIA/19119* (last accessed 17 May 2021).

Delsaut, Y., 'Ephémère 68: A propos de Reprise, de Hervé Le Roux', *Actes de la Recherche en Sciences Sociales*, 3/158 (2005), 62–95.

Depardon, R., *Errance* (Paris: Editions Points, 2003).

Depardon, R., *Images politiques* (Paris: Editions La Fabrique, 2004).

Depardon, R., 'Interview with Raymond Depardon and Claudine Nougaret', Press Kit *Modern Life* (2009), *https://medias.unifrance.org/medias/84/144/36948/presse/la-vie-moderne-dossier-de-presse-anglais.pdf* (last accessed 17 May 2021).

Deranty, J. P., 'Work and the Precarization of Existence', *European Journal of Social Theory*, 11/4 (2008), 443–63.

Deranty, J. P., D. Petherbridge, J. Rundell and R. Sinnerbrink (eds), *Recognition, Work, Politics: New Directions in French Critical Theory* (Leiden and Boston: Brill, 2007).

DeRoo, R. J., *Agnès Varda Between Film, Photography, and Art* (Berkeley: University of California Press, 2017).

Derrida, J., 'Politics of Friendship', trans. Gabriel Motzkin and Michael Syrotinski, with Thomas Keenan, *American Imago*, 50/3 (Fall 1993), 353–91.

Derrida, J., *Specters of Marx*, trans. Peggy Kamuf (London, New York: Routledge, 1994).

Derrida, J., 'Archive Fever: A Freudian Impression', *Diacritics*, 25/2 (Summer 1995), 9–63.

Derrida, J., and Dufourmantelle, A., *Of Hospitality*, trans. Rachel Bowlby (Stanford: Stanford University Press, 2000).

Derrida, J. and E. Roudinesco, *For what tomorrow …: A Dialogue* (Stanford: Stanford University Press, 2004).

Derrida, J., and D. Willis, 'The Animal That Therefore I Am (More to Follow)', *Critical Inquiry*, 28/2 (Winter 2002), 369–418.

Didi-Huberman, G., *Survival of the Fireflies*, trans. Lia Swope Mitchell (Minneapolis: University of Minnesota Press, 2018).

Downing, L., and L. Saxton (eds) *Film and Ethics: Foreclosed Encounters* (London: Routledge, 2009).

Dubosc, D., 'Les films insérés', *http://www.dominiquedubosc.com/TEXTES/GREVE/greve01.pdf?-session=natio:42D08B54331C363E938 D40BDB4317A41* (link removed).

Edelblutte, S., 'Que reste-t-il du textile vosgien?', *L'Information Géographique*, 72 (2008), 66–88.

Edelblutte, S., *Paysages et territoires de l'industrie en Europe: héritages et renouveaux* (Paris, Ellipses, 2010).

Edelblutte, S., 'Le paysage est-il un lieu de mémoire', *France Culture*, 'Planète Terre' (17 octobre 2012), *http://www.franceculture.fr/emissions/planete-terre/le-paysage-est-il-un-lieu-de-memoire* (last accessed 17 May 2021).

Elayoubi, F., *Prière à la lune* (Paris: Editions Bachari, 2006).

Elkaïm, S., and L. Estrade, 'Denis Gheerbrant, l'arpenteur', *Critikat* (6 octobre 2009), *https://www.critikat.com/panorama/entretien/denis-gheerbrant/* (last accessed 17 May 2021).

Elsässer, T., *European Cinema and Continental Philosophy: Film as Thought Experiment* (Edinburgh: Edinburgh University Press, 2014).

Fleckinger, H. (ed.), Carole Roussopoulos: *Caméra militante. Luttes de libération des années 1970* (Geneva: Editions MétisPresses, 2010).

Flinn, M. C., *The Social Architecture of French Cinema, 1929–1939* (Liverpool: Liverpool University Press, 2014).

Flitterman-Lewis, S., *To Desire Differently: Feminism and the French Cinema* (Urbana-Champaign: University of Illinois Press, 1990).

Foucault, M., 'Of Other Space' (1967), *https://foucault.info/documents/heterotopia/foucault.heteroTopia.en/* (last accessed 17 May 2021).

Frodon, J. M., 'Avec *Les Habitants* de Depardon, la parole est à la "France du centre"', *Slate.fr* (7 novembre 2016), *http://www.slate.fr/story/117205/habitants-depardon-cinema* (last accessed 17 May 2021).

Froger, M., 'Don et image de don: esthétique documentaire et communauté', *Intermédialités: Histoire et théorie des arts, des lettres et des techniques*, 4 (Fall 2004), 115–40.

Froger, M., *Le cinéma à l'épreuve de la communauté* (Montreal: Presses de l'Université de Montréal, 2009).

Gaines, J. M., 'Political Mimesis', in Jane M. Gaines and Michael Renov (eds), *Collecting Visible Evidence* (Minneapolis: University of Minnesota Press, 1999), pp. 84–102.

Gaines, J. M., 'Documentary radicality', *Revue Canadienne d'Etudes Cinématographiques/Canadian Journal of Film Studies*, 16/1 (2007), 5–24.

Gaon, S., 'Communities in Question: Sociality and Solidarity in Nancy and Blanchot', *Journal for Cultural Research*, 9/4 (October 2005), 387–403.

Gauthier, G., *Un siècle de documentaires français: des tourneurs de manivelle aux voltigeurs du multimédia* (Paris: Editions Armand Colin, 2004).

Gheerbrant, D., 'La République Marseille: une suite cinématographique par Denis Gheerbrant', in *La République Marseille* (Editions Montparnasse, 2009).

Gilligan, C., *In a Different Voice* (Cambridge, MA: Harvard University Press, 1982).

Gilligan, C., 'Le care, éthique féminine ou éthique féministe? Entretien', *Multitudes*, 2/37–8 (2009), 76–8.

Gleiberman, O., 'Film Review: *Faces Places* (*Visages Villages*)', *Variety* (26 May 2017), *https://variety.com/2017/film/reviews/visages-villages-review-agnes-varda-1202444461/* (last accessed 17 May 2021).

Gonzalez, S., 'La République Marseille – Denis Gheerbrant', *Grenouille: Radio & Création* (11 juin 2009), *http://www.radiogrenouille.com/ audiotheque/la-republique-marseille-denis-gheerbrant-presente-sa-collection-de-huit-films-documentaires/* (last accessed 17 May 2021).

Gordon, D. A., *Immigrants and Intellectuals: May '68 and the Rise of Anti-racism in France* (London: Merlin Press, 2012).

Grant, P. D., *Cinéma Militant: Political Filmmaking and May 1968* (New York: Wallflower Press, 2018).

Guattari, F., *The Three Ecologies*, trans. Ian Pindar and Paul Sutton (London: Bloomsbury, 2000).

Guilly, J. C., *La France périphérique: comment on a sacrifié les classes populaires* (Paris: Editions Flammarion, 2014).

Haddad, S., *Derrida and the Inheritance of Democracy* (Bloomington: Indiana University Press, 2013).

Hanotiaux, G., 'Rêver sous le capitalisme', *Ensemble*, 96 (avril 2018), 42–6, *http://www.asbl-csce.be/journal/Ensemble96chomage42* (last accessed 28 May 2021).

Hayes, G., and M. O'Shaughnessy (eds), *Cinéma et engagement* (Paris: L'Harmattan, 2005).

Hirigoyen, M. F., *Le harcèlement moral au travail* (Paris: Presses Universitaires de France, 2014).

Irigaray, L., 'Toward a Mutual Hospitality' in T. Claviez (ed.), *The Conditions of Hospitality: Ethics, Politics, and Aesthetics on the Threshold of the Possible* (Bronx: Fordham University Press, 2013), pp. 42–54.

Kelly, V., 'Cinéma Engagé: Activist Filmmaking in French and Francophone Contexts', *South Central Review*, 17/3 (Autumn 2000), special issue: 'Cinéma Engagé: Activist Filmmaking in French and Francophone Contexts', 1–6.

Kline, T. J. (ed.), *Agnès Varda Interviews* (Jackson: University Press of Mississippi, 2014).

Lane, J. F., *Republican Citizens, Precarious Subjects: Representations of Work in Post-Fordist France* (Liverpool: Liverpool University Press, 2020).

Laugier, S., 'L'éthique du care en trois subversions', *Multitudes*, 3/2 (2010), 112–25.

Le Blanc, G., *Vies ordinaires, vies précaires* (Paris: Le Seuil, 2007).

Le Blanc, G., *Que faire de notre vulnérabilité?* (Paris: Editions Bayard, 2011).

Leblanc, G., 'Militantisme et esthétique', *CinémAction*, 110 (2004), special issue: 'Le Cinéma militant reprend le travail', 30–4.

Leboutte, P., 'Jean-Louis Comolli – Sur la parole filmée d'une femme de ménage. La parole libère', *Des Images* (25 mai 2005), *http://www.desimages.be/spip.php?article137* (last accessed 17 May 2021).

Le Coadic, R., 'Brittany's New "Bonnets Rouges" and their Critics', in L. A. Brannelly, G. Darwin, P. McCoy and K. O'Neill, *Proceedings of the Harvard Celtic Colloquium, 34* (Cambridge, MA: Harvard University Press, 2015).

Lewis, T., 'The Politics of "Hauntology" in Derrida's *Specters of Marx*', in Michael Sprinker (ed.), *Ghostly Demarcations: A Symposium on Jacques Derrida's Specters of Marxism* (New York: Verso, 1999), pp. 134–67.

Lhénoret, S., 'Le dernier soupir du "village fantôme" de Pirou', *Le Monde* (12 décembre 2016), *https://www.lemonde.fr/francaises-francais/visuel/2016/12/12/le-dernier-soupir-du-village-fantome-de-pirou_5047734_4999913.html* (last accessed 17 May 2021).

Linhart, D., 'Les formes modernes de l'emprise managériale' (2019), *https://doi.org/10.1590/ES0101-73302019219374* (last accessed 15 July 2021).

Linhart, D., 'Modernisation et précarisation de la vie au travail', Papeles del CIEC, 43/1 (2009), *https://identidadcolectiva.es/pdf/43.pdf* (last accessed 12 July 2021).

Linhart, D. and Mauchamp, N., *Le travail* (Paris: Le Cavalier Bleu, 2009).

Llorey, I., *State of Insecurity: Government of the Precarious* (New York: Verso, 2015).

Lussault, M., 'La condition périurbaine', in Joseph Confavreux (ed.), *Le fond de l'air est jaune: Comprendre une révolte inédite* (Paris: Editions du Seuil, 2019), pp. 171–9.

Macé, Marielle, '"Let Us Connect": On a Political Pronoun', trans. Emelyn Lih, *La Deleuziana – Online Journal of Philosophy*, 7 (2018), 173–84.

Magagnoli, P., *Documents of Utopia: The Politics of Experimental Documentary* (New York: Columbia University Press, 2015).

Maggiori, R., and J. B. Marongiu, 'Entretien avec Pierre Bourdieu', *Libération* (11 février 1993), *http://www.homme-moderne.org/societe/socio/bourdieu/misere/libe0293.html* (last accessed 28 May 2021).

Mal, C., 'David Dufresne: "Avec le cinéma, on n'est plus dans l'actualité, on entre dans l'Histoire"', *Le Blog Documentaire* (22 septembre 2020), *http://leblogdocumentaire.fr/david-dufresne-cinema-on-nest-plus-lactualite-on-entre-lhistoire/* (last accessed 17 May 2021).

Marchart, O., 'Democracy and Minimal Politics: The Political Difference and its Consequences', *The South Atlantic Quarterly*, 110/4 (Fall 2011), 965–73.

Mariette, A., '"Silence, on ferme!" Regard documentaire sur des fermetures d'usine', *Ethnologie Française*, 35/4 (2005), 653–66.

Marshall, B., 'Rancière and Deleuze: Entanglements in Film Theory', in O. Davis (ed.), *Rancière Now* (London: Polity, 2013).

Martinez, D., 'Le travail à cœur: entretien avec Yves Clot', *La Nouvelle Vie Ouvrière* (16 juillet 2010), 44–7, *http://www.snupfen.org/IMG/pdf/ Le_travail_a_coeur-Yves-Clot.pdf* (last accessed 17 May 2021).

Massey, D., *For Space* (London: Sage, 2005).

Mauffrey, N. 'Un imaginaire collectif au féminin/masculin: *Les Veuves de Noirmoutier* d'Agnès Varda', *Studies in French Cinema*, 19/2 (2019), 135–49.

May, T., 'Jacques Rancière and the Ethics of Quality', *SubStance*, 36/2 (2007), 'Issue 113: The Future of Anarchism', 20–36.

Merklen, D., *Quartiers populaires, quartiers politiques* (Paris: La Dispute, 2009).

Michel, M., 'Ville moyenne, ville-moyen', *Annales de Géographie*, 478 (novembre–décembre 1977), 641–85.

Mitterrand, A., 'La dernière classe', *Critikat* (23 septembre 2014), *https://www.critikat.com/actualite-cine/critique/on-a-greve/* (last accessed 28 May 2021).

Molinier, P., 'Formaliser et politiser les récits du care', *revue ¿Interrogations?*, 11 – Varia (décembre 2010), (online), *https://www.revue-interrogations.org/Formaliser-et-politiser-les-recits* (last accessed 28 May 2021).

Molinier, P., 'Souffrance, défenses, reconnaissance. Le point de vue du travail', *Nouvelle Revue de Psychosociologie*, 10/2 (2010), 99–110.

Molinier, P., and Flottes, A. (eds), 'Travail et santé mentale: approches cliniques', *Travail et Emploi*, 129 (2012), 51–66.

Molinier, P., S. Laugier and P. Paperman (eds), *Qu'est-ce que le care? Souci des autres, sensibilité, responsabilité* (Paris: Petite Bibliothèque Payot, 2009).

Moucharik, S., 'Le film *Rêve d'usine*: une conception singulière de la "lutte"', *Ethnologie Française*, 38/4 (2008), 723–35.

Murcia, C., 'Soi et l'autre (Les Glaneurs et la glaneuse)', in A. Fiant, R. Hamery and E. Thouvenel (eds), *Agnès Varda: Le cinéma et au-delà* (Rennes: Presses Universitaires de Rennes, 2014), pp. 43–8.

Murray Levine, A. J., *Vivre Ici: Space, Place, and Experience in Contemporary French Documentary* (Liverpool: Liverpool University Press, 2018).

Muyan, W., 'We can be heroes: Interview with Agnès Varda', *Film Comment* (September–October 2017), 24–30.

Nancy, J. L., *The Birth to Presence*, trans. B. Holmes and others (Stanford: Stanford University Press, 1994).

Nancy, J. L., 'The Political and/or Politics', trans. C. Sander, *Oxford Literary Review*, 36/1, 'The Present of Deconstruction' (2014), 5–17.

Nancy, J. L., *Portrait*, trans. S. Clift and S. Sparks (Bronx: Fordham University Press, 2018).

Nichols, B., *Representing Reality* (Bloomington: Indiana University Press, 1991).

Noiriel, G., *Les gilets jaunes à la lumière de l'histoire* (Paris : Editions de l'Aube, 2019).

Nora, P., 'Between Memory and History: Les Lieux de Mémoire', *Representations*, 26, Special Issue: 'Memory and Counter-Memory' (Spring 1989), 7–24.

Offredi, C., 'La précarité des années 1980 ou un phénomène social en gestation dans la société', *International Review of Community Development/Revue Internationale d'Action Communautaire*, 19 (1988), 21–31.

O'Shaughnessy, M., *The Face of Political Cinema: Commitment in French Film since 1995* (New York: Berghahn, 2007).

O'Shaughnessy, M., 'French Film and Work', *Framework*, 53/1 (Spring 2012), 155–71.

Ostria, V., 'Et la vie/Le voyage à la mer', *Les Inrockuptibles* (1er janvier 2002), *https://www.lesinrocks.com/cinema/films-a-l-affiche/et-la-vie-le-voyage-a-la-mer/* (last accessed 17 May 2021).

Paperman, P., 'Ethique du care: un changement de regard sur la vulnérabilité', *Gérontologie et Société*, 33/2 (2010), 51–61.

Paperman, P., C. Ibos, A. Damamme and P. Molinier (eds), *Vers une société du care: une politique de l'intention* (Paris: Editions Le Cavalier Bleu, 2019).

Paperman, P., and S. Laugier (eds), *Le Souci des autres. Ethique et Politique du care* (Paris: Editions de l'Ecole des Hautes Etudes en Sciences Sociale, 2005).

Paperman, P., and P. Molinier, 'L'éthique du *care* comme pensée de l'égalité', *Travail, Genre et Sociétés*, 26 (novembre 2011), 189–93.

Paugam, S., 'Face au mépris social, la revanche des invisibles', in Coll. «Gilets jaunes»: *Hypothèse sur un mouvement* (Paris: La Découverte, 2019), pp. 37–42.

Peigne-Giuly, A., 'Lussas en croisade pour le réel', *Libération* (27 août 2002), *https://www.liberation.fr/culture/2002/08/26/lussas-en-croisade-pour-le-reel_413438/* (last accessed 28 May 2021).

Pelluchon, C., *Eléments pour une éthique de la vulnérabilité* (Paris: Les Editions du Cerf, 2011).

Péron, D., 'La tournée des papotes', *Libération* (19 mai 2017), *https://next.liberation.fr/cinema/2017/05/19/la-tournee-des-pap otes_1570887* (last accessed 17 May 2021).

Perron, T., 'Les origines du cinéma militant (ou le cinéma militant et la mort)' (2004), *http://www.peripherie.asso.fr/mouvement-ouvrier-et-cinema/le-cinema-militant* (last accessed 17 May 2021).

Perron, T., 'Portrait de Marcel Trillat', *Histoire d'un film, mémoire d'une lutte*, 'Etranges étrangers' (Editions Scope-Périphérie, 2009), *http://www.peripherie.asso.fr/patrimoine-marcel-trillat/portrait-de-marcel-trillat* (last accessed 17 May 2021).

Perron, T., 'Le territoire des images: Pratiques du cinéma et luttes ouvrières', *Le Mouvement social*, 1/230 (2010), 127–43.

Pezé, M., *Ils ne mouraient pas tous mais tous étaient frappés: Journal de la consultation Souffrance et Travail 1997–2008* (Paris: Editions Flammarion, 2010).

Pezé, M., 'Le territoire, pas la carte', *Souffrance et Travail* (12 février 2016), *https://www.souffrance-et-travail.com/magazine/emploi-chomage/marie-peze-le-territoire-pas-la-carte* (last accessed 28 May 2021).

Pitti, L., 'Peñarroya 1971–1979: "Notre santé n'est pas à vendre!"', *Plein Droit*, 83 (2009), *http://www.gisti.org/spip.php?article4461* (last accessed 17 May 2021)

Prédal, R., 'La mise en scène de La vie moderne (ou le portrait de l'artiste en paysan cévenol)', in D. Coureau (ed.), *Raymond Depardon: L'immobilité et le mouvement du monde* (Paris: L'Harmattan, 2015), pp. 29–52.

Pressmann, F., 'Docus en crise: Jean-Pierre Thorn et Denis Gheerbrant', *arteradio* (24 mars 2004), *https://www.arteradio.com/son/2147/docus_ en_crise* (link no longer active).

Puar, J., 'Precarity Talk: A Virtual Roundtable with Lauren Berlant, Judith Butler, Bojana Cvejic, Isabell Lorey, Jasbir Puar, and Ana Vujanovic', *The Drama Review*, 56/4 (Winter 2012), 163–77.

Rachlin, N., 'L'Exclusion au cinéma: le cas d'Agnès Varda', *Women in French Studies*, special issue (2006), 88–111.

Rachlin, N., 'The Last Working-Class City in France: Gheerbrant's *La République Marseille* and Post-Global Cinema', *Substance*, 43/1 (2014), 44–62.

Ragel, P., '"Nul, après nous, ne témoignera que nous avons été"', in D. Coureau (ed.), *Raymond Depardon: L'immobilité et le mouvement du monde* (Paris: L'Harmattan, 2015), pp. 53–70.

Rancière, J., *The Emancipated Spectator*, trans. Gregory Elliott, (New York: Verso, 2008).

Rancière, J., *The Intervals of Cinema*, trans. John Howe (London; New York: Verso, 2014).

Reid, D., *Opening the Gates: The Lip Affair, 1968–1981* (New York: Verso, 2018).

Renault, E., *Souffrances sociales. Philosophie, psychologie et politique* (Paris: La Découverte, 2008).

Robert-Diard, P., 'Une certaine France vue par Raymond Depardon', *Le Monde* (13 novembre 2013), *https://www.lemonde.fr/a-la-une/article/2005/06/09/les-bouts-de-france-de-raymond-depardon_660146 _3208.html* (last accessed 17 May 2021).

Roger, P., 'Critique – *Ils ne mouraient pas tous*', *Etudes: Revue de Culture Contemporaine*, 4/404 (2006), 534–5.

Rolston III, H., 'Value and the Nature of Value', in Robin Attfield and Andrew Belsey (eds), *Philosophy and the Natural Environment* (Cambridge: Cambridge University Press, 1994), pp. 13–30.

Ross, K., *May 68 and its Afterlives* (Chicago: University of Chicago Press, 2002).

Rothberg, M., D. Sanyal and M. Silverman (eds), special issue of *Yale French Studies*, *Noeuds de mémoire: Multidirectional Memory in Postwar French and Francophone Culture*, 118–19 (2010).

Rouaud, C., 'Que reste-t-il de ces beaux jours ?' (2007), press kit *Les Lip: L'imagination au pouvoir*, *https://medias.unifrance.org/medias/103/ 106/27239/presse/les-lip-l-imagination-au-pouvoir-presskit-french.pdf* (last accessed 17 May 2021).

Roy, A., 'Denis Gheerbrant: Le cinéaste de la parole', *24 images*, 152 (juin–juillet 2011), 49–53.

Salman, S., 'Fortune d'une catégorie: la souffrance au travail chez les médecins du travail', *Varia*, 50/1 (janvier–mars 2008), 31–47.

Sauder, R., 'Forbach trahit sa mémoire car nous avons trahi Forbach', *Libération* (24 mars 2014), *https://www.liberation.fr/france/2014/03/24/forbach-trahit-sa-memoire-car-nous-avons-trahi-forbach_989787* (last accessed 17 May 2021).

Scandura, J., *Down in the Dumps* (Durham, NC: Duke University Press, 2008).

Simon, P., 'Sophie Bruneau et Marc-Antoine Roudil à propos de *Ils ne mouraient pas tous …* ', *cinergie.be* (février 2006), *https://www.cinergie. be/actualites/sophie-bruneau-et-marc-antoine-roudil-a-propos-de-ils-ne-mouraient-pas-tous* (last accessed 17 May 2021).

Smith, A., *Agnès Varda* (Manchester: Manchester University Press, 1998).

Still, J., '*Sharing the World*: Luce Irigaray and the Hospitality of Difference', *L'Esprit Créateur*, 52/3 (2012), 40–51.

Soullard, C., 'Visages Paysans: A propos de Raymond Depardon', *Revue des Deux Mondes* (septembre 2008), 147–52.

Stafford, A., *Photo-texts: Contemporary French Writing of the Photographic Image* (Liverpool: Liverpool University Press, 2010).

Standing, G., *The Precariat: The New Dangerous Class* (London: Bloomsbury, 2011).

Stewart, K., *Ordinary Affects* (Durham, NC: Duke University Press, 2007).

Thépenier, C., 'Entretien avec Nicolas Burlaud', press kit *La Fête est finie* (2013), *http://lafeteestfinie.primitivi.org/wp-content/uploads/2015/09/lfef_doc_press.pdf* (last accessed 28 May 2021).

Tourette, L., '*Coming for a Visit*: press kit' (prod. Vezfilm, 2009), *http://static1.1.sqspcdn.com/static/f/408586/21168367/1354653777093/Coming+for+a+visit+-+Press+kit.pdf?token=gQYG%2Bus0Vy%2BDZ9Hdt8IVWcnmP6U%3D* (last accessed 17 May 2021).

Vidal, B., *Heritage Film: Nation, Genre, and Representation* (New York: Columbia University Press, 2012).

Vigna, X., *L'insubordination ouvrière dans les années 68. Essai d'histoire politique des usines* (Rennes: Presses Universitaires de Rennes, 2007).

Ward, J., 'Ethique de la responsabilité et éthique du *care*: quelles logiques pour fonder une éthique de l'intervention sociale?' *L'Harmattan* (avril 2010), *https://www.editions-harmattan.fr/index.asp?navig=catalogue&obj= article&no=14495&razSqlClone=1* (last accessed 17 May 2021).

Waters, S., 'Disappearing bodies: the workplace and documentary film in an era of pure money', *French Cultural Studies*, 26/3 (2015), 289–301.

Waters, S., *Suicide Voices: Labour Trauma in France* (Liverpool: Liverpool University Press, 2020).

Widemann, D., 'Régis Sauder : «J'avais rendez-vous avec Forbach»', *L'Humanité* (19 avril 2017), *https://www.humanite.fr/regis-sauder-javais-rendez-vous-avec-forbach-634953* (last accessed 28 May 2021).

Witt, M., 'The Renaissance of Documentary Filmmaking in France in the 1980s and 1990s', *Critical Studies in Television*, 7/2 (Autumn 2012), 10–29.

Worms, F., *Le Moment du soin. A quoi tenons-nous?* (Paris: Presses Universitaires Françaises, 2010).

# Index

❧